MONEY
FOR
PERFORMING
ARTISTS

MONEY
FOR
PERFORMING ARTISTS

Edited by Suzanne Niemeyer

American Council for the Arts
New York, New York

Copublished with Allworth Press

93 92 91   5 4 3 2 1

Book and Cover Design by Celine Brandes, *Photo Plus Art*
Typesetting by *The Desktop Shop*, Baltimore, MD

Printing by *Capital City Press, Inc.*

Director of Publishing: Robert Porter
Associate Director of Publishing: Doug Rose
Publishing Assistant: Tiffany Chez Robinson

Library of Congress Cataloging-in-Publication Data:

Money for performing artists / edited by Suzanne Niemeyer.
     p.   cm.
    Includes indexes.
    ISBN 0-915400-96-0: $14.95
    1. Performing arts — United States — Scholarships, fellowships, etc. — Directories. 2. Performing arts — Canada — Scholarships, fellowships, etc. — Directories. I. Niemeyer, Suzanne.
PN2293.E35M66 1992
791'.079 — dc20   91-29393
                                                       CIP

TABLE OF CONTENTS

ACKNOWLEDGMENTS

This publication would not have been possible without the hard work and support of many people. Special thanks goes to Doug Oxenhorn, a tireless and diligent researcher. Thanks also to David Bosca, Library Director at the Arts Resource Consortium Library, who provided space and support during the research for this volume, and to his assistant Eleanor Zimmer. Finally, the many individuals who took time out of their busy schedules to respond to our surveys deserve special gratitude. Without their help this book would not exist.

—*S.N.*

HOW TO USE THE GUIDE

In this single volume, we have assembled a unique resource compendium of the myriad programs of support and assistance for professional, individual performing artists in the U.S. and Canada. We have found programs geared for performing artists of every stripe—dancers, choreographers, musicians, composers, actors, playwrights, directors, and performance artists.

What we have learned in assembling the 223 organization profiles that appear on the following pages is that support for performing artists comes in a wide variety of forms and from diverse sources. We have uncovered programs that offer several million dollars in fellowships, touring opportunities, commissions, or competitions for emerging musicians. Other programs offer playwrights workshop opportunities to develop scripts with professional actors and directors. Some operate on an international scale, while others provide service community wide. We've tried to collect information from the largest government agencies to the smaller nonprofit groups. You may be surprised at the many places that can provide help.

There are, of course, many additional organizations that provide support to performing artists. In this volume, we have attempted to identify the organizations that offer the greatest benefits to the most artists. We have also included the organizations able to lead you to those sources of support that, for space reasons, could not be included here. Our hope is that this volume becomes the primary reference to organizations that can help you the most.

This book is intended to simplify your search for the various kinds of assistance that you need to advance your career. We have arranged the profiles alphabetically by organization name. Each entry includes detailed sections about the organization's specific programs for performing artists. Following the name, address, phone number, and contact person for the organization, each entry is divided into three sections for quick reference.

The "Profile of Financial Support to Artists" is intended to give you an idea of the size and scope of the program. It includes the total amount of funding and value of in-kind support that the organization gives to individual artists, the total number of applications for funding that the organization receives from individual artists, the number of individuals that receive funding, and the dollar range of grants to individuals. At a glance, you will be able to determine how many opportunities exist and how many people compete for them.

The "Direct Support Programs" section details fellowships, competitions, project grants, professional development grants, emergency assistance, script development workshops, and residency programs that serve individual performing artists. Commissions and arts-in-education programs may also be included here, depending on the scope of the program, the standardization of the application and selection process, and the availability of direct funds for individual artists. This section also outlines each program's eligibility requirements, scope, and application selection process. *When considering a particular grant, artists should consider how their projects correspond to the stated purpose of the program.* A careful examination of the information provided under the eligibility heading can save time and effort. Citizenship, residency, age, art forms, and other special requirements can all affect your eligibility. I the description of the application/selection process, you will find information on deadlines; the organization's preferred method for making an initial contact; the application procedure, including required support materials; the selection process; the notification process; and reporting requirements. The deadlines supplied here are subject to change, and you should always contact the organization to confirm dates.

The "Technical Assistance Programs and Services" section encompasses a wide range of activities that benefit performing artists. These include touring and performance opportunities, artist registries, festivals, showcases and booking conferences, and arts-in-education programs.

Many organizations confine their programs to artists living in certai areas or to specific types of support. Not all programs are for everyone. To help you find the programs for which you are eligible and which bes match your needs and interests, we have provided four indexes. The Alphabetical Index of Organizations lets you quickly locate the organiza tions you are most interested in researching. The Index of Organization by Geographic Area lists the organizations according to the area served: listings include individual states, the U.S., Canada, and international service organizations. The Index of Organizations by Discipline lists organizations by the art forms they serve: dance, interdisciplinary, music, musical theater/opera, theater, or all performing arts. The Index of Orga izations by Type of Support lists organizations according to the services they provide:

- APPRENTICESHIPS/INTERNSHIPS. Organizations that fund apprentice ships or internships. Most programs focus on folk arts, but a few offer theater apprenticeships for directors or designers.

- ARTISTS' COLONIES/RETREATS. Organizations that provide a working retreat for artists. Some request that residents pay a fee but offer stipends or full or partial fee waivers to artists in financial need. Residencies in this category are generally most appropriate for performing artists working on the early phases of individual creative projects such as playwriting or music composition.
- ARTS IN EDUCATION/COMMUNITY RESIDENCIES. Organizations that sponsor, administer, or select artists for school/community residency and visiting artist programs.
- COMMISSIONS. Organizations that commission works directly or that fund commissions by performers or presenters.
- COMPETITIONS. Organizations that sponsor competitions for performers, usually instrumentalists or vocalists. Most competitions aim to launch the careers of emerging professionals. Prizes may include cash, concert tours, or free management.
- EMERGENCY ASSISTANCE. Organizations that provide financial support for artists facing work-related or personal emergencies.
- FELLOWSHIPS/AWARDS. Organizations that offer financial support to artists based on past accomplishments or on potential for future success. These grants generally carry few or no restrictions.
- FESTIVALS. Organizations that sponsor festivals featuring performing artists.
- FINANCE. Organizations that provide information on or assistance with taxes, recordkeeping, accounting, or financial management.
- HEALTH. Organizations that offer group health plans for artists or information on healthcare options or art hazards.
- INTERNATIONAL OPPORTUNITIES/EXCHANGE PROGRAMS. Organizations that sponsor residencies or independent work or study abroad.
- JOB OPPORTUNITIES/CAREER DEVELOPMENT. Organizations that maintain job banks, publicize employment opportunities, or conduct career development workshops.
- LEGAL ASSISTANCE AND ADVICE. Organizations that provide information or referrals on legal matters.
- LIVE/WORK SPACE. Organizations that offer low-cost or free live/work space to artists or that offer information on such opportunities.
- MARKETING/PUBLIC RELATIONS/DISTRIBUTION. Organizations that offer information on or assistance with marketing, public relations, or distribution.
- PERFORMANCE OPPORTUNITIES. Organizations that regularly hire performers for concert series or other programs.
- PRESENTERS, INFORMATION. Organizations that publish or provide information on presenting organizations.

- PRODUCTION/DEVELOPMENT ASSISTANCE AND RESIDENCIES. Organizations that offer funding, residencies, facilities, or workshops to assist artists in preparing original works for production. Residency programs listed here provide performing artists with time and facilities to rehearse and often culminate with a public performance. Script development workshops give playwrights a chance to work with professional actors, directors, and designers. Organizations offering workshops often produce selected works as well. Composers may compete for opportunities to have their work rehearsed and premiered by major orchestras.

- PROFESSIONAL DEVELOPMENT/TECHNICAL ASSISTANCE GRANTS. Organizations that provide financial support for general professional development activities such as travel to conferences or seminars, consultation fees, and promotional efforts. Sometimes these grants may be used for the production or exhibition of work deemed critical to an artist's career.

- PROJECT SUPPORT. Organizations that offer grants for the development, production, or completion of a specific project.

- REGISTRIES. Organizations that maintain registries or directories of individual artists.

- STUDY GRANTS. Organizations that offer grants for independent study, workshop attendance, or study at an institution. Artists interested in study grants should also consult the Professional Development/Technical Assistance Grants heading.

- TOURING OPPORTUNITIES. Organizations that administer or fund performing arts tours. Many state and regional arts councils audition performers for touring rosters and then provide fee support to organizations presenting rostered artists.

- TRAVEL GRANTS. Organizations that offer grants for travel, often for project development or professional development purposes. Artists interested in travel grants should also consult the Professional Development/Technical Assistance Grants heading.

One last thing. You can help us and other artists by showing what you have learned on your own. If you know of programs that aren't listed here, please complete and return the card inserted in this book so that we can include them in the next edition.

Good luck!

Suzanne Niemeyer
Editor

August 9, 1991

THE GUIDE

ACTORS THEATRE OF LOUISVILLE (ATL)

316 West Main Street
Louisville, KY 40202-4218
502-584-1265
CONTACT: LITERARY STAFF

DIRECT SUPPORT PROGRAMS

➤ **HUMANA FESTIVAL OF NEW AMERICAN PLAYS**

Purpose: To discover and recognize new playwrights of unique artistic merit and to produce new plays of social relevance

Eligibility:

   Special Requirements: Focus is on works by U.S. citizens or residents; must apply through agent or with a letter of recommendation from a literary manager or artistic director of a professional theater

   Art Forms: Playwriting

Type of Support: Production of play; playwright receives housing, travel, and stipend

Scope of Program: 6-8 productions annually

Competition for Support: 900 applications annually

Application/Selection Process:

   Deadline: Ongoing (decisions made in the fall)

   Preferred Initial Contact: Call or write for guidelines

   Application Procedure: Submit script, letter of recommendation

   Selection Process: Staff review, outside readers, producing director

   Notification Process: Letter

➤ **THE NATIONAL TEN-MINUTE PLAY CONTEST**

Purpose: To recognize potential and established writers for American theater

Eligibility:

   Art Forms: Playwriting

Type of Support: $500-$1,000; possible production at spring or fall showcase by apprentice company of actors, or at Humana Festival (Equity production)

Scope of Program: 1 or 2 awards, totalling $1,000, per year

Competition for Support: 2,000 applications annually

Application/Selection Process:

   Deadline: December 1

   Preferred Initial Contact: Call or write for guidelines

   Application Procedure: Submit script

   Selection Process: Staff review, outside readers

   Notification Process: Letter to finalists, letter and phone call to winners

ACTS INSTITUTE, INC.

P.O. Box 10153
Kansas City, MO 64111
816-753-0208
CONTACT: CHARLOTTE PLOTSKY

DIRECT SUPPORT PROGRAMS
➤ **CASH GRANT PROGRAM FOR COLONY RESIDENCIES**

Purpose: To serve as a last resort for artists who have been accepted at an artists'/writers' colony and need financial assistance that the colony is unable to provide

Eligibility:
  Age: 18 or older
  Special Requirements: Applicant must have been accepted at an artists' colony and been unable to procure financial support from the National Endowment for the Arts and from his or her state arts council
  Art Forms: All disciplines

Type of Support: $700-$1,000 toward cost of residency

Scope of Program: $1,400-$5,000 awarded annually

Application/Selection Process:
  Deadline: December 1 (summer residencies), June 1 (winter residencies)
  Preferred Initial Contact: Write for application/guidelines; enclose SASE
  Application Procedure: Submit application form, $10 fee, samples of work, project budget, acceptance letter from colony, rejections for financial aid from the National Endowment for the Arts and state arts council, artists' statement, references

TECHNICAL ASSISTANCE PROGRAMS AND SERVICES

Programs of Special Interest: The ACTS Institute publishes "Havens for Creatives," a directory of 85 artist colony programs available worldwide.

AFFILIATE ARTISTS, INC. (AAI)

37 West 65th Street
New York, NY 10023
212-580-2000
CONTACT: CAROL WOLFF, DIRECTOR, ARTIST AFFAIRS

TECHNICAL ASSISTANCE PROGRAMS AND SERVICES

Programs of Special Interest: U.S. performing artists with 3-10 years professional experience may apply for the opportunity to audition for AAI's artist roster ($20 application fee; selected artists are invited to New York City for auditions). Singers, instrumentalists, actors, dancers, choreographers, and mimes appearing on the roster are eligible for 1- to 6-week Affiliate Artists Residencies, which place solo performers in a community to meet and perform for the public in various locations. The Affiliate Artists Conductors Program places rostered conductors in full-season residencies with orchestras and opera companies, and Affiliate Artists' Xerox Pianists Program provides rostered pianists with a series of 2-week residencies with American symphony orchestras. Resident artists' fees and expenses are paid by corporate sponsors.

ALABAMA STATE COUNCIL ON THE ARTS (ASCA)

One Dexter Avenue
Montgomery, AL 36130
205-242-4076
CONTACT: RANDY SHOULTS, COMMUNITY DEVELOPMENT PROGRAM MANAGER

PROFILE OF FINANCIAL SUPPORT TO ARTISTS
Total Funding/Value of In-Kind Support: $56,750 for FY 1990-91
Competition for Funding: Total applications, 90; total individuals funded/provided with in-kind support, 21
Grant Range: $750-$5,000

DIRECT SUPPORT PROGRAMS
➤ **FELLOWSHIPS**
Purpose: To encourage professional development of individual Alabama artists
Eligibility:
  Citizenship: U.S.
  Residency: Alabama
  Special Requirements: Previous grantees ineligible for 3 years
  Art Forms: Dance (performance, choreography), media/photography, music (vocal performance, instrumental performance, composition, conducting/musical direction), literature, theater (acting, design, directing, playwriting, mime, puppetry), visual arts/crafts
Type of Support: $2,500-$5,000
Scope of Program: 14 awards in FY 1990-91
Application/Selection Process:
  Deadline: May 1
  Preferred Initial Contact: Call or write for application/guidelines

Application Procedure: Submit application form, samples of work, resumé

Selection Process: Professional advisory panel, ASCA council and staff

Notification Process: 4 months after deadline

Formal Report of Grant Required: Yes

➤ TECHNICAL ASSISTANCE GRANTS

Purpose: To provide funds for artists in need of assistance in marketing their work, establishing a portfolio, learning tax laws and accounting basics, grantseeking, or perfecting a particular artistic technique

Eligibility:
  Citizenship: U.S.
  Residency: Alabama
  Special Requirements: Artists may submit only 1 technical assistance application per grant period
  Art Forms: All disciplines

Type of Support: Up to $1,500 for attending workshops or seminars, studying under another artist, or other educational opportunities except for pursuit of a college degree

Scope of Program: Limited funds

Application/Selection Process:
  Deadline: While funds last (fiscal year begins in October)
  Preferred Initial Contact: Call or write for application/guidelines
  Application Procedure: Submit application form, samples of work, resumé, project budget
  Selection Process: Professional advisory panel, ASCA council and staff
  Notification Process: 4 months after receipt of application
  Formal Report of Grant Required: Yes

➤ FOLK ARTS APPRENTICESHIPS

CONTACT: JOEY BRACKNER, FOLKLIFE PROGRAM MANAGER

Purpose: To ensure the transmission of folk skills by providing financial assistance to masters willing to take students

Eligibility:
  Residency: Alabama
  Special Requirements: Apprentices must locate master artist before applying; masters may apply alone or with apprentice
  Art Forms: Folk arts (includes visual arts and crafts, traditional music and dance, regional foodways, folk architecture, beliefs, myths, and medicinal practices)

Type of Support: Up to $5,000 for apprenticeship

Scope of Program: 7 awards in 1990-91

Application/Selection Process:
  Deadline: April 1, October 1

Preferred Initial Contact: Consult program manager before applying
Application Procedure: Submit application form, samples of work, resumé
Selection Process: Professional advisory panel, ASCA council and staff
Formal Report of Grant Required: Yes

TECHNICAL ASSISTANCE PROGRAMS AND SERVICES
Programs of Special Interest: ASCA reviews in-state and out-of-state artists for school and community residencies (contact Barbara George, Arts in Education Program Manager), and subsidizes, through the Presenter Program, the booking of performances and exhibitions. The semi-annual Alabama Artist Showcase promotes the state's established dance, music, and theater artists. The council also invites individual performing artists and companies to perform at state functions. A peer review panel selects artists for such performance opportunities (contact Bill Bates, Deputy Director).

ALASKA STATE COUNCIL ON THE ARTS (ASCA)

411 West 4th Avenue
Suite 1E
Anchorage, AK 99501-2343
907-279-1558
CONTACT: G. JEAN PALMER, GRANTS OFFICER

PROFILE OF FINANCIAL SUPPORT TO ARTISTS
Total Funding/Value of In-Kind Support: $47,880 for FY 1991
Competition for Funding: Total applications, 103; total individuals funded/provided with in-kind support, 33
Grant Range: Up to $5,000

DIRECT SUPPORT PROGRAMS
➤ INDIVIDUAL ARTIST FELLOWSHIP GRANTS
Purpose: To assist experienced, professional artists in the creation of original works of art and in the development of their careers
Eligibility:
Residency: Alaska
Special Requirements: Originating artists only; no full-time students; previous grantees ineligible for 3 years, preference given to artists who have never received an ASCA fellowship; collaborative projects ineligible

Art Forms: Visual arts, crafts, photography, traditional Native American art eligible in odd-numbered years; music composition, choreography, media arts, literature (including playwriting) eligible in even-numbered years

Type of Support: $5,000

Scope of Program: 6 awards in FY 1991

Application/Selection Process:
  Deadline: October 1
  Preferred Initial Contact: Call or write for application/guidelines
  Application Procedure: Submit application form, samples of work
  Selection Process: Peer panel of artists, board of directors
  Notification Process: Letter in late November
  Formal Report of Grant Required: Yes

➤ **ARTIST TRAVEL GRANTS**

Purpose: To enable individual artists to attend events that will enhance their artistic skills or professional standing

Eligibility:
  Residency: Alaska
  Special Requirements: Originating artists only; no full-time students; previous grantees ineligible for 1 year; preference given to artists who have never received Travel Grant
  Art Forms: Visual arts, photography, media arts, literature (including playwriting), musical composition, choreography, and other arts involving the creation of new works

Type of Support: Maximum $600 to cover up to two-thirds of travel costs to attend workshops, conferences, or seminars, or to undertake projects

Scope of Program: 22 grants, totalling $8,868, awarded in FY 1989

Application/Selection Process:
  Deadline: 30 days before departure; awards made on first-come, first-served basis (fiscal year begins in July)
  Preferred Initial Contact: Call or write for application/guidelines
  Application Procedure: Submit application form, resumé, samples of work
  Notification Process: Letter within 2 weeks of application's receipt
  Formal Report of Grant Required: Yes

➤ **MASTER ARTIST AND APPRENTICE GRANTS IN TRADITIONAL NATIVE ARTS**

Purpose: To support and encourage the maintenance and development of the traditional arts of Alaska's Native peoples

Eligibility:
  Residency: Alaska (apprentice)
  Special Requirements: Master and apprentice must apply together; priority given to apprentices studying within their own cultural traditions; applications where master and apprentice belong to same immediate family are discouraged

Art Forms: Any traditional Native Americanart form, including but not limited to visual arts, crafts, music, dance, storytelling, and singing

Type of Support: Up to $2,000 to cover master's fees and apprentice's supplies

Scope of Program: 7 apprenticeships, totalling $10,979, in FY 1989

Application/Selection Process:

Deadline: May 1, October 1 (more funding available for May 1 applications)

Preferred Initial Contact: Call or write for application/guidelines

Application Procedure: Submit application form, samples of work, letters of recommendation (optional), project budget

Selection Process: Traditional Native Arts Advisory Panel, ASCA council

Notification Process: Letter in late July or mid-November

Formal Report of Grant Required: Yes

TECHNICAL ASSISTANCE PROGRAMS AND SERVICES

Programs of Special Interest: The Artists in Schools Program provides matching funds to Alaskan schools to support artists' residencies.

THE EDWARD F. ALBEE FOUNDATION

14 Harrison Street
New York, NY 10013
212-226-2020

DIRECT SUPPORT PROGRAMS

➤ **RESIDENCY**

Purpose: To provide residencies for talented artists in need of time and space to work on a specific project

Eligibility:

Art Forms: Painting, sculpture, playwriting, screenwriting, poetry, fiction, nonfiction, music composition

Type of Support: 1-month residency, including room and board, at the William Flanagan Memorial Creative Persons Center in Montauk, NY

Scope of Program: 6 residencies per month, June 1-October 1

Application/Selection Process:

Deadline: January 1-April 1

Preferred Initial Contact: Write for application/guidelines

Application Procedure: Submit application form, samples of work, project proposal, resumé, 2 letters of recommendation

Notification Process: May 15

ALBERTA FOUNDATION FOR THE ARTS

Beaver House
10158 - 103 Street
Edmonton, Alberta
Canada T5J OX6
403-427-9968

DIRECT SUPPORT PROGRAMS
➤ **ARTS STUDY GRANTS—PERFORMING ARTS**
CONTACT: MELISSA CABLE, ARTS CONSULTANT

Purpose: To help talented Albertans to offset the costs of further training and the improvement of skills

Eligibility:
   Residency: Alberta
   Special Requirements: Professional artists, students, and arts administrators are eligible
   Art Forms: Music, theater, dance

Type of Support: Up to $2,000

Scope of Program: 211 grants, totalling $108,711, in FY 1988-89

Application/Selection Process:
   Deadline: February 15, August 1
   Preferred Initial Contact: Call or write for application/guidelines
   Application Procedure: Submit application form, other materials as requested
   Selection Process: Jury
   Notification Process: Letter
   Formal Report of Grant Required: Yes

TECHNICAL ASSISTANCE PROGRAMS AND SERVICES

Programs of Special Interest: The annual Alberta Showcase gives performing artists an opportunity to perform for presenters, agents, and managers. Performance Plus is an annual series of showcase performances at Alberta Teachers' Conventions featuring performers with educational programs. The Performing Artists in Schools Program provides fee support to schools for artists' residencies. Alberta performing artists accepted into the Educational Touring Grants Program receive matching grants for performance presentations in Alberta schools (deadline, June 30; contact Niki Munro, Consultant). The annual On Stage Program, held in Edmonton and Calgary, provides emerging performers interested in touring with an opportunity to demonstrate their concert programs and to participate in follow-up workshops and consultations. The biennial Alberta Performing Artists Directory lists performing artists and groups who are interested in touring, and the annual Community Presenters Profiles furnishes information on

Alberta community presenting organizations and their facilities, series formats, and contact names. Touring planning and career development advisory services cover targeting audiences, tour booking and promotional materials, contract negotiations, and technical considerations. International cultural relations advisory services are available for artists interested in international tours, festivals, competitions, or conferences.

AMERICAN ACADEMY AND INSTITUTE OF ARTS AND LETTERS

633 West 155th Street
New York, NY 10032-7599
212-368-5900

DIRECT SUPPORT PROGRAMS

➤ **THE RICHARD RODGERS PRODUCTION AWARD/ DEVELOPMENT GRANTS**

Purpose: To subsidize a production by a not-for-profit theater group of a work by composers and writers who are not already established in the field of musical theater

Eligibility:
  Citizenship: U.S. (permanent residents also eligible)
  Special Requirements: Previous grantees ineligible; collaborative groups or sole creators may apply; works already produced by a professional theater company before paying audiences must have received no more than 21 performances by a for-profit company or 50 performances by a not-for-profit company; productions must take place in New York City
  Art Forms: Musical theater

Type of Support: Production costs (any profits derived from initial production are distributed 50% to the author(s) and 50% to the Rodgers Fund); semi-finalists may be selected to receive professional readings (Development Grants)

Scope of Program: Up to 1 Production Award, up to 4 Development Grants per year

Application/Selection Process:
  Deadline: November
  Preferred Initial Contact: Write for application/guidelines; enclose SASE
  Application Procedure: Submit application form, work (book, lyrics, 1-page plot summary, cassette)
  Selection Process: Selection Committee including artists, Academy members, and individuals from outside of the organization
  Notification Process: Letter
  Formal Report of Grant Required: Yes

AMERICAN ACADEMY IN ROME (AAR)

41 East 65th Street
New York, NY 10021-6508
212-517-4200
CONTACT: JANE FRIEDMAN, FELLOWSHIPS COORDINATOR

DIRECT SUPPORT PROGRAMS
➤ **ONE-YEAR ROME PRIZE FELLOWSHIPS IN THE SCHOOL OF FINE ARTS**

Purpose: To provide artists, architects, composers, and scholars the opportunity to pursue independent work and research in Rome

Eligibility:
    Citizenship: U.S.
    Special Requirements: Must hold a B.A. or equivalent in field
    Art Forms: Architecture, landscape architecture, visual arts, music composition

Type of Support: 1-year residency including room, partial board, studio, $7,000 stipend, $1,300 travel allowance

Scope of Program: 10 awards (2 in music composition) per year

Application/Selection Process:
    Deadline: November 15
    Preferred Initial Contact: Call or write for application/guidelines
    Application Procedure: Submit application form, $30 fee, samples of work, letters of recommendation; finalists are interviewed
    Selection Process: Peer panels of artists, board of directors
    Notification Process: Letter in March or April
    Formal Report of Grant Required: Yes

AMERICAN BALLET COMPETITION (ABC)

P.O. Box 328
Philadelphia, PA 19105
215-829-9800
CONTACT: RANDOLPH SWARTZ, EXECUTIVE DIRECTOR

DIRECT SUPPORT PROGRAMS
➤ **ABC STIPEND PROGRAM**

Purpose: To provide dancers participating in international ballet competitions with travel stipends, per diems, technical and artistic support, and administrative services

Eligibility:
    Citizenship: U.S.
    Art Forms: Dance (ballet, modern)

Type of Support: Average $500-$5,000 toward travel costs, per diem expenses

Scope of Program: Average 4 awards per year

Application/Selection Process:
 Preferred Initial Contact: Call or write for application/guidelines
 Application Procedure: Submit application form, $50 fee, references; audition required
 Selection Process: Individuals outside of organization
 Notification Process: Phone call or letter
 Formal Report of Grant Required: No

AMERICAN FEDERATION OF MUSICIANS

1501 Broadway
Suite 600
New York, NY 10036
212-869-1330

CONTACT: LOCAL CHAPTER OF AMERICAN FEDERATION OF MUSICIANS

DIRECT SUPPORT PROGRAMS
➤ **LESTER PETRILLO MEMORIAL FUND FOR DISABLED MUSICIANS**

Purpose: To provide emergency assistance to members whose physical or mental disabilities prevent them from earning their livelihood as musicians

Eligibility:
 Special Requirements: Must be current member in good standing of American Federation of Musicians (fees involved)
 Art Forms: Music

Type of Support: Emergency assistance grant averaging $300 ($100-$1,000 range in 1990)

Scope of Program: 269 grants in 1990

Competition for Support: 272 applications in 1990

Application/Selection Process:
 Deadline: None
 Preferred Initial Contact: Call or write local chapter for application/guidelines
 Application Procedure: Submit application form, doctor's certificate, confirmation from local chapter
 Selection Process: Staff
 Notification Process: Letter

AMERICAN GUILD OF ORGANISTS (AGO)

475 Riverside Drive, Suite 1260
New York, NY 10115
212-870-2310
CONTACT: DANIEL N. COLBURN II, EXECUTIVE DIRECTOR

PROFILE OF FINANCIAL SUPPORT TO ARTISTS

Total Funding/Value of In-Kind Support: $9,600 for FY 1989-90

Competition for Funding: Total applications, n/a; total individuals funded/provided with in-kind support, 8

Grant Range: $500-$2,000

DIRECT SUPPORT PROGRAMS

➤ **HOLTKAMP-AGO AWARD IN ORGAN COMPOSITION**

Eligibility:
    Citizenship: U.S., Canada, Mexico
    Special Requirements: Work must be unpublished organ solo 8-10 minutes in length
    Art Forms: Music composition (organ)

Type of Support: $2,000, publication, and performance at biennial National Convention of the American Guild of Organists

Scope of Program: 1 award every 2 years

Application/Selection Process:
    Deadline: June 1 (odd-numbered years)
    Preferred Initial Contact: Write for application/guidelines
    Application Procedure: Submit application form, work, $5 for return postage
    Selection Process: Peer panel of artists

➤ **MOLLER-AGO AWARD IN CHORAL COMPOSITION**

Eligibility:
    Citizenship: U.S., Canada, Mexico
    Special Requirements: Work must be based on a text selected by AGO; work must be unpublished composition for SATB chorus and organ, 2 1/2 to 5 minutes in length, in which the organ plays a distinctive role
    Art Forms: Music composition (choral and organ)

Type of Support: $2,000, publication, performances at Regional Conventions of the American Guild of Organists

Scope of Program: 1 award every 2 years

Application/Selection Process:
    Deadline: July 31
    Preferred Initial Contact: Write for application/guidelines
    Application Procedure: Submit application form, work
    Selection Process: Peer panel of artists

➤ **AGO NATIONAL COMPETITION IN ORGAN IMPROVISATION (NCOI)**

Purpose: To promote the art of improvisation through a 3-level competition consisting of a preliminary round, semi-final round, and final round

Eligibility:
>   **Special Requirements:** Must be member of the American Guild of Organists or the Royal Canadian College of Organists
>   **Art Forms:** Music performance (organ improvisation)

Type of Support: 1st place, $2,000; 2nd place, $1,000; 3rd place, $500

Scope of Program: Biennial competition

Application/Selection Process:
>   **Deadline:** February 1 of even-numbered years
>   **Preferred Initial Contact:** Write for application/guidelines
>   **Application Procedure:** Submit application form, $25 fee; applicant's work is recorded by an approved AGO proctor during preliminary round (early March); up to 7 semi-finalists compete at the AGO Pedagogy Conference (late June); 3 finalists compete at the AGO National Conference (late June; semi-finalists and finalists receive travel expenses and per diems)
>   **Selection Process:** Panels of 3 judges at each level
>   **Notification Process:** Semi-finalists announced by April 15; finalists and winners announced at competitions

➤ **NATIONAL YOUNG ARTISTS COMPETITION IN ORGAN PERFORMANCE (NYACOP)**

Purpose: Division I of NYACOP provides a 2-level competition, beginning at the chapter level and concluding at the regional level; Division II provides a 3-level competition, consisting of chapter competitions, regional competitions, and national finals

CONTACT: JOHN HERR, DIRECTOR, NYACOP

Eligibility:
>   **Age:** 22 or younger (Division I), 35 or younger (Division II)
>   **Special Requirements:** Division II competitors must be AGO members (dues are $15-$46)
>   **Art Forms:** Music performance (organ)

Type of Support: Division II National Level awards are $2,000 and recital opportunities nationwide (1st place), $1,000 (2nd place), $500 (3rd place); cash prizes are also available for Division I and Division II at some chapter and regional competitions

Scope of Program: Biennial competition

Application/Selection Process:
>   **Deadline:** February 1 (odd-numbered years)
>   **Preferred Initial Contact:** Call or write for application/guidelines
>   **Application Procedure:** Submit application form, $20 fee to enter chapter level competition; 1st place winners in each division compete in competitions at AGO regional conventions (competitors receive free accommodations, meals, and local

transportation); Division II 1st place winners compete at the AGO National Convention (competitors' expenses are paid)
Selection Process: Peer panel of artists
Notification Process: Winners announced at competitions; competitions take place in March (chapter level) and August of odd-numbered years; national finals for Division II take place in late June of even-numbered years

TECHNICAL ASSISTANCE PROGRAMS AND SERVICES
Programs of Special Interest: AGO administers Professional Certification Exams ($35-$75 fees) and provides cash awards to high scorers. Group health insurance and a tax-sheltered annuity retirement plan are available to members. AGO publishes the monthly *American Organist* and a Professional Concerns Handbook. (Membership fees range from $15 to $46.)

AMERICAN MUSIC CENTER, INC. (AMC)

30 West 26th Street
Suite 1001
New York, NY 10010-2011
212-366-5260

DIRECT SUPPORT PROGRAMS
➤ **MARGARET FAIRBANK JORY COPYING ASSISTANCE PROGRAM**
CONTACT: DEBORAH STEINGLASS, DIRECTOR OF MARGARET FAIRBANK JORY COPYING ASSISTANCE PROGRAM
Purpose: To assist American composers with the expenses of extraction and reproduction of parts for a premiere performance that serves to advance the composer's professional career
Eligibility:
    Citizenship: U.S. (permanent residents also eligible)
    Special Requirements: Applicant must have written commitment for at least 1 public performance of the work by a professional ensemble of recognized artistic merit in the U.S. or abroad; funds for the copying of full scores are restricted to performances in which all performers read from the full score; works must be at least 10 minutes in length and require 7 or more performers
    Art Forms: Music composition (ensemble)
Type of Support: Up to $2,000 for copying costs (average grant, $750)
Scope of Program: 75 awards, totalling $60,000, in 1991
Competition for Support: 130 applications in 1991

Application/Selection Process:
    Deadline: February 1, May 1, October 1
    Preferred Initial Contact: Call or write for application/guidelines
    Application Procedure: Submit application form, complete
    score, resumé, copyist's estimate, confirmation of performance
    Selection Process: Peer panel of artists
    Notification Process: Letter 4 weeks after deadline
    Formal Report of Grant Required: No

TECHNICAL ASSISTANCE PROGRAMS AND SERVICES

CONTACT: LIBRARY AND INFORMATION SERVICES
Phone: 212-366-5263

Programs of Special Interest: The Library of Contemporary Music holds more than 30,000 scores, as well as recordings, and is used by performers seeking new works. Monthly Opportunity Updates describe competitions, grants, job openings, and performance and study opportunities. The AMC newsletter publicizes member premieres, commissions, and new recordings. Staff consultation is available on career development, funding for new music, commissioning sources, publishers, performing ensembles, and composer organizations. AMC members are eligible for group health and life insurance. (Membership fees are $40 for individuals or small ensembles.)

AMERICAN PIANISTS ASSOCIATION, INC.

Clowes Memorial Hall
Butler University
4600 Sunset Avenue
Indianapolis, IN 46208
CONTACT: DR. AILEEN JAMES, AUDITIONS DIRECTOR

DIRECT SUPPORT PROGRAMS

➤ **NATIONAL BEETHOVEN FELLOWSHIP AUDITIONS**
Purpose: To support the careers of America's rising young pianists
Eligibility:
    Citizenship: U.S.
    Age: 18-30
    Special Requirements: Previous fellows ineligible
    Art Forms: Piano performance
Type of Support: 3-year fellowship including $2,500 annually, national performance engagements, master classes, $2,500 sponsorship for international competitions abroad, promotional and marketing assistance
Scope of Program: 3 awards per biennial competition
Competition for Support: 60 applications per competition

Application/Selection Process:
Deadline: July (even-numbered years)
Preferred Initial Contact: Call or write for application/guidelines
Application Procedure: Submit application form; regional auditions held in Chicago, San Francisco, and Philadelphia in October of even-numbered years; main auditions held the following March in Indianapolis
Selection Process: Staff, panels of music professionals
Notification Process: Letter for preliminary rounds

THE AMERICAN-SCANDINAVIAN FOUNDATION (ASF)

725 Park Avenue
New York, NY 10021
212-879-9779
CONTACT: DELORES DI PAOLA, DIRECTOR OF EXCHANGE

DIRECT SUPPORT PROGRAMS
➤ **AWARDS FOR STUDY IN SCANDINAVIA**
Purpose: To encourage advanced study and research in Scandinavia
Eligibility:
Citizenship: U.S. (permanent residents also eligible)
Special Requirements: Must have completed undergraduate education; language competence (as necessary), the special merit of pursuing the project in Scandinavia, and evidence of confirmed invitation or affiliation are important factors; conference attendance and study at English-language institutions are ineligible for support
Art Forms: All disciplines and scholarly fields
Type of Support: $2,000 grant for short visit to Scandinavia; $10,000 fellowship for a full academic year of research or study
Scope of Program: $170,500 available for 1991-92
Application/Selection Process:
Deadline: November 1
Preferred Initial Contact: Call or write for application/guidelines
Application Procedure: Submit application form, $10 fee, samples of work, resumé, project description
Selection Process: Committee
Notification Process: Letter by mid-April
Formal Report of Grant Required: Yes

AMERICAN SOCIETY OF COMPOSERS, AUTHORS AND PUBLISHERS (ASCAP)

One Lincoln Plaza
New York, NY 10023
212-621-6327
CONTACT: FRANCES RICHARD, DIRECTOR, SYMPHONIC AND CONCERT DEPARTMENT

PROFILE OF FINANCIAL SUPPORT TO ARTISTS

Total Funding/Value of In-Kind Support: $25,000 per year
(composers' competition and grants)
Competition for Funding: Total applications, 860; total individuals
funded/provided with in-kind support, 48 (all programs)
Grant Range: Up to $5,000

DIRECT SUPPORT PROGRAMS

➤ **ASCAP FOUNDATION GRANTS TO YOUNG COMPOSERS**
Purpose: To encourage the development of talented young
American composers
Eligibility:
    Citizenship: U.S. (permanent residents also eligible)
    Age: Under 30
    Special Requirements: Works that have received awards or
    prizes in any other national competition or grant-giving program
    are ineligible; arrangements are ineligible
    Art Forms: Music composition
Type of Support: $500-$1,250
Scope of Program: Approximately $20,000 available
Application/Selection Process:
    Deadline: March 15
    Preferred Initial Contact: Call or write for application/guidelines
    Application Procedure: Submit application form, sample of
    work, biographical information, 1 professional recommendation
    Selection Process: Screening Panel of music authorities; Selec-
    tion Committee
    Notification Process: Letter by June 1
    Formal Report of Grant Required: Yes

➤ **ASCAP/RUDOLF NISSIM COMPOSERS COMPETITION**
Purpose: To award an annual prize to a serious composer member
of ASCAP
Eligibility:
    Special Requirements: Must be member of ASCAP ($10 member-
    ship fee); work must require a conductor and must not have been
    performed professionally; score may be published or unpublished

Art Forms: Music composition (for orchestra, chamber orchestra, or large ensemble)

Type of Support: $5,000; additional funds available for rehearsal preparation if award-winning work receives its first public performance by a leading American orchestra or ensemble

Scope of Program: 1 award per year

Application/Selection Process:
Deadline: November 15
Preferred Initial Contact: Call or write for application/guidelines
Application Procedure: Submit sample of work under pseudonym, separate cover letter and biography
Selection Process: Committee of conductors
Notification Process: Letter

➤ **MUSICAL THEATRE WORKSHOP**

CONTACT: MICHAEL KERKER, DIRECTOR OF MUSICAL THEATRE
Phone: 212-621-6234

Purpose: To identify and develop the future great American musical composers and lyricists

Eligibility:
Special Requirements: Composer and lyricist must apply together
Art Forms: Composition for musical theater

Type of Support: 10 weekly workshop meetings with professional directors, producers, choreographers, performers, and composers; workshop culminates in 10- to 15-minute presentations of participants' work for panel critique

Scope of Program: 12 recipients in 1990

Application/Selection Process:
Deadline: August
Preferred Initial Contact: Call or write for guidelines
Application Procedure: Submit 4 songs from and synopsis of musical, biographies
Selection Process: Panel review
Notification Process: Phone call to recipients, letter to nonrecipients

ARIZONA COMMISSION ON THE ARTS

417 West Roosevelt Street
Phoenix, AZ 85003
602-255-5882
CONTACT: TOMÁS C. HERNÁNDEZ, PERFORMING ARTS DIRECTOR

PROFILE OF FINANCIAL SUPPORT TO ARTISTS
Total Funding/Value of In-Kind Support: $73,900 for FY 1990

Competition for Funding: Total applications, 494; total individuals funded/provided with in-kind support, 18

Grant Range: $3,300-$5,000

DIRECT SUPPORT PROGRAMS

➤ **PERFORMING ARTS FELLOWSHIPS**

Purpose: To allow individual artists to set aside time to work, to purchase supplies and materials, to achieve specific artistic career goals, and to further their professional development

Eligibility:

Residency: Arizona

Age: 18 or older

Special Requirements: No students enrolled for more than 3 credit hours at college or university; previous recipients ineligible for following 3 years

Art Forms: Performing arts; eligible disciplines rotate on 3-year cycle among choreography (1991), music composition (1992), playwriting (1993)

Type of Support: $5,000-$7,500

Scope of Program: $60,000 budgeted for 1991 fellowships in creative writing, performing arts, and visual arts; budget divided among disciplines in proportion to number of applicants

Application/Selection Process:

Deadline: September 14

Preferred Initial Contact: Call or write for application/guidelines

Application Procedure: Submit application form, samples of work, resumé/biography

Selection Process: Panel of out-of-state arts professionals

Notification Process: April

➤ **ARTIST PROJECTS**

Purpose: To support artist projects that allow the artist increased time to research and develop ideas or new works, that stretch the artist's work or seek to advance the art form, that bear relevance to the artist's community, or that involve interdisciplinary collaborations with other artists or non-artists

Eligibility:

Residency: Arizona

Age: 18 or older

Special Requirements: No students enrolled in more than 3 credit hours at a college or university; previous grantees not eligible; funds may not be used for self-presenting

Art Forms: All disciplines, innovative work encouraged

Type of Support: Up to $5,000 for project-related costs

Scope of Program: $20,000 allotted for 1991

Application/Selection Process:

Deadline: September 14

Preferred Initial Contact: Call or write for application/guidelines

Application Procedure: Submit application forms, biographies of artists involved, samples of work

Selection Process: Panel of out-of-state artists

Notification Process: April

Formal Report of Grant Required: Yes

➤ PROFESSIONAL DEVELOPMENT GRANTS

Purpose: To provide Arizona artists and organizations representing artists assistance in attending out-of-state conferences that will contribute to their professional growth

Eligibility:

Residence: Arizona

Special Requirements: Artists usually limited to 1 Professional Development Grant per year; assistance usually not provided for artist to attend same conference for 2 successive years

Art Forms: All disciplines

Type of Support: Up to $500

Scope of Program: n/a

Application/Selection Process:

Deadline: 6 weeks before conference

Application Procedure: Submit materials describing conference (if available) and letter of request outlining conference date and location, how attendance would be beneficial, total costs involved, amount and sources of other financial assistance

TECHNICAL ASSISTANCE PROGRAMS AND SERVICES

Programs of Special Interest: Individual artists and companies may apply for inclusion on the selective Artists Roster, which provides information to community sponsors interested in the Artists in Residence: Schools; Artists in Residence: Communities, and Bicultural Arts programs. The commission's Arts Services Program and Arts Resource Center furnish artists with information about business-related issues, including marketing, contracts, taxes, copyright, and insurance. Meet the Composer/Arizona offers funds for composers' fees to Arizona organizations presenting events featuring composers and their works.

ARKANSAS ARTS COUNCIL (AAC)

The Heritage Center
Suite 200
225 East Markham
Little Rock, AR 72201
501-371-2539
CONTACT: SALLY A. WILLIAMS, ARTIST PROGRAMS COORDINATOR

DIRECT SUPPORT PROGRAMS
➤ **FELLOWSHIP PROGRAM**

Purpose: To enable artists to set aside time for creating their art, to improve their skills, or to enhance their artistic careers

Eligibility:
    Residency: Arkansas, 1 year
    Age: 18 or older
    Special Requirements: Must not be degree-seeking student during fellowship period; previous grantees ineligible for 3 years
    Art Forms: Literature, music composition/choreography, visual arts (eligible categories within these disciplines rotate annually)

Type of Support: $5,000

Scope of Program: Up to 10 awards

Competition for Support: 45 applications in 1991

Application/Selection Process:
    Deadline: February 15
    Preferred Initial Contact: Call or write for application/guidelines
    Application Procedure: Submit application form, samples of work, project/enhancement goals description
    Selection Process: Peer panel of artists, board of directors
    Notification Process: Letter in late May
    Formal Report of Grant Required: No

TECHNICAL ASSISTANCE PROGRAMS AND SERVICES

Programs of Special Interest: The Folk Arts Program offers apprenticeships, and the AAC's Resource Guide for Arkansas Folk Arts includes sections on financial and technical assistance (contact the Folk Arts Coordinator). The Individual Artist Directory links artists with professional opportunities. Artists may apply for inclusion in the AAC's Artists-in-Education or Arkansas Touring Program rosters. The AAC assists artists who cannot afford legal services through referrals to the University of Arkansas at Little Rock Law School Legal Clinic. The Arts Council Library offers a wide selection of reference materials.

ART AWARENESS, INC.

Route 42, Box 177
Lexington, NY 12452
518-989-6433

DIRECT SUPPORT PROGRAMS
➤ **PERFORMING ARTISTS RESIDENCIES**

Purpose: To promote the creation of new work and the presentation of new or established work at the Art Awareness New Lex Theater

Eligibility:
  Special Requirements: Professional artists only; no students
  Art Forms: Theater, music (chamber and jazz), dance, performance art, literature

Type of Support: 2-week to 3-month summer residency including up to $8,000 project budget (most projects range from $2,000 to $5,000), lodging and cooking facilities for groups of up to 12 (additional lodging for larger groups available at nearby facilities at prevailing rates); residents create a new work and perform the newly commissioned work or earlier works

Scope of Program: n/a

Application/Selection Process:
  Deadline: October 15
  Application Procedure: Submit project proposal and budget, samples of work, resumé, supporting materials
  Notification Process: Spring

ARTISTS FOUNDATION

8 Park Plaza
Boston, MA 02116
617-227-2787
CONTACT: BERT SEAGER, MUSIC PERFORMANCE COORDINATOR

PROFILE OF FINANCIAL SUPPORT TO ARTISTS

Total Funding/Value of In-Kind Support: $389,000 for FY 1990

Competition for Funding: Total applications, 2,050; total individuals funded/provided with in-kind support, 112

Grant Range: $1,000-$10,000

DIRECT SUPPORT PROGRAMS

➤ **MASSACHUSETTS ARTISTS FELLOWSHIP PROGRAM**

CONTACT: KATHLEEN BRANDT, FELLOWSHIP DIRECTOR

Purpose: To nurture the work of Massachusetts' best individual artists by recognizing exceptional, completed work

Eligibility:

Residency: Massachusetts, 6 months

Age: 18 or older

Special Requirements: Originating artists only; no undergraduate students; no graduate students enrolled in program related to category of application; previous grantees ineligible for 3 years

Art Forms: Disciplines rotate on 2-year cycle between artists' books/choreography/crafts/drawing/film/interarts/music composition/new genres/photography/printmaking/sculpture/video and design in the built environment/fiction/folk & ethnic arts/nonfiction/painting/playwriting/poetry

Type of Support: $10,000 fellowship awards, $1,000 finalist awards (amounts may change depending on availability of funds)

Scope of Program: 17 fellowship awards, 50 finalist awards for FY 1991

Application/Selection Process:

Deadline: December

Preferred Initial Contact: Call or write for application/guidelines

Application Procedure: Submit application form, samples of work

Selection Process: Peer panel of artists

Notification Process: Letter in June

Formal Report of Grant Required: No

➤ **ARTISTS EMERGENCY ASSISTANCE PROGRAM**

Purpose: To provide grants to artists confronted by medical emergencies, fire, or unexpected catastrophes, and to provide loans when emergency funds are needed to complete an arts project

Eligibility:

Residency: Massachusetts, 1 year

Special Requirements: Professional artists only; no students enrolled in degree-granting programs

Art Forms: Artists' books, choreography, crafts, drawing, film, interarts, music composition, new genres, photography, printmaking, sculpture, video, design in the built environment, fiction, folk & ethnic arts, nonfiction, painting, playwriting, poetry

Type of Support: Up to $500 grant or loan

Scope of Program: n/a

Application/Selection Process:

Deadline: Funds distributed on first-come, first-served basis (fiscal year begins in July)

Preferred Initial Contact: Call to check on availability of funds

Application Procedure: Submit application form, references, proof of status as artist (e.g., samples of work, resumé, reviews)
Notification Process: 5 days after receipt of application

TECHNICAL ASSISTANCE PROGRAMS AND SERVICES
Programs of Special Interest: The Health Education Program provides publications and seminars on hazards in the arts; Arts at CityPlace provides noncommercial performance space and a daily concert series; Volunteer Lawyers for the Arts are available for pro bono and reduced-rate legal services.

ARTIST TRUST

512 Jones Building
1331 Third Avenue
Seattle, WA 98101
206-467-8734
CONTACT: EXECUTIVE DIRECTOR

PROFILE OF FINANCIAL SUPPORT TO ARTISTS
Total Funding/Value of In-Kind Support: $65,000 for FY 1990
Competition for Funding: Total applications, 650; total individuals funded/provided with in-kind support, 50
Grant Range: $300-$5,000

DIRECT SUPPORT PROGRAMS
➤ ARTIST TRUST FELLOWSHIPS
Purpose: To allow individual artists time to create
Eligibility:
  Citizenship: U.S. (resident aliens eligible)
  Residency: Washington State, 1 year
  Special Requirements: Originating artists only; must be Washington State registered voter (except resident aliens); no students
  Art Forms: Dance (choreography), design arts, theater, visual arts, crafts, literature, media arts, music composition
Type of Support: $5,000; recipient must participate in and report on a "Meet the Artist" activity outside of his or her community
Scope of Program: 16 awards (2 in each discipline)
Application/Selection Process:
  Deadline: Multiple deadlines depending on discipline
  Preferred Initial Contact: Call or write for application/guidelines
  Application Procedure: Submit application form, samples of work, resumé

Selection Process: Peer panel of artists, board of directors
Notification Process: Letter 8-12 weeks after deadline
Formal Report of Grant Required: Yes

➤ GAP (GRANTS FOR ARTIST PROJECTS)
Purpose: To allow artists to pursue their own creative development through projects such as development, completion, or presentation of a new work; publication; travel for artistic research or to present or complete work; workshops for professional development
Eligibility:
Residency: Washington State, 1 year
Special Requirements: Must be Washington State registered voter; no students
Art Forms: All disciplines
Type of Support: $100-$750 for specific project
Scope of Program: 41 grants in FY 1990
Application/Selection Process:
Deadlines: 2 per year, usually in spring and fall
Preferred Initial Contact: Call or write for application/guidelines
Application Procedure: Submit application form, samples of work, resumé, project budget
Selection Process: Committee of artists and arts professionals
Notification Process: Letter 8-12 weeks after deadline
Formal Report of Grant Required: Yes

TECHNICAL ASSISTANCE PROGRAMS AND SERVICES
Programs of Special Interest: Artist Trust maintains an information clearinghouse of programs and services of interest to Washington State artists. Extensive data on healthcare options is available. A quarterly journal for artists is also available.

ARTPARK

Box 371
Lewiston, NY 14092
716-745-3377 (Oct-Mar)/716-754-9001 (Apr-Sep)
CONTACT: JOAN McDONOUGH, PARK PROGRAMS DIRECTOR

DIRECT SUPPORT PROGRAMS
➤ ARTPARK RESIDENCIES
Purpose: To offer artists opportunities to experiment, collaborate, and develop their work
Eligibility:
Citizenship: U.S. (workshop visa holders also eligible)

Special Requirements: Practicing professional artists only; no students

Art Forms: Dance, music (band, chamber, choral, new, ethnic, jazz), theater, visual arts, crafts, photography, media arts, interdisciplinary

Type of Support: 1- to 6-week residency including $450 weekly fee, $200 weekly living allowance, and allowances for travel and materials; residents work as project, craft, workshop, or performing artists; performing artists may conduct public performances (often including audience participation, open rehearsals, and discussion groups) or develop new works; most performing artists have a 1- or 2-week run with 2 or more sessions a day

Scope of Program: 100-150 residencies per year

Competition for Support: 600 applications in 1990

Application/Selection Process:

Deadline: Fall

Preferred Initial Contact: Call or write for guidelines

Application Procedure: Submit $20 fee, resumé, samples of work (project, craft, and performing artists), description of proposed work or workshop (craft, workshop, and performing artists)

Selection Process: ArtPark staff (craft, workshop, and performing artists)

Notification Process: Letter in mid-March

Formal Report of Grant Required: Yes

THE ARTS AND HUMANITIES COUNCIL OF TULSA (AHCT)

2210 South Main Street
Tulsa, OK 74114
918-584-3333

DIRECT SUPPORT PROGRAMS
➤ **INDIVIDUAL ARTIST/HUMANITIES GRANTS**

CONTACT: GEORGIA WILLIAMS

Purpose: To allow artists, writers, and scholars to create new works, complete works in progress, or to pursue new avenues of artistic expression and scholarly endeavor

Eligibility:

Residency: Tulsa metropolitan area, 1 year

Art Forms: All disciplines in the arts and humanities

Type of Support: Up to $1,000

Scope of Program: $5,000 awarded annually

Application/Selection Process:
Deadline: April 15
Preferred Initial Contact: Call or write for application/guidelines after March 1
Application Procedure: Submit application form, support material
Selection Process: Board panel
Notification Process: Letter
Formal Report of Grant Required: Yes

TECHNICAL ASSISTANCE PROGRAMS AND SERVICES

Programs of Special Interest: The council sponsors an Artists-in-the-Schools Program (contact Georgia Williams); the Tulsa International Mayfest Arts Festival featuring performing, visual, and literary arts; a workshop series that addresses areas such as grantwriting and marketing; and entertainment hotlines that promote local artists and activities. The Tulsa SummerArts Program hires professional artists to teach talented middle school students (contact Ann Rubenstein).

ARTS AND SCIENCE COUNCIL OF CHARLOTTE/ MECKLENBURG, INC. (ASC)

214 North Church Street
Suite 100
Charlotte, NC 28203
704-372-9667

CONTACT: BECKY W. ABERNETHY, ASSOCIATE DIRECTOR, ARTS EDUCATION/GRANTS

DIRECT SUPPORT PROGRAMS

➤ **EMERGING ARTIST PROGRAM (EAP)**

Purpose: To enable established, professional artists to further their careers and pursue their artistic goals
Eligibility:
Residency: Mecklenburg County, 1 year
Age: 18 or older
Special Requirements: No students; previous grantees ineligible
Art Forms: Dramatic arts, literary arts (includes screenwriting/playwriting), music, dance, visual arts, multi-disciplinary, interdisciplinary

Type of Support: $200-$1,200 to support project that furthers artist's career

Scope of Program: $10,000-$13,500 awarded annually (12 grants, totalling $11,627, in 1991)

Competition for Support: 22 applications in 1991

Application/Selection Process:
  Deadline: Late summer/early fall
  Preferred Initial Contact: Call or write for application/guidelines
  Application Procedure: Submit application form, samples of work, letters of recommendation
  Selection Process: Panel of artists, ASC board and staff
  Notification Process: Letter 2-3 months after application
  Formal Report of Grant Required: No

TECHNICAL ASSISTANCE PROGRAMS AND SERVICES

Programs of Special Interest: ASC staff offer grantwriting assistance for ASC's Emerging Artist Program, North Carolina Arts Council grant programs, and other select local grant programs that the artist has researched; call at least 1 week in advance for appointment. The Cultural Education Research Handbook lists artists who are qualified to teach or perform in local schools; artists who live within a 200-mile radius of Charlotte/Mecklenburg are eligible for inclusion.

THE ARTS ASSEMBLY OF JACKSONVILLE, INC.

128 East Forsyth Street
3rd Floor
Jacksonville, FL 32202
904-358-3600
CONTACT: PAGE D. MANKIN, GRANTS AND SERVICES MANAGER

DIRECT SUPPORT PROGRAMS

➤ **ART VENTURES FUND CAREER OPPORTUNITY GRANTS FOR ARTISTS**

Purpose: To assist artists in attaining the "next level" of their professional development by funding expenses such as materials, advanced study with a mentor, contracting professional services for a project, travel, equipment rental or purchase, living expenses during pursuit of a specific project

Eligibility:
  Citizenship: U.S.
  Residency: First Coast area of Florida (Duval, St. Johns, Baker, Clay, Nassau counties), 1 year
  Age: 18 or older
  Special Requirements: No students
  Art Forms: All disciplines

Type of Support: Up to $5,000

Scope of Program: 11 awards, totalling $25,000, in FY 1990-91

Competition for Support: 44 applications in 1990-91

Application/Selection Process:

    Deadline: June 1

    Preferred Initial Contact: Call or make appointment to seek technical assistance

    Application Procedure: Submit application form, samples of work, 2 letters of recommendation, resumé, project budget; evaluation panel may schedule on-site visits to applicants

    Selection Process: Panel of artists and foundation staff members, Art Ventures Fund Advisory Committee

    Notification Process: Letter in September

    Formal Report of Grant Required: Yes

➤ **FLORIDA TIMES-UNION ARTS EDUCATION MATCHING GRANT PROGRAM**

Purpose: To provide matching funds for schools, PTAs, arts organizations, and artists who wish to provide Duval County school students with basic arts education experiences as a supplement to the basic curriculum

Eligibility:

    Citizenship: U.S.

    Residency: Duval County

    Special Requirements: School principal must agree to present project; must have 1:1 matching funds

    Art Forms: All disciplines

Type of Support: Up to $500 matching grant

Scope of Program: 20 grants in 1991

Application/Selection Process:

    Preferred Initial Contact: Call or write for information

    Application Procedure: Attend workshops, meetings for program development

    Selection Process: Peer panel review

    Notification Process: Letter

    Formal Report of Funding Required: Yes

TECHNICAL ASSISTANCE PROGRAMS AND SERVICES

Programs of Special Interest: The Arts Assembly of Jacksonville administers an Artist in Residence Program for Duval County schools and distributes to First Coast Schools a resource guide publicizing arts education programs available from individual artists. The organization showcases 1,500 artists in the annual multi-disciplinary Arts Mania Festival, which includes special programming by and for the disabled. An annual arts education conference also provides a showcase opportunity for artists.

ARTS COUNCIL FOR CHAUTAUQUA COUNTY

116 East 3rd Street
Jamestown, NY 14701
716-664-2465
CONTACT: PATRICE DANIELSON, DIRECTOR OF ARTISTS SERVICES

DIRECT SUPPORT PROGRAMS

➤ **FUND FOR THE ARTS PROJECTS POOL**
FELLOWSHIPS/DECENTRALIZATION GRANTS
CONTACT: SHARON BARTOO, ASSISTANT TO THE DIRECTOR

Purpose: Fellowships, awarded solely on the basis of creative excellence, assist the career development of Chautauqua County artists; decentralization grants expand and upgrade the arts and cultural programming in Chautauqua and Cattaraugus counties

Eligibility:
   Residency: Chautauqua County, 1 year (Cattaraugus County residents also eligible for decentralization grants)
   Age: 18 or older
   Special Requirements: Decentralization grant applicants must be sponsored by nonprofit organization; previous grantees ineligible for 1 year
   Art Forms: All disciplines

Type of Support: $1,000 fellowships, up to $3,000 decentralization grants

Scope of Program: 5 fellowships and 2 decentralization grants, totalling $6,500, to individuals in FY 1990

Competition for Support: 11 applications in 1990

Application/Selection Process:
   Deadline: October 17
   Preferred Initial Contact: Call or write for application/guidelines
   Application Procedure: Submit application form, samples of work, references, resumé, project budget, proof of residency
   Selection Process: Individuals outside of organization, board
   Notification Process: Letter
   Formal Report of Grant Required: Yes

TECHNICAL ASSISTANCE PROGRAMS AND SERVICES

Programs of Special Interest: The council offers a Group Health Program for working artists and their families; an Artist-in-Residence Program that places rostered artists in county schools for up to 2 weeks; and a reference library and workshops that address artist's needs. The council refers artists to local organizations to hold workshops and lectures/demonstrations.

Arts Council of Hillsborough County

1000 North Ashley
Suite 316
Tampa, FL 33602
813-229-6547
CONTACT: SUSAN EDWARDS, DIRECTOR, PROGRAM SERVICES

Direct Support Programs
➤ **EMERGING ARTIST GRANTS**

Purpose: To assist promising local artists and arts groups in advancing their careers

Eligibility:
   Residency: Hillsborough County
   Special Requirements: Previous grantees ineligible for 2 years
   Art Forms: All disciplines

Type of Support: Up to $1,500 for a specific career development project (includes presentation, equipment, travel, advanced study)

Scope of Program: 33 awards, totalling $25,843, in FY 1990

Competition for Support: 75 applications in 1990

Application/Selection Process:
   Deadline: 2 per year
   Preferred Initial Contact: Call or write for application/guidelines
   Application Procedure: Submit application form, samples of work, resumé, project budget, supporting materials (e.g., reviews, catalogs)
   Selection Process: Panel of artists and arts professionals, board of directors
   Notification Process: Letter 5 weeks after deadline
   Formal Report of Grant Required: Yes

Technical Assistance Programs and Services

Programs of Special Interest: The council sponsors workshops for artists in areas such as basic business matters, marketing, public relations, fundraising, grantwriting, and taxes. The council also offers tax and insurance planning services, and acts as a liaison between artists and those seeking their services and as an arts advocate in legislative and policy matters. Graphics services are offered to artists and nonprofit art groups at nominal rates, and the Arts Library holds a wide reference collection on arts issues. The Arts Directory covers almost 200 arts organizations, and the Facilities Guide provides information about space available for exhibitions and presentations. The council administers an Artists in the Schools Program and sponsors artist lectures and performances.

ARTS COUNCIL OF INDIANAPOLIS (ACI)

47 South Pennsylvania
Suite 703
Indianapolis, IN 46204
317-631-3301
CONTACT: NORMAN BRANDENSTEIN, DIRECTOR OF SERVICES

DIRECT SUPPORT PROGRAMS

➤ **INDIVIDUAL ARTIST FELLOWSHIPS/RECOGNITION GRANTS**

Purpose: To foster the professional development and recognition of established and emerging artists living and working in Indianapolis/Marion County

Eligibility:
  Residency: Marion County, 1 year
  Age: 18 or older
  Special Requirements: No students; previous grantees ineligible; must have 3 years professional stature for fellowship, less than 3 years professional experience for recognition grant
  Art Forms: Performing arts (music, dance, theater, performing folk arts), literary arts, visual arts (including performance art)

Type of Support: $5,000 fellowship, $1,000 recognition grant; recipients conduct community service activity and public forum discussion of fellowship activities

Scope of Program: 3 fellowships (1 in each category), 3 recognition grants (1 in each category)

Competition for Support: 59 applications in 1990

Application/Selection Process:
  Preferred Initial Contact: Call or write for application/guidelines
  Application Procedure: Submit application form, samples of work, artist's statement, resumé, supporting materials (optional)
  Selection Process: Peer panel of artists
  Notification Process: Letter 7 weeks after deadline
  Formal Report of Grant Required: Yes

TECHNICAL ASSISTANCE PROGRAMS AND SERVICES

Programs of Special Interest: The council offers professional development workshops and maintains the unjuried Indianapolis Artist Registry and a project pool for artists.

ARTS COUNCIL OF SANTA CLARA COUNTY

4 North Second Street
Suite 505
San Jose, CA 95113
408-998-2787
CONTACT: LAWRENCE THOO, ASSOCIATE DIRECTOR

DIRECT SUPPORT PROGRAMS
➤ **INDIVIDUAL ARTIST ACCOMPLISHMENT AWARDS**

Purpose: To secure for the South Bay a robust cultural environment equal to the dynamism, pluralism, and spirit of adventure that characterize life in Silicon Valley

Eligibility:
    Residency: Santa Clara County
    Age: 18 or older
    Art Forms: All; eligible disciplines rotate

Type of Support: $1,000-$1,500

Scope of Program: 7 awards, totalling $9,000, in FY 1990

Application/Selection Process:
    Preferred Initial Contact: Call or write for application/guidelines
    Application Procedure: Submit application form, samples of work, financial statement, project budget
    Selection Process: Peer panel of artists

TECHNICAL ASSISTANCE PROGRAMS AND SERVICES

Programs of Special Interest: A registry of individual Santa Clara County artists is in development.

ARTS FOR GREATER ROCHESTER, INC. (AGR)

335 E. Main Street
Suite 200
Rochester, NY 14604
716-546-5602
CONTACT: GINNA MOSESON, PROGRAM DIRECTOR

DIRECT SUPPORT PROGRAMS
➤ **AGR DECENTRALIZATION GRANT PROGRAM**

Purpose: To enable nonprofit community organizations and arts groups to sponsor arts-related projects of community interest that are open to the public

Eligibility:
    Citizenship: U.S.

Residency: Monroe County
Age: 18 or older
Special Requirements: Artists must apply through a Monroe County nonprofit organization
Art Forms: All disciplines
Type of Support: Up to $5,000 for a specific project
Scope of Program: 24 grants, totalling $39,300, awarded to organizations in 1990
Application/Selection Process:
Deadline: Late August
Preferred Initial Contact: Call or write for application/guidelines; attend application seminar
Application Procedure: Sponsor submits application form, financial statement, project budget, artist's resumé, samples of work
Selection Process: Peer panel of artists and community representatives
Notification Process: Letter 3-4 months after deadline
Formal Report of Grant Required: Yes

TECHNICAL ASSISTANCE PROGRAMS AND SERVICES
Programs of Special Interest: AGR's Volunteer Lawyers for the Arts Program provides legal assistance to Monroe County artists with annual incomes below $15,000 a year and nonprofit organizations who bring in less than $100,000 a year. AGR maintains a reference library, and offers group insurance for artists and networking opportunities through weekly breakfasts and an annual "artist to artists" event. The organization has also launched an arts-in-education program.

ARTS FOUNDATION OF MICHIGAN (AFM)

1553 Woodward Avenue
Suite 1352
Detroit, MI 48226
313-964-2244
CONTACT: KIMBERLY ADAMS, EXECUTIVE DIRECTOR

DIRECT SUPPORT PROGRAMS
➤ **MICHIGAN ARTS AWARDS/GENERAL GRANTS PROGRAM**
Purpose: Michigan Arts Awards recognize individual and groups of artists in Michigan for consistent dedication and vision in advancing standards of creativity and excellence in the fine and performing arts; General Grants fund new works by individual artists that demonstrate the quality, originality, and professional execution of the artist
Eligibility:
Residency: Michigan

Special Requirements: Professional artists only; must apply with nonprofit sponsoring organization (General Grants); project must involve the creation of a new work and be accessible to the public (General Grants); limit 1 General Grant per year to an artist or sponsoring organization; Michigan Arts Awards by nomination only

Art Forms: All disciplines

Type of Support: $5,000 Michigan Arts Awards (winner must give brief presentation at awards ceremony in Detroit); General Grants average $1,500 to fund salaries of artists working on specific project

Scope of Program: 3 Michigan Arts Awards in 1991; 10 General Grants, totalling $17,670, in 1990

Application/Selection Process:

Preferred Initial Contact: Call or write for information

Application Procedure: Michigan Arts Awards by nomination only (nominator submits nomination form, samples of artist's work, letters of recommendation); for General Grants, sponsoring organization submits application form, financial statement, project narrative and budget

Selection Process: Board of directors

Notification Process: Letter

Formal Report of Funding Required: Yes

TECHNICAL ASSISTANCE PROGRAMS AND SERVICES

Programs of Special Interest: AFM has co-published the Michigan Arts Resource Guide, which includes information on technical assistance, career development, sources of funding, internships, and fellowships. The Competition Program supplies funds for cash prizes to Michigan organizations sponsoring arts competitions.

ARTS INTERNATIONAL (AI)

Institute of International Education
809 United Nations Plaza
New York, NY 10017
212-984-5370

PROFILE OF FINANCIAL SUPPORT TO ARTISTS

Total Funding/Value of In-Kind Support: $785,000 in FY 1990 (includes Fund for U.S. Artists grants to organizations)

Competition for Funding: Total applications, n/a; total individuals funded/provided with in-kind support, 63

Grant Range: Up to $10,000

DIRECT SUPPORT PROGRAMS

➤ **THE FUND FOR U.S. ARTISTS AT INTERNATIONAL FESTIVALS AND EXHIBITIONS—PERFORMING ARTS GRANTS**

Purpose: To make grants to individual performing artists and organizations that have been invited to participate in international festivals

Eligibility:

Citizenship: U.S. (permanent residents also eligible)

Special Requirements: No students; preference to applicants who have not received support from the Fund for U.S. Artists in the past year; proposals that reflect the cultural and regional diversity of the U.S. are encouraged; festival must be truly international in scope, reach a diverse audience, and be substantially performance-oriented

Art Forms: Performing arts

Type of Support: $500-$2,500 for individuals

Scope of Program: 27 grants to individuals in 1990

Application/Selection Process:

Deadline: February 1, June 1, November 1 (apply to deadline that falls at least 2 months before festival begins)

Preferred Initial Contact: Call or write for application/guidelines

Application Procedure: Submit application form, samples of work, letter of invitation, project description and budget, biographies of artists involved

Selection Process: Panel of experts in the performing arts and presenters with international experience

Notification Process: Letter

Formal Report of Grant Required: Yes

➤ **MUSICA INTERNATIONAL TRAVEL GRANTS FOR MUSICIANS AND COMPOSERS**

Purpose: To provide travel grants for U.S. musicians and composers to participate in international competitions, workshops/symposia, and composer premieres

Eligibility:

Citizenship: U.S. (permanent residents also eligible)

Special Requirements: Musicians must be participating in an international competition or attending a workshop/symposium; composers must be attending a premiere of their work abroad; musicians who have received Musica grants in previous years are ineligible

Art Forms: Music (composition and performance); eligible categories rotate

Type of Support: Up to $1,000 for travel

Scope of Program: 24 grants, totalling $15,000, in 1990

Application/Selection Process:

Deadline: January, June

Preferred Initial Contact: Call or write for application/guidelines

Application Procedure: Submit application form, samples of work, 2 letters of recommendation, photocopy of application or letter of invitation to event
Selection Process: Peer panel of artists and art professionals
Notification Process: Letter 7-9 weeks after deadline
Formal Report of Grant Required: Yes

➤ **CINTAS FELLOWSHIPS**
CONTACT: VANESSA PALMER, PROGRAM OFFICER
Phone: 212-984-5564

Purpose: To acknowledge demonstrated creative accomplishments and to encourage the professional development of talented creative artists
Eligibility:
   Citizenship: Cuba (artists with Cuban parent or grandparent also eligible)
   Residency: Outside of Cuba
   Special Requirements: Originating, professional artists only; fellowships not awarded more than twice to the same person
   Art Forms: Architecture, literature, music composition, visual arts
Type of Support: $10,000; recipients contribute or dedicate 1 work completed during fellowship to the Cintas Foundation
Scope of Program: $120,000 awarded in 1990
Application/Selection Process:
   Deadline: March 1
   Preferred Initial Contact: Write for application/guidelines
   Application Procedure: Submit application form, samples of work, letters of recommendation, artist's statement
   Selection Process: Peer panel of artists
   Notification Process: Letter in August
   Formal Report of Grant Required: Yes

ARTS MIDWEST

528 Hennepin Avenue, Suite 310
Minneapolis, MN 55403
612-341-0755
CONTACT: JEANNE LAKSO, SENIOR PROGRAM DIRECTOR

DIRECT SUPPORT PROGRAMS
➤ **JAZZ MASTERS AWARDS**
CONTACT: JANIS LANE-EWART

Purpose: To honor regional jazz artists for outstanding artistry as performers and educators, lifelong achievements in jazz, and continuous contributions to jazz and their communities
Eligibility:
   Residency: Illinois, Indiana, Iowa, Michigan, Minnesota, North Dakota, Ohio, South Dakota, Wisconsin

Special Requirements: Artist must be nominated by a member of his or her community

Art Forms: Music (jazz)

Type of Support: $5,000

Scope of Program: 3 awards per year

Competition for Support: 50 nominations in 1990

Application/Selection Process:

Preferred Initial Contact: Call or write for information

Application Procedure: Nominator submits samples of work

Selection Process: Peer panel of artists

Notification Process: Phone call or letter

TECHNICAL ASSISTANCE PROGRAMS AND SERVICES

Programs of Special Interest: Meet the Composer/Midwest provides fee support to midwestern organizations presenting composers in conjunction with performances of the composers' works (deadlines, May 1, October 31). The computerized Jazz Referral Service network links musicians, jazz support organizations, jazz educators, jazz media, and jazz recording distributors. The Jazz Program also publishes a series of how-to booklets for the jazz community, a free monthly Jazz Calendar, and the free quarterly Jazzletter (contact Janis Lane-Ewart, Senior Program Director). The Performing Arts Touring Program provides funding to midwestern presenting organizations to sponsor performances by rostered artists. To be eligible for the program's roster, artists must reside in the Midwest and have at least 2 years professional performance experience (contact Bobbi Morris, Program Associate). The Dance on Tour Program provides fee support to midwestern organizations presenting out-of-region or out-of-state professional dance artists/companies (contact Bobbi Morris, Program Associate). The Midwest Presenters Directory profiles college and community performing arts spaces and presenting organizations. The computerized Local Arts Agency/Community Arts Agency Directory describes the programs and services of over 300 agencies.

ARTS UNITED OF GREATER FORT WAYNE

114 East Superior Street
Fort Wayne, IN 46802
219-424-0646
CONTACT: ROBERT BUSH, PRESIDENT

DIRECT SUPPORT PROGRAMS

➤ **INDIVIDUAL ARTIST FELLOWSHIPS**

Purpose: To foster the development of northeast Indiana's artists by funding activities significant to an artist's professional growth and recognition or for creation or completion of a project

Eligibility:
   Residency: Northeast Indiana (Adams, Allen, DeKalb, Huntington, LaGrange, Noble, Steuben, Wabash, Wells, and Whitely counties), 1 year
   Special Requirements: Previous grantees ineligible for 1 cycle; Master Fellowship applicants must have significant professional record of working, exhibiting, or performing in their art form
   Art Forms: Eligible disciplines rotate on a 2-year cycle between dance/music/theater/literature/performing folk arts (1991-92) and visual arts/crafts/media arts/design arts/visual folk arts (1992-93)
Type of Support: Master Fellowships, up to $1,000; Associate Fellowships, up to $500
Scope of Program: 6 awards in 1990
Competition for Support: 18 applications in 1990
Application/Selection Process:
   Deadline: April 1
   Application Procedure: Submit application form, samples of work, resumé, programs or reviews (if available)
   Selection Process: Panel of experts in eligible disciplines, board of directors
   Notification Process: 2 months after deadline
   Formal Report of Grant Required: Yes

AUGUSTA SYMPHONY ORCHESTRA

P.O. Box 579
Augusta, GA 30903
404-826-4705

DIRECT SUPPORT PROGRAMS
➤ **WILLIAM S. BOYD COMPETITION FOR YOUNG PIANISTS**
Purpose: To encourage young pianists by providing financial assistance and audience exposure
Eligibility:
   Age: 16-30
   Art Forms: Music performance (piano)
Type of Support: 1st prize, $5,000 and engagement with Augusta Symphony; 2nd prize, $3,000; 3rd prize, $2,000
Scope of Program: Biennial competition
Competition for Support: 25 applications in 1991
Application/Selection Process:
   Deadline: February 1 (odd-numbered years)
   Preferred Initial Contact: Call or write for application/guidelines

Application Procedure: Submit application form, samples of work; 6 semi-finalists invited to competition
Selection Process: Peer panel of artists
Notification Process: Letter
Formal Report of Grant Required: No

GINA BACHAUER INTERNATIONAL PIANO FOUNDATION

P.O. Box 11664
Salt Lake City, UT 84147
801-521-9200
CONTACT: PAUL C. POLLEI, ARTISTIC DIRECTOR/FOUNDER

DIRECT SUPPORT PROGRAMS

➤ **GINA BACHAUER INTERNATIONAL PIANO COMPETITION**
Purpose: To recognize and encourage superb artistry and to assist career development for deserving young pianists
Eligibility:
    Age: 19-32
    Art Forms: Music performance (piano)
Type of Support: 1st prize, $3,000, grand piano, New York debut, management, concert engagements; 2nd prize, $5,000, concert engagements; 3rd prize, $3,000; other finalists and semi-finalists receive cash awards
Scope of Program: Triennial competition (10 cash awards in 1991)
Competition for Support: 300 applications
Application/Selection Process:
    Deadline: January 1 (1994, 1997)
    Preferred Initial Contact: Call or write for application/guidelines (available 18 months before competition)
    Application Procedure: Submit application form, $35 fee, resumé; taped or live audition required (live auditions held 1 year before competition); artists invited to participate in June competition pay $75 fee
    Selection Process: Panels of judges
    Notification Process: Letter by February 15 (preliminaries), winners announced at competition

Baltimore Opera

101 West Read Street
Suite 605
Baltimore, MD 21201
301-727-0592
CONTACT: JAMES HARP

Direct Support Programs

➤ **BALTIMORE OPERA VOCAL COMPETITION FOR AMERICAN OPERATIC ARTISTS**

Purpose: To award and encourage outstanding operatic talent

Eligibility:
  Citizenship: U.S.
  Age: 20-35
  Special Requirements: Previous 1st prize winners ineligible; applicants who have performed or are contracted to perform a lead role with an OPERA America member company with an annual budget in excess of $2,000,000 are ineligible
  Art Forms: Vocal performance (opera)

Type of Support: 1st prize, $12,500; 2nd prize, $7,000; 3rd prize, $5,000; 4th, 5th, and 6th prizes, $1,000; prizes must be used for career development; semi-finalists receive stipend

Scope of Program: Annual competition

Competition for Support: 121 applications in 1991

Application/Selection Process:
  Deadline: May 15
  Preferred Initial Contact: Write for application/guidelines
  Application Procedure: Submit application form, $35 fee, 2 letters of recommendation; auditions in June
  Selection Process: Baltimore Opera Auditions Committee selects semi-finalists; national panel of judges selects finalists and winners
  Notification Process: Letter for preliminaries

BRITISH COLUMBIA MINISTRY OF MUNICIPAL AFFAIRS, RECREATION AND CULTURE-CULTURAL SERVICES BRANCH (CSB)

800 Johnson Street
Sixth Floor
Victoria, British Columbia
Canada V8V 1X4
604-356-1728
CONTACT: KATE WILKINSON, COORDINATOR, ARTS AWARDS PROGRAMS

PROFILE OF FINANCIAL SUPPORT TO ARTISTS

Total Funding/Value of In-Kind Support: n/a

Competition for Funding: Total applications, 700; total individuals funded/provided with in-kind support, 400

Grant Range: $200-$25,000 for FY 1991-92

DIRECT SUPPORT PROGRAMS

➤ **PROFESSIONAL DEVELOPMENT ASSISTANCE PROGRAM**

Purpose: To assist tuition and course-related costs for the purposes of upgrading and improving the skills of practicing professional artists or arts managers

Eligibility:

Citizenship: Canada (landed immigrants also eligible)

Residency: Preference to applicants who have resided in British Columbia for at least 1 year

Special Requirements: Minimum 2 years professional experience; artists who are changing disciplines must have minimum 5 years' professional experience; limit 1 grant per year

Art Forms: Arts administration, literature, dance (performance, choreography), film/video, multi-disciplinary, musicological and conservation studies, music (performance, composition), book publishing studies, theater (acting, directing, technical), visual arts

Type of Support: Maximum $1,500 for up to 50% of tuition and course-related costs for concentrated period of study at recognized educational institution

Scope of Program: n/a

Application/Selection Process:

Deadline: May 15, September 15, January 15

Preferred Initial Contact: Consult with Arts Awards Coordinator before applying

Application Procedure: Submit application form, samples of work, letters of reference, letter of acceptance from institution, project description and budget, resumé

Selection Process: Organization staff

Notification Process: Letter 2 months after deadline
Formal Report of Grant Required: Yes

➤ **PERFORMING ARTS RECOMMENDOR PROGRAM**

Purpose: To provide support to independent performing artists for the creation of new work

Eligibility:
    Citizenship: Canada (landed immigrants also eligible)
    Residency: British Columbia, 1 year
    Special Requirements: Must have completed all basic training and have had at least 1 work produced professionally; must apply through approved recommendor company for support; artist must control expenditure of project funds
    Art Forms: Choreography, music composition, playwriting

Type of Support: $500-$5,000

Scope of Program: $120,000 in 1991

Application/Selection Process:
    Preferred Initial Contact: Call or write for list of recommendor companies
    Application Procedure: Depends on recommendor company
    Selection Process: Recommendor company
    Formal Report of Grant Required: Yes

➤ **INTERNATIONAL TOURING**

CONTACT: PROGRAM COORDINATOR
Phone: 604-356-1718

Purpose: To provide assistance to professional British Columbia artists or arts organizations touring outside of Canada to develop a proven or potential international market for the artist

Eligibility:
    Citizenship: Canada (landed immigrants also eligible)
    Residency: British Columbia
    Special Requirements: Professional artists only; tour must have a diversified revenue base, including a significant percentage of earned income; priority to requests received a year or more in advance; attendance at international conferences, competitions, or symposia ineligible
    Art Forms: All disciplines (priority to artists who, by the nature of their work, must tour)

Type of Support: Average $2,000-$5,000

Scope of Program: 8 awards in 1991

Application/Selection Process:
    Deadline: At least 6 months prior to start of tour (preference to applications received at least 1 year before tour begins)
    Preferred Initial Contact: Call program coordinator before applying
    Application Procedure: Submit letter of request, tour itinerary, confirmations of engagement (if possible), tour budget

Selection Process: Committee review
Notification Process: Letter 3 months after application
Formal Report of Grant Required: Yes

TECHNICAL ASSISTANCE PROGRAMS AND SERVICES
Programs of Special Interest: The Artists in Schools Program provides matching funds to British Columbia schools to sponsor performances or 3-day to 4-month residencies by professional artists. The Arts Resource Touring Subsidy (ARTS) Program provides matching funds to British Columbia nonprofit community organizations that wish to sponsor visiting Canadian professional performing arts events.

BROADCAST MUSIC, INC. (BMI)

320 West 57th Street
New York, NY 10019
212-586-2000

TECHNICAL ASSISTANCE PROGRAMS AND SERVICES
Programs of Special Interest: Lyricists, librettists, and composers for musical theater may apply to the BMI-Lehman Engel Theater Workshop series, a free 2- to 3-year program of weekly workshops with experienced musical theater professionals (contact Norma Grossman, Director, Musical Theater; deadlines are May 1 for librettists, August 1 for composers and lyricists). Jazz composers may apply to the BMI Jazz Composers Workshops, a free 2- to 3-year biweekly series; some participants' works are performed in BMI-sponsored concerts (contact Burt Korall, Director of Jazz Composers Workshops; deadline, early August).

BRONX COUNCIL ON THE ARTS (BCA)

1738 Hone Avenue
Bronx, NY 10461
212-931-9500
CONTACT: BETTI-SUE HERTZ

PROFILE OF FINANCIAL SUPPORT TO ARTISTS
Total Funding/Value of In-Kind Support: $27,000 for FY 1990
Competition for Funding: Total applications, 190; total individuals funded/provided with in-kind support, 18
Grant Range: $1,500

DIRECT SUPPORT PROGRAMS

➤ **BRONX RECOGNIZES ITS OWN (BRIO)**

Purpose: To assist the career development of Bronx artists

Eligibility:
    Residency: Bronx County
    Age: 18 or older
    Special Requirements: No degree-seeking students; previous grantees ineligible for 1 year
    Art Forms: Architecture, choreography, crafts, fiction, film, interpretive performance, music composition, nonfiction literature, painting, performance art/emergent forms, photography, playwriting/screenwriting, poetry, printmaking/drawing/artists' books, sculpture, video

Type of Support: $1,500; recipients must perform public service activity

Scope of Program: 16 awards in 1990

Application/Selection Process:
    Deadline: Mid-January
    Preferred Initial Contact: Call or write for application/guidelines
    Application Procedure: Submit application form, samples of work, resumé
    Selection Process: Peer panel of artists
    Notification Process: Letter in April
    Formal Report of Grant Required: Yes

➤ **COMMUNITY REGRANTS PROGRAM**

CONTACT: ED FRIEDMAN, DIRECTOR OF ARTS SERVICES

Purpose: To fund ongoing programs of local community-based organizations that meet high standards of artistic quality and provide needed community service; programs developed by arts and community organizations that reach unserviced or underserved areas of the Bronx; and programs that serve or sponsor individual artists

Eligibility:
    Special Requirements: Individual artists must find nonprofit organization to apply on their behalf
    Art Forms: All disciplines

Type of Support: $350-$3,000 awards to organizations in 1990

Scope of Program: $110,000 total funding in 1990

Application/Selection Process:
    Deadline: August 15
    Preferred Initial Contact: Call or write for application/guidelines
    Application Procedure: Sponsoring organization submits application form, financial statement, project budget, samples of artist's work, artist's resume
    Selection Process: Individuals from outside of BCA
    Notification Process: Letter 5 months after deadline
    Formal Report of Grant Required: Yes

TECHNICAL ASSISTANCE PROGRAMS AND SERVICES

Programs of Special Interest: The council provides seminars in such areas as management, fundraising, marketing and public relations, and offers the arts constituency graphic and public relations services, fundraising assistance, computer services, and special mailing privileges. BCA conducts arts-in-education programs and holds summer neighborhood festivals.

THE MARY INGRAHAM BUNTING INSTITUTE OF RADCLIFFE COLLEGE

34 Concord Avenue
Cambridge, MA 02138
617-495-8212
CONTACT: CHIHO TOKITA, FELLOWSHIP COORDINATOR

DIRECT SUPPORT PROGRAMS

➤ **BUNTING FELLOWSHIP PROGRAM**

Purpose: To support women who wish to advance their careers through independent work in academic and professional fields and in the creative arts

Eligibility:
  Special Requirements: Women only; artists must demonstrate significant professional accomplishments (participation in group or one-person shows) and must reside in Cambridge/Boston area during residency
  Art Forms: Visual arts, film/video, performing arts, literary arts (scholars in any field also eligible)

Type of Support: 1-year residency including $21,500 stipend for FY 1991-92, studio space, access to most Harvard/Radcliffe resources; fellows present work-in-progress at public colloquia or in exhibitions

Scope of Program: 10 awards per year (4 to artists in 1991-92)

Competition for Support: 138 applications in 1991-92

Application/Selection Process:
  Deadline: October 15
  Preferred Initial Contact: Call or write for application/guidelines
  Application Procedure: Submit application form, $40 fee, samples of work, resumé, references
  Selection Process: Peer panel of artists, interdisciplinary final selection committee
  Notification Process: Letter in April

TECHNICAL ASSISTANCE PROGRAMS AND SERVICES
Programs of Special Interest: The Affiliation Program offers appointees the use of studio space and other resources available to Bunting Fellows for 1 year. Applicants must meet same eligibility requirements as Bunting Fellows.

THE BUSH FOUNDATION

E-900 First National Bank Building
332 Minnesota Street
St. Paul, MN 55101
612-227-0891
CONTACT: SALLY DIXON, DIRECTOR, BUSH ARTIST FELLOWSHIPS

DIRECT SUPPORT PROGRAMS
➤ **BUSH ARTIST FELLOWSHIPS**
Purpose: To allow Minnesota, North Dakota, South Dakota, and western Wisconsin artists a significant period of uninterrupted time for work in their chosen form
Eligibility:
  Residency: Minnesota, North Dakota, South Dakota, western Wisconsin
  Age: 25 or older
  Special Requirements: No students or nonprofessionals; previous grantees ineligible for 5 years
  Art Forms: Visual arts, film/video, scriptworks (playwriting/screenwriting), choreography, music composition, literature; scriptworks, music composition, and choreography eligible in alternating years only
Type of Support: $26,000 total stipend for 12-18 months' work on projects outlined in applicant's proposal, plus up to $7,000 for production and travel costs
Scope of Program: 15 awards, totalling $495,000, in 1989-90
Competition for Support: 460 applications in 1989-90
Application/Selection Process:
  Deadline: Fall
  Preferred Initial Contact: Call or write for application/guidelines
  Application Procedure: Submit application, samples of work, resumé, references
  Selection Process: Peer panel of artists, interdisciplinary panel
  Notification Process: Letter 1 week after panel deliberations
  Formal Report of Grant Required: Yes

CALIFORNIA ARTS COUNCIL (CAC)

2411 Alhambra Boulevard
Sacramento, CA 95817
916-739-3186

PROFILE OF FINANCIAL SUPPORT TO ARTISTS

Total Funding/Value of In-Kind Support: $1,912,925 for FY 1989-90
Competition for Funding: Total applications, 2,065; total individuals funded/provided with in-kind support, 273
Grant Range: n/a

DIRECT SUPPORT PROGRAMS

➤ **ARTISTS FELLOWSHIP PROGRAM**

CONTACT: ANNE BOURGET, PROGRAM ADMINISTRATOR

Purpose: To recognize and honor the work and careers of California artists who are primary creators of their art

Eligibility:
   Residency: California, 1 year
   Special Requirements: Must be originating, professional artist with at least 5 years experience; no students enrolled in degree-granting programs; previous applicants ineligible for 3 years; previous grantees ineligible for 7 years; collaborations limited to 2 artists
   Art Forms: Disciplines rotate on 4-year cycle among media arts/new genres, 1991-92; literature, 1992-93; visual arts, 1993-94; performing arts (choreography, music composition, playwriting), 1994-95

Type of Support: $5,000

Scope of Program: 63 fellowships in FY 1989-90

Application/Selection Process:
   Deadline: October
   Application Procedure: Submit application form, resumé, artist's statement (optional), samples of work
   Selection Process: Peer panel of artists and arts professionals
   Notification Process: Letter in July
   Formal Report of Grant Required: Yes

➤ **ARTIST IN RESIDENCE PROGRAM**

CONTACT: BRENDA BERLIN, ARTISTS IN SCHOOLS; ANDREA S. TEMKIN, ARTISTS SERVING SPECIAL CONSTITUENTS; LUCERO ARELLANO, ARTISTS IN COMMUNITIES

Purpose: To offer long-term interaction of professional artists in many disciplines with the public in workshops sponsored by schools, non-profit arts organizations, government units, and tribal councils

Eligibility:
   Special Requirements: Professional artists with at least 3 years experience; artist must apply with sponsor; no full-time students in degree programs

Art Forms: All disciplines

Type of Support: 3- to 11-month residencies; artists earn $1,300 per month for 80 hours project time

Scope of Program: 185 residencies, totalling $1,405,555, in FY 1989-90

Application/Selection Process:
   Deadline: February
   Preferred Initial Contact: Call or write for application/guidelines; 30-minute Artist in Residence video available
   Application Procedure: Submit application form, artist's statement, sponsor organization statement, project description and budget, supporting materials (e.g., reviews, performance programs), letters of support, samples of work
   Selection Process: Peer panel of artists and arts professionals
   Notification Process: 4-6 months after deadline

➤ **TRADITIONAL FOLK ARTS PROGRAM**
CONTACT: BARBARA LAPAN RAHM, FOLKLORIST

Purpose: To identify, assist, encourage, and honor those traditional folk artists whose community- or family-based arts have endured through several generations, carry a sense of community aesthetic, and demonstrate the highest artistic excellence

Eligibility:
   Residency: California
   Special Requirements: Must be a member of the cultural community—family, ethnic, tribal, religious—where the art form originates
   Art Forms: Folk arts

Type of Support: Funds for apprenticeship

Scope of Program: 13 apprenticeships, totalling $32,370, in FY 1989-90

Application/Selection Process:
   Deadline: May 1
   Preferred Initial Contact: Call or write for application/guidelines

TECHNICAL ASSISTANCE PROGRAMS AND SERVICES
CONTACT: PHILIP HORN, TOURING AND PRESENTING PROGRAM MANAGER
Phone: 916-445-9688

Programs of Special Interest: The Touring/Presenting Program publishes the annual California Touring Artists Directory of California performing artists and companies, which is distributed to presenting organizations nationwide. Artists included in the directory are eligible for CAC fee subsidies through presenting organizations. The Touring/Presenting Program staff offer consultations, seminars, and workshops to artists.

CALIFORNIA COMMUNITY FOUNDATION

606 South Olive Street
Suite 2400
Los Angeles, CA 90014
213-413-4042
CONTACT: SUSAN FONG, PROGRAM OFFICER

DIRECT SUPPORT PROGRAMS
➤ **BRODY ARTS FUND FELLOWSHIPS**

Purpose: To strengthen and encourage emerging artists representing communities often outside the mainstream

Eligibility:
   Residency: Los Angeles County
   Age: No undergraduate students or younger
   Special Requirements: No students; preference given to ethnic and other minorities (e.g., disabled, gay)
   Art Forms: Disciplines rotate on a 3-year cycle among literature/ media arts, 1991; visual arts, 1992; performing arts (including dance performance or choreography, acting, directing, music performance or composition, conducting)

Type of Support: $2,500

Scope of Program: 10 awards in 1989-90

Application/Selection Process:
   Deadline: September 15
   Preferred Initial Contact: Call or write for application/guidelines
   Application Procedure: Submit application form, samples of work, resumé, supporting materials (e.g., reviews, references)
   Selection Process: Multi-disciplinary panels, staff
   Notification Process: Phone call and follow-up letter in December
   Formal Report of Grant Required: Yes

TECHNICAL ASSISTANCE PROGRAMS AND SERVICES

Programs of Special Interest: The California Community Foundation maintains the Funding Information Center, a collection focusing on regional grant and fellowship opportunities. Grantseekers should call for reservations.

CAMARGO FOUNDATION

P.O. Box 32
East Haddam, CT 06423
CONTACT: JANE VIGGIANI, EXECUTIVE SECRETARY

DIRECT SUPPORT PROGRAMS
➤ RESIDENCY GRANTS

Purpose: To provide residencies on the French Riviera to artists
Eligibility:
    Citizenship: U.S., Canada (permanent residents also eligible)
    Art Forms: Music composition, photography, visual arts
Type of Support: 4-month spring or fall residency, including housing and work space
Scope of Program: 2 residencies per year in each discipline
Application/Selection Process:
    Deadline: March 15
    Preferred Initial Contact: Write for application/guidelines
    Application Procedure: Submit application form, samples of work, letters of recommendation
    Selection Process: Committee
    Notification Process: Letter by April 15
    Formal Report of Grant Required: Yes

THE CANADA COUNCIL/CONSEIL DES ARTS DU CANADA (CC/CAC)

99 Metcalfe Street
P.O. Box 1047
Ottawa, Ontario
Canada K1P 5V8
613-598-4365
CONTACT: INFORMATION OFFICER, COMMUNICATIONS SECTION

PROFILE OF FINANCIAL SUPPORT TO ARTISTS
Total Funding/Value of In-Kind Support: n/a
Competition for Funding: Total applications, n/a; total individuals funded/provided with in-kind support, 1,200
Grant Range: n/a

DIRECT SUPPORT PROGRAMS
➤ DANCE—ARTS GRANTS "A"/ARTS GRANTS "B"
CONTACT: DANCE OFFICER, ARTS AWARDS SERVICE
Phone: 613-598-4315

Purpose: To help individual dance artists working with classical forms, modern dance, and experimental dance pursue their personal development through research, the creation of new work, or the undertaking of further study past basic training

Eligibility:
>   **Citizenship:** Canada (permanent residents also eligible)
>   **Age:** 18 or older
>   **Special Requirements:** Applicants must have completed basic training and be professionals or on the threshold of a professional career; choreographers must have had at least 5 works performed in public; applicants training to become dance teachers must have been professional dancers, and former ballet dancers must be enrolled in a teacher-training course in a professional school; ballet teachers must be teaching at a nonprofit institution that trains full-time students planning professional careers in dance; modern dance teachers must teach dance professionals or students within the framework of a professional program; individuals training to become dance therapists are ineligible; Arts Grants "A" applicants must have made a nationally or internationally recognized contribution to dance over a number of years
>   **Art Forms:** Dance (dancers, choreographers, teachers, notators, curators, critics, technicians, historians, accompanists, and administrators are eligible)

Type of Support: Arts Grants "A" up to $32,000 for living expenses (up to $2,500 per month) and project costs, and up to $2,800 for travel costs; Arts Grants "B" up to $18,000 for living expenses (up to $1,500 a month) project costs, and travel costs

Scope of Program: 2 Arts Grants "A", 22 Arts Grants "B" in FY 1989-90

Application/Selection Process:
>   **Deadline:** April 1 (Arts Grants "B" only), October 1
>   **Preferred Initial Contact:** Call or write for guidelines; submit project description and resumé before applying
>   **Application Procedure:** Submit application form, biography, 3 letters of appraisal, samples of work, project budget; Arts Grants "B" applicants in performing, choreography, and teaching are also auditioned and interviewed
>   **Selection Process:** Staff, peer panel of artists, board
>   **Notification Process:** Letter
>   **Formal Report of Grant Required:** Yes

> ➤ **DANCE—SHORT-TERM GRANTS/TRAVEL GRANTS**

CONTACT: DANCE OFFICER, ARTS AWARDS SERVICE
Phone: 613-598-4315

Purpose: Short-Term Grants help individual dance artists working with classical forms, modern dance, and experimental dance pursue creative work or artistic development projects; Travel Grants assist these individuals with travel expenses on occasions important to their careers

Eligibility:
Citizenship: Canada (permanent residents also eligible)
Age: 18 or older
Special Requirements: Applicants must have completed basic training and be professionals or on the threshold of a professional career; choreographers must have had at least 5 works performed in public; applicants training to become dance teachers must have been professional dancers, and former ballet dancers must be enrolled in a teacher-training course in a professional school; ballet teachers must be teaching at a nonprofit institution that trains full-time students planning professional careers in dance; modern dance teachers must teach dance professionals or students within the framework of a professional program; individuals training to become dance therapists are ineligible
Art Forms: Dance (dancers, choreographers, teachers, notators, curators, critics, technicians, historians, accompanists, and administrators are eligible)
Type of Support: Short-Term Grants up to $4,000 for living expenses (up to $1,500 per month) and project costs, plus travel allowance up to $2,800; Travel Grants up to $2,800 for travel, plus living and local transportation expenses up to $500
Scope of Program: 32 Short-Term Grants, 3 Travel Grants in FY 1989-90
Application/Selection Process:
Deadline: March 1, April 1, September 1, October 15
Preferred Initial Contact: Call or write for guidelines; submit project description and resumé before applying
Application Procedure: Submit application form, biography, 3 letters of appraisal, samples of work, project budget; applicants in performing, choreography, and teaching are also auditioned and interviewed
Selection Process: Staff, peer panel of artists, board
Notification Process: Letter
Formal Report of Grant Required: Yes

➤ **MUSIC I GRANTS—ARTS GRANTS "B"**
CONTACT: MUSIC OFFICER, ARTS AWARDS SERVICE
Phone: 613-598-4316

Purpose: To assist singers and instrumentalists in classical music to pursue advanced study with a private teacher or at a teaching institution
Eligibility:
Citizenship: Canada (permanent residents also eligible)
Age: 17 or older
Special Requirements: Must have completed basic training (instrumentalists must have an undergraduate degree) and be embarking on either advanced studies or a professional career
Art Forms: Classical music performance
Type of Support: Up to $18,000 for living expenses (up to $1,500 a month) and project costs, plus travel costs up to $2,800

Scope of Program: n/a

Application/Selection Process:

Deadline: December 1

Preferred Initial Contact: Call or write for guidelines; submit project description and resumé before applying

Application Procedure: Submit application form, project description and budget, samples of work, 3 letters of appraisal; selected candidates must also audition

Selection Process: Staff, peer panel of artists, board

Notification Process: Letter 3-5 months after deadline

Formal Report of Grant Required: Yes

➤ ARTISTS IN MID-CAREER GRANTS

CONTACT: MUSIC OFFICER, ARTS AWARDS SERVICE

Phone: 613-598-4316

Purpose: To assist performers of classical music who are in mid-career and need time for renewal

Eligibility:

Citizenship: Canada (permanent residents also eligible)

Special Requirements: Must have completed studies at least 5 years ago, have performed for a minimum of 5 years, have an active professional career, and have an established national reputation; any proposal, except completion of a graduate degree, that meets the applicant's artistic needs is eligible

Art Forms: Classical music performance (singing, instrumental)

Type of Support: Up to $18,000 for living expenses (up to $1,500 a month) project costs, and travel costs (grants for 2 collaborative artists up to $25,000; for 3 artists up to $30,000)

Scope of Program: n/a

Application/Selection Process:

Deadline: May 1

Preferred Initial Contact: Call or write for guidelines; submit project description and resumé before applying

Application Procedure: Submit application form, project description and budget, samples of work, critical notices, 3 letters of appraisal

Selection Process: Staff, peer panel of artists, board

Notification Process: Letter 3 months after deadline

➤ MUSIC I—SHORT-TERM GRANTS/TRAVEL GRANTS

CONTACT: MUSIC OFFICER, ARTS AWARDS SERVICE

Phone: 613-598-4316

Purpose: Short-Term Grants assist singers and instrumentalists in classical music to pursue advanced study with a private teacher or at a teaching institution, and assist voice teachers of professional singers with projects to improve their teaching methods; Travel Grants assist these individuals with travel expenses on occasions important to their careers

Eligibility:
   Citizenship: Canada (permanent residents also eligible)
   Age: 17 or older
   Special Requirements: Must have completed basic training (instrumentalists must have undergraduate degree) and be embarking on either advanced studies or a professional career; Travel Grant applicants intending to attend an international competition must have been a finalist in a recognized national competition; grants may not be used to pay recording costs, promotional costs, or production costs
   Art Forms: Classical music performance (instrumentalists, singers, and teachers of professional singers are eligible)

Type of Support: Project Grants up to $4,000 for living expenses (up to $1,500 per month) and project costs, plus travel allowance up to $2,800; Travel Grants up to $2,800 for travel, plus living and local transportation expenses up to $500

Scope of Program: n/a

Application/Selection Process:
   Deadline: March 1, June 1, September 1
   Preferred Initial Contact: Call or write for guidelines; submit project description and resumé before applying
   Application Procedure: Submit application form, project description and budget, samples of work, repertoire list, 3 letters of appraisal; selected candidates must also audition
   Selection Process: Staff, peer panel of artists, board
   Notification Process: Letter 6-8 weeks after deadline
   Formal Report of Grant Required: Yes

➤ **MUSIC II—ARTS GRANTS "A"/ARTS GRANTS "B"**
CONTACT: MUSIC OFFICER, ARTS AWARDS SERVICE
Phone: 613-598-4317

Purpose: Arts Grants "A" provide free time for personal artistic activity to artists who have made nationally or internationally recognized contributions in music; Arts Grants "B" support personal creative activity over a period of time

Eligibility:
   Citizenship: Canada (permanent residents also eligible)
   Age: 17 or older
   Special Requirements: Composers of classical music must have completed basic training and be embarking on either advanced studies or a professional career; composers or performers of nonclassical music must have at least 2 years professional experience; choral conductors must have completed basic training and conducted outside of the institution where they trained; grants may not be used for recording costs, promotional costs, or production costs
   Art Forms: Classical music (composition), nonclassical music (performance, lyricizing, composition), choral conducting, instrument-making

Type of Support: Arts Grants "A" up to $32,000 for living expenses (up to $2,500 per month) and project costs, and up to $2,800 for travel costs; Arts Grants "B" up to $18,000 for living expenses (up to $1,500 a month) project costs, and travel costs

Scope of Program: n/a

Application/Selection Process:

   Deadline: Arts Grants "A", October 1; Arts Grants "B", April 1, October 1 (choral conductors only)

   Preferred Initial Contact: Call or write for guidelines; submit project description and resumé before applying

   Application Procedure: Submit application form, samples of work (except conductors; instrument-makers submit slides), project budget; choral conductors must audition; selected instrument-makers present instruments to jury

   Selection Process: Staff, peer panel of artists, board

   Notification Process: Letter 3-5 months after deadline

   Formal Report of Grant Required: Yes

➤ **MUSIC II—SHORT-TERM GRANTS/TRAVEL GRANTS**

CONTACT: MUSIC OFFICER, ARTS AWARDS SERVICE

Phone: 613-598-4317

Purpose: Project Grants support artists who need a short period of time in which to pursue their own creative work or artistic development; Travel Grants assist artists who need to travel on occasions important to their careers

Eligibility:

   Citizenship: Canada (permanent residents also eligible)

   Age: 17 or older

   Special Requirements: Composers of classical music must have completed basic training and be embarking on either advanced studies or a professional career; composers or performers of nonclassical music must have at least 2 years professional experience; choral conductors must have completed basic training and conducted outside of the institution where they trained; grants may not be used for recording costs, promotional costs, or production costs; Travel Grant applicants planning to attend an international competition must already have been finalists in a recognized national competition

   Art Forms: Classical music (composition), nonclassical music (performance, lyricizing, composition), choral conducting, instrument-making

Type of Support: Short-Term Grants up to $4,000 for living expenses (up to $1,500 per month) and project costs, plus travel allowance up to $2,800; Travel Grants up to $2,800 for travel, plus living and local transportation expenses up to $500

Scope of Program: n/a

Application/Selection Process:

   Deadline: 2-4 per year, depending on field

Preferred Initial Contact: Call or write for guidelines; submit project description and resumé before applying

Application Procedure: Submit application form, samples of work (except conductors; instrument-makers submit slides), project description and budget; conductors must audition; selected instrument-makers present instruments to jury

Selection Process: Staff, peer panel of artists, board

Notification Process: Letter 6-8 weeks after deadline

Formal Report of Grant Required: Yes

➤ **COMMISSIONING OF CANADIAN COMPOSITIONS PROGRAM**
CONTACT: MUSIC AND OPERA SECTION
Phone: 613-598-4352

Purpose: To encourage the creation of new works by Canadian composers through providing grants to artists/companies to cover composers' fees and copying costs

Eligibility:
  Citizenship: Composer must be Canadian citizen or permanent resident
  Special Requirements: Artists or groups of artists may apply to commission a work for a premiere performance; commissions for functional music by dance companies, independent choreographers, theater companies, and multi-media groups are also eligible (functional music projects must generally involve innovative use of music); composers may not apply for grant themselves; film scores are ineligible; premiere performance date and location must be set
  Art Forms: Music composition

Type of Support: $296-$20,000 grant range in 1989-90

Scope of Program: 94 commissions in 1989-90

Application/Selection Process:
  Deadline: March 1, September 1, November 1
  Preferred Initial Contact: Call or write for information
  Application Procedure: Commissioner submits application form, samples of work, and other materials as requested
  Selection Process: Jury of music professionals
  Notification Process: Letter 2 months after deadline

➤ **THEATER—ARTS GRANTS "A"/ARTS GRANTS "B"**
CONTACT: THEATRE OFFICER, ARTS AWARDS SERVICE
Phone: 613-598-4314

Purpose: To support theater artists' professional development projects such as study, research, apprenticeships, internships, residencies, or the creation of new works

Eligibility:
  Citizenship: Canada (permanent residents also eligible)
  Age: 18 or older
  Special Requirements: Must have worked for the equivalent of 2 years or more with 1 or more professional theater companies, or

in independent professional productions; teachers must be working with professionals or teaching in institutions recognized by the Canada Council as offering professional training; composers must have written music for at least 2 professional theater productions; Arts Grants "A" applicants must have made nationally or internationally recognized contributions in their field over a number of years; grants may not be used for full production of a completed work

Art Forms: Theater and musical theater (actors, administrators, clowns, composers, critics, designers, dramaturgs, mimes, movement teachers, playwrights, production personnel, puppeteers, stage managers, and voice teachers are eligible)

Type of Support: Arts Grants "A" up to $32,000 for living expenses (up to $2,500 per month) and project costs, and up to $2,800 for travel costs; Arts Grants "B" up to $18,000 for living expenses (up to $1,500 a month) project costs, and travel costs

Scope of Program: 4 Arts Grants "A", 40 Arts Grants "B" in FY 1989-90

Application/Selection Process:

Deadline: April 1, October 15 (Arts Grants "B" only)

Preferred Initial Contact: Call or write for guidelines; submit project description and resumé before applying

Application Procedure: Submit application form, project description and budget, resumé, 3 letters of recommendation, samples of work (designers, playwrights, critics only)

Selection Process: Staff, peer panel of artists, board

Notification Process: 3-5 months after deadline

Formal Report of Grant Required: Yes

➤ **THEATRE—SHORT-TERM GRANTS/TRAVEL GRANTS**

CONTACT: THEATRE OFFICER, ARTS AWARDS SERVICE

Phone: 613-598-4314

Purpose: Short-Term Grants support theater artists' professional development projects such as study, research, apprenticeships, internships, residencies, or the creation of new works; Travel Grants support theater artists who need to travel on occasions important to their careers

Eligibility:

Citizenship: Canada (permanent residents also eligible)

Age: 18 or older

Special Requirements: Must have worked for the equivalent of 2 years or more with 1 or more professional theater companies, or in independent professional productions; teachers must be working with professionals or teaching in institutions recognized by the Canada Council as offering professional training; composers must have written music for at least 2 professional theater productions; grants may not be used for full production of a completed work

Art Forms: Theater and musical theater (actors, administrators, clowns, composers, critics, designers, dramaturgs, mimes, movement teachers, playwrights, production personnel, puppeteers, stage managers, and voice teachers are eligible)

Type of Support: Short-Term Grants up to $4,000 for living expenses (up to $1,500 per month) and project costs, plus travel allowance up to $2,800; Travel Grants up to $2,800 for travel, plus living and local transportation expenses up to $500

Scope of Program: 62 Project Grants, 24 Travel Grants in FY 1989-90

Application/Selection Process:
    Deadline: January 15, May 1, September 15
    Preferred Initial Contact: Call or write for guidelines; submit project description and resumé before applying
    Application Procedure: Submit application form, project description and budget, resumé, 3 letters of recommendation, samples of work (designers, playwrights, critics only)
    Selection Process: Staff, peer panel of artists, board
    Notification Process: 8 weeks after deadline

➤ **INTERDISCIPLINARY WORK AND PERFORMANCE ART—ARTS GRANTS "A"/ARTS GRANTS "B"**

CONTACT: ANNE-MARIE HOGUE, ARTS AWARDS SERVICE

Phone: 613-598-4318

Purpose: Arts Grants "A" provide free time for personal artistic activity to artists who have made nationally or internationally recognized contributions in interdisciplinary work or performance art; Arts Grants "B" support personal creative activity over a period of time

Eligibility:
    Citizenship: Canada (permanent residents also eligible)
    Age: 18 or older
    Special Requirements: Professional artists only; must have completed formal training, accomplished a body of work, and had at least 1 professional exhibition, publication, or production of an interdisciplinary or performance work
    Art Forms: Interdisciplinary, performance art

Type of Support: Arts Grants "A" up to $40,000 for materials and services (up to $10,000) and living expenses (up to $2,500 per month); Arts Grants "B" up to $18,000 for living expenses (up to $1,500 per month), project costs, and travel costs (Arts Grants "B" for 2 collaborative artists up to $25,000; for 3 artists up to $30,000)

Scope of Program: 2 Arts Grants "A", 4 Arts Grants "B" in FY 1989-90

Application/Selection Process:
    Deadline: April 1 (Arts Grants "B" only), October 1
    Preferred Initial Contact: Call or write for guidelines; submit project description and resumé before applying
    Application Procedure: Submit application form, samples of work, references, project budget
    Selection Process: Peer panel of artists, organization staff, board of directors
    Notification Process: Letter 3-5 months after deadline
    Formal Report of Grant Required: Yes

➤ **INTERDISCIPLINARY WORK AND PERFORMANCE ART—SHORT-TERM GRANTS/TRAVEL GRANTS**

CONTACT: ANNE-MARIE HOGUE, ARTS AWARDS SERVICE

Phone: 613-598-4318

Purpose: Short-Term Grants support artists who need a short period of time in which to pursue their own creative work or artistic development; Travel Grants assist artists who need to travel on occasions important to their careers

Eligibility:
   Citizenship: Canada (permanent residents also eligible)
   Age: 18 or older
   Special Requirements: Professional artists only; must have completed formal training, accomplished a body of work, and had at least 1 professional exhibition, publication, or production of an interdisciplinary or performance work; previous applicants ineligible for 1 year
   Art Forms: Interdisciplinary, performance art

Type of Support: Project Grants up to $4,000 for living expenses (up to $1,500 per month) and project costs, plus travel allowance up to $2,800; Travel Grants up to $2,800 for travel, plus living and local transportation expenses up to $500

Scope of Program: 15 Project Grants, 5 Travel Grants in FY 1989-90

Application/Selection Process:
   Deadline: May 1, October 1
   Preferred Initial Contact: Call or write for guidelines; submit project description and resumé before applying
   Application Procedure: Submit application form, samples of work, references, project budget
   Selection Process: Peer panel of artists, organization staff, board of directors
   Notification Process: Letter 6-8 weeks after deadline
   Formal Report of Grant Required: Yes

➤ **PARIS STUDIOS**

CONTACT: ANNE-MARIE HOGUE, ARTS AWARDS SERVICE

Phone: 613-598-4318

Purpose: To provide studios at the Cité Internationale des Arts to Canadian visual artists and musicians wishing to pursue creative work, and to musicians wishing to pursue advanced studies

Eligibility:
   Citizenship: Canada (permanent residents also eligible)
   Age: 18 or older
   Special Requirements: Must have completed basic training
   Art Forms: Visual arts, music

Type of Support: Studio space and living accommodations at the Cité Internationale des Arts for 3 months to 1 year at a moderate cost, stipend for living and travel expenses

Scope of Program: 7 awards in FY 1989-90

Application/Selection Process:
 Deadline: December 1 (singers and instrumentalists in classical music), April 1 (all other applicants)
 Preferred Initial Contact: Call or write for application
 Selection Process: Staff, peer panel of artists, board
 Notification Process: Letter in July

➤ **EXPLORATIONS PROGRAM GRANTS**
 Phone: 613-598-4337 (British Columbia and the Prairie Provinces); 613-598-4340 (Ontario); 613-598-4338 (Québec); 613-598-4339 (Atlantic Provinces and Northern Canada)

Purpose: To provide emerging artists, professional artists who are changing disciplines, and new arts organizations with project grants in support of innovative approaches to artistic creation and new developments in the arts

Eligibility:
 Citizenship: Canada (permanent residents also eligible)
 Special Requirements: Grantees of other Canada Council programs generally ineligible
 Art Forms: All disciplines

Type of Support: Up to $16,000 for living expenses (maximum $1,100 per month for up to 9 months) and project expenses

Scope of Program: 97 grants, totalling $1,061,269, awarded in September 1990 competition

Application/Selection Process:
 Deadline: January 15, May 1, September 15
 Preferred Initial Contact: Call or write for guidelines; submit project description and resumé before applying
 Application Procedure: Submit application form, 3 references, project budget, samples of work (optional)
 Selection Process: Regional jury
 Notification Process: Letter 4 months after deadline
 Formal Report of Grant Required: Yes

TECHNICAL ASSISTANCE PROGRAMS AND SERVICES

Programs of Special Interest: Touring Grants provide financial assistance to Canadian performing artists, ensembles, and companies undertaking regional or national tours (contact Touring Office: 613-598-4395 (dance, theater); 613-598-4396 (music)). The Dance Section's Independance Program provides performing opportunities for independent Canadian choreographers by supporting presenters of new and innovative dance who are working in small-scale situations. The Dance Section also offers a small number of project grants to independent ballet, modern, and experimental dance artists who are incorporated as nonprofit organizations (contact 613-598-4360). The Touring Office's Concerts Canada Program offers grants to artists' managers to develop the careers of Canadian classical musicians (contact Micheline Lesage, 613-598-4396). The Music and Opera Section offers Grants for Sound Recording to independent Canadian producers and Canadian record companies to support the recording of classical and contemporary music performed or composed by Canadians; Grants for the Production of New Works in Opera and Musical Theater to producing groups to support commissions, workshopping of works-in-progress, and artistic and production costs; and Assistance to Community Choirs to retain the services of professional musicians.

CATHEDRAL ARTS

47 South Pennsylvania
Suite 401
Indianapolis, IN 46204
317-637-4574
CONTACT: THOMAS BECZKIEWICZ, EXECUTIVE DIRECTOR

DIRECT SUPPORT PROGRAMS

➤ **THE INTERNATIONAL VIOLIN COMPETITION OF INDIANAPOLIS**

Purpose: To launch young violinists on major international careers

Eligibility:
Age: 18-30
Art Forms: Music performance (violin)

Type of Support: 1st prize, $20,000, Carnegie Hall recital and 75 other recital and major orchestra engagements in North America and Europe; 2nd prize, $15,000; 3rd prize, $10,000; 4th prize, $5,000; 5th prize, $4,000; 6th prize, $3,000; semi-finalists, $500; other cash prizes, $350-$1,000

Scope of Program: Competition held every 4 years

Competition for Support: 200 applications in 1990

Application/Selection Process:
Deadline: February 1994 for September 1994 competition
Preferred Initial Contact: Write for application/guidelines
Application Procedure: Submit application form, $25 fee, certified samples of work, 3 letters of recommendation, certificate of musical education or equivalent, printed programs, reviews; selected applicants attend 3-week competition in Indianapolis (free round-trip airfare available from 1 European and 1 Far Eastern city; housing, meals, and in-city travel provided)
Selection Process: Jury
Notification Process: Letter to applicants selected to compete; winners announced at competition

CENTER FOR CONTEMPORARY OPERA, INC. (CCO)

Gracie Station
P.O. Box 1350
New York, NY 10028-0010
212-308-6728
CONTACT: RICHARD MARSHALL, DIRECTOR

DIRECT SUPPORT PROGRAMS
➤ **THE INTERNATIONAL OPERA SINGERS COMPETITION**

Purpose: To assist singers who are ready for careers in gaining recognition and to acquaint them with the contemporary operatic repertory written in English

Eligibility:
  Special Requirements: Previous 1st place winners are ineligible
  Art Forms: Music performance (opera vocal)

Type of Support: 1st prize, $1,000 and recital at Carnegie Hall's Weill Recital Hall; 2nd prize, $500; 3rd prize, $250; $300 award for vocal artistry; $300 award for best performance of contemporary aria; master class for finalists

Scope of Program: Annual competition

Competition for Support: 85 applications in 1991

Application/Selection Process:
  Deadline: January 15
  Preferred Initial Contact: Call or write for application/guidelines
  Application Procedure: Submit application form, samples of work, $30 fee; semi-finalists invited to May competition in New York
  Selection Process: 3 panels of music professionals
  Notification Process: Letter (preliminaries)

CENTRUM

Fort Worden State Park
P.O. Box 1158
Port Townsend, WA 98368
206-385-3102

DIRECT SUPPORT PROGRAMS
➤ **ARTIST RESIDENCIES**

Purpose: To provide artists with privacy, freedom from everyday obligations, and time to create

Eligibility:
  Special Requirements: Previous recipients ineligible for 1 year
  Art Forms: Architecture, interdisciplinary collaborative projects, visual arts, performing arts, literature

Type of Support: Individuals may apply for 1-month music (composition or performance) residency that includes housing, a piano, and $75 weekly stipend; individuals or groups may apply for performing arts residencies lasting up to 1 month that include housing, working facilities, and $75 total weekly stipend

Scope of Program: 32 residencies in 1990 (5 to performing artists)

Application/Selection Process:

    Deadline: April 1 (September-January), October 1 (February-May)

    Application Procedure: Submit application form, project proposal, resumé, samples of work

    Selection Process: Peer panel of artists

    Notification Process: Within 2 months of deadline

CHANGE, INC.

P.O. Box 705
Cooper Station
New York, NY 10276
212-473-3742
CONTACT: DENISE LE BEAU, BOARD MEMBER

DIRECT SUPPORT PROGRAMS

➤ **EMERGENCY ASSISTANCE**

Purpose: To assist artists in need of emergency financial aid

Eligibility:

    Special Requirements: Professional artists only; no students; applicants must require emergency financial aid; no previous recipients

    Art Forms: All disciplines

Type of Support: $100-$500; medical treatment, including free hospitalization, also available for qualified applicants from facilities working with Change, Inc.

Scope of Program: 75 grants, totalling $37,500, in 1990

Competition for Support: 200 applications in 1990

Application/Selection Process:

    Deadline: None

    Preferred Initial Contact: Request guidelines by mail or phone, or write letter of application

    Application Procedure: Submit letter detailing financial emergency, documentation of emergency (e.g., copies of eviction notice, outstanding bills), resumé, samples of work, reviews, performance announcements, 2 letters of recommendation from individuals in field verifying professional status

    Selection Process: Board of directors

    Notification Process: Letter within a few days if necessary

    Formal Report of Grant Required: No

CHICAGO DEPARTMENT OF CULTURAL AFFAIRS

Cultural Grants
78 East Washington Street
Chicago, IL 60602
312-744-1742
CONTACT: MARY E. YOUNG, DIRECTOR OF CULTURAL GRANTS

PROFILE OF FINANCIAL SUPPORT TO ARTISTS

Total Funding/Value of In-Kind Support: $367,400 for FY 1990 (includes project support to small arts organizations)

Competition for Funding: Total applications, 483; total individuals funded/provided with in-kind support, 343

Grant Range: $1,000-$4,000

DIRECT SUPPORT PROGRAMS

➤ **COMMUNITY ARTS ASSISTANCE PROGRAM**

CONTACT: COMMUNITY ARTS ASSISTANCE STAFF

Phone: 312-744-6630

Purpose: To promote Chicago's new and emerging multi-ethnic artists and nonprofit arts organizations by funding technical assistance, professional, or organizational development projects that address a specific need or problem

Eligibility:
   Citizenship: U.S. (permanent residents also eligible)
   Residency: Chicago, 6 months
   Age: 21 or older
   Art Forms: All disciplines

Type of Support: Up to $1,500 for project

Scope of Program: 268 grants in FY 1990 (includes grants to organizations)

Application/Selection Process:
   Deadline: January
   Preferred Initial Contact: Call or write for application/guidelines
   Application Procedure: Submit application form, samples of work
   Selection Process: Panel of artists and arts professionals
   Notification Process: Letter 4-5 months after deadline
   Formal Report of Grant Required: Yes

➤ **NEIGHBORHOOD ARTS PROGRAM (NAP)**

CONTACT: NEIGHBORHOOD ARTS STAFF

Phone: 312-744-6630

Purpose: To encourage and support the presentation of high-quality instructional arts projects that benefit youth, elderly, and disabled participants in Chicago's low- and moderate-income neighborhoods

Eligibility:
   Citizenship: U.S. (permanent residents also eligible)
   Residency: Chicago, 6 months
   Age: 21 or older
   Special Requirements: 1 project per applicant per funding year
   Art Forms: All disciplines
Type of Support: Up to $4,000 for project materials, artists' salaries, and support services
Scope of Program: 75 grants in FY 1990
Application/Selection Process:
   Deadline: August
   Preferred Initial Contact: Call or write for application/guidelines
   Application Procedure: Submit application forms, samples of work
   Selection Process: Panel of artists and arts professionals
   Notification Process: Letter 4-5 months after deadline
   Formal Report of Grant Required: Yes

TECHNICAL ASSISTANCE PROGRAMS AND SERVICES

Programs of Special Interest: The Performing Arts Registry is a referral service for individuals and groups. Arts Resource Workshops and Special Events, conducted by professional consultants, are offered to artists, students, and arts administrators for nominal fees or free. The Arts Technical Assistance Guide outlines local and regional nonprofit arts organizations that provide technical assistance and funding opportunities for artists and arts administrators.

CITY OF RALEIGH ARTS COMMISSION (CORAC)

305 South Blount Street
Raleigh, NC 27601
919-831-6234
CONTACT: ELAINE LORBER, EXECUTIVE DIRECTOR

DIRECT SUPPORT PROGRAMS
➤ **EMERGING ARTISTS PROGRAM**

Purpose: To recognize and provide financial support for committed, accomplished artists in their formative years, enabling them to advance their work and careers as developing professionals
Eligibility:
   Residency: Wake County, 1 year
   Age: 18 or older
   Special Requirements: Previous grantees ineligible for 3 years
   Art Forms: All disciplines

Type of Support: $250-$1,000 for specific professional development projects (e.g., expenses for training, travel, space, supplies)

Scope of Program: 10 awards in 1989-90

Application/Selection Process:
  Deadline: November 8
  Preferred Initial Contact: Call for application/guidelines
  Application Procedure: Confer with executive director before applying; submit application form, project proposal and budget, resumé, letters of recommendation, references, samples of work, supporting materials (optional)
  Notification Process: Letter 6-7 weeks after deadline
  Formal Report of Grant Required: Yes

THE CLEVELAND INSTITUTE OF MUSIC

11021 East Boulevard
Cleveland, OH 44106
216-791-5165
CONTACT: KAREN KNOWLTON, EXECUTIVE DIRECTOR

DIRECT SUPPORT PROGRAMS
➤ **ROBERT CASADESUS INTERNATIONAL PIANO COMPETITION**

Purpose: To promote pianistic excellence, clarity of expression, and the highest level of musicianship as exemplified by the French pianist Robert Casadesus

Eligibility:
  Age: 17-32
  Art Forms: Music performance (piano)

Type of Support: 1st prize, $10,000, New York debut, 2 years of free management, engagements with the Cleveland Orchestra and others; 2nd prize, $4,000; 3rd prize, $3,000; 4th prize, $2,000; 5th prize, $1,500; 6th prize, $1,000; other cash prizes, $500-$1,000

Scope of Program: Biennial competition

Competition for Support: 180 applications in 1991

Application/Selection Process:
  Deadline: Spring (odd-numbered years)
  Preferred Initial Contact: Call or write for application/guidelines
  Application Procedure: Submit application form, $30 fee, samples of work; selected applicants compete in Cleveland (all competitors receive free room and board for duration of competition)
  Selection Process: Screening committee, international panel of judges
  Notification Process: Letter to preliminary applicants; winners announced at competition

VAN CLIBURN FOUNDATION

2525 Ridgmar Boulevard
Suite 307
Fort Worth, TX 76116
817-738-6536
CONTACT: DENISE CHUPP, ARTISTIC ADMINISTRATOR

DIRECT SUPPORT PROGRAMS

➤ VAN CLIBURN INTERNATIONAL PIANO COMPETITION

Purpose: To provide an opportunity for the most gifted and communicative musicians to rise to the top and gain recognition

Eligibility:

Age: 19-30

Special Requirements: Must be a very advanced pianist with a large active repertoire and rather considerable performance experience; previous 1st prize winners ineligible

Art Forms: Music performance (piano)

Type of Support: 1st prize, $15,000, Carnegie Hall recital, concert tours, recording opportunities; 2nd prize, $10,000, New York recital, concert tours, recording opportunities; 3rd prize, $7,500, concert tours, recording opportunities; 4th prize, $5,000; 5th prize, $3,500; 6th prize, $2,000; Best Performance of Chamber Music, $1,000; Highest Ranking Pianist of the United States, $1,000; Jury Discretionary Award, $4,000

Scope of Program: 1 competition every 4 years

Competition for Support: 250 applications in 1988-89

Application/Selection Process:

Deadline: Next competition to be held in 1993 (application deadline in 1992)

Preferred Initial Contact: Call or write for application/guidelines

Application Procedure: Submit application form, application fee, references, professional biography, repertoire list, press clippings; audition also required (auditions are held at several sites worldwide; videotapes of performances are reviewed in Fort Worth)

Selection Process: Individuals outside of organization

Notification Process: Applicants invited to competition are notified by phone and letter

Formal Report of Grant Required: No

COLORADO COUNCIL ON THE ARTS AND HUMANITIES (CCAH)

750 Pennsylvania Street
Denver, CO 80203-3699
303-894-2619
CONTACT: DANIEL A. SALAZAR, DIRECTOR, INDIVIDUAL ARTIST PROGRAM

PROFILE OF FINANCIAL SUPPORT TO ARTISTS

Total Funding/Value of In-Kind Support: $62,000 for FY 1990

Competition for Funding: Total applications, 200; total individuals funded/provided with in-kind support, 26

Grant Range: Up to $4,000

DIRECT SUPPORT PROGRAMS

➤ **INDIVIDUAL ARTIST PROGRAM CREATIVE FELLOWSHIPS**

Purpose: To recognize outstanding accomplishments among creative artists

Eligibility:
　　Citizenship: U.S.
　　Residency: Colorado, 1 year
　　Age: 18 or older
　　Special Requirements: Originating artists only; no full-time students enrolled in degree programs; previous grantees ineligible for 1 round
　　Art Forms: Choreography, music composition, performance art, visual arts, crafts, photography, media arts, interdisciplinary, folk arts, fiction, poetry, playwriting; eligible disciplines rotate on 3-year cycle

Type of Support: $4,000 and assistance in promoting work

Scope of Program: 12 awards in 1990

Application/Selection Process:
　　Deadline: November 15
　　Preferred Initial Contact: Call or write for application/guidelines
　　Application Procedure: Submit application form, samples of work
　　Selection Process: Panel of artists and arts professionals
　　Notification Process: Letter by May
　　Formal Report of Grant Required: Yes

➤ **COLORADO VISIONS PROJECT GRANTS FOR INDIVIDUAL ARTISTS (COVISIONS)**

Purpose: To provide direct financial support for artists to produce and showcase within their community art work that reflects the community's culture, history, and architecture, that fosters respect for diverse cultures, and that explores contemporary social issues

Eligibility:
  Citizenship: U.S.
  Residency: Colorado
  Age: 18 or older
  Special Requirements: Originating artists only
  Art Forms: Media arts (film, video, audio), performing arts (choreography, music composition, performance art), visual arts, design arts, folk arts, literature
Type of Support: Up to $2,000 project grant
Scope of Program: $20,000 budget for 1991
Application/Selection Process:
  Deadline: December 10
  Preferred Initial Contact: Call or write for application/guidelines
  Application Procedure: Submit application form, samples of work, project proposal and budget
  Selection Process: Community Arts Development panel including artists
  Notification Process: Letter in February
  Formal Report of Grant Required: Yes

➤ **FOLK ARTS MASTER APPRENTICE PROGRAM**

Purpose: To support the maintenance and development of the traditional art forms as found in Colorado
Eligibility:
  Citizenship: U.S.
  Residency: Colorado
  Special Requirements: Master and apprentice must apply together; apprentice must have experience in art form
  Art Forms: Folk arts (performing, visual)
Type of Support: Up to $2,000 for 2-month apprenticeship ($1,000 master's fees, $1,000 for apprentice's essential materials and travel)
Scope of Program: 17 apprenticeships in 1991
Application/Selection Process:
  Deadline: September 1
  Preferred Initial Contact: Call or write for application/guidelines
  Application Procedure: Submit application form, samples of work, project description and budget, references
  Selection Process: Panel of folklorists and folk artists
  Notification Process: Letter in November
  Formal Report of Grant Required: Yes

TECHNICAL ASSISTANCE PROGRAMS AND SERVICES

Programs of Special Interest: Artists accepted to the CCAH Resource List are eligible for 1-week to 5-month residencies in schools through the Artist in Residence Program (contact Patty Ortiz, Artists in Residence Program Director, Young Audiences, Inc., 1415 Larimer Street, Denver, CO 80202; 303-825-3650).

COLUMBIA UNIVERSITY

Department of Music
703 Dodge Hall
New York, NY 10027
212-854-3825
CONTACT: LISA DAVENPORT, ADMINISTRATIVE AIDE

DIRECT SUPPORT PROGRAMS
➤ JOSEPH H. BEARNS PRIZE IN MUSIC
Purpose: To encourage young American composers
Eligibility:
  Citizenship: U.S.
  Age: 18-25
  Art Forms: Music composition
Type of Support: $1,500-$2,500 in 1991
Scope of Program: 2 awards, totalling $4,000, in 1991
Competition for Support: 73 applications in 1991
Application/Selection Process:
  Deadline: Early February
  Preferred Initial Contact: Call or write for information
  Selection Process: Panel
  Notification Process: Letter

COMMONWEALTH COUNCIL FOR ARTS AND CULTURE (CCAC)

P.O. Box 553, CHRB
Saipan, MP 96950
670-322-9982/9983
CONTACT: ANA S. TEREGEYO, EXECUTIVE DIRECTOR

DIRECT SUPPORT PROGRAMS
➤ GRANTS-IN-AID
Eligibility:
  Citizenship: U.S.
  Residency: Northern Mariana Islands
  Art Forms: Dance, media arts, music (performance, composition), photography, theater, visual arts, literature, folk arts
Type of Support: $200-$2,000
Scope of Program: 6-9 awards per year

Application/Selection Process:
Deadline: 90 days before project begins
Preferred Initial Contact: Call or write the CCAC main office on
Saipan or CCAC board representatives for application/guidelines

CONCERT ARTISTS GUILD (CAG)

850 Seventh Avenue
New York, NY 10019
212-333-5200

DIRECT SUPPORT PROGRAMS
➤ THE NEW YORK COMPETITION

Purpose: To develop the performing careers of emerging musical artists
Eligibility:
Special Requirements: Artists under full-service U.S. management ineligible (except singers who are under management for
opera only); chamber ensembles, except duo pianists, must
generally consist of at least 3 artists; previous grantees ineligible
Art Forms: Classical instrumentalists (except organists),
vocalists, chamber ensembles

Type of Support: $2,500, New York recital, free 2-year management
by CAG, commissioned work written by composer of artist's
choice, recording contract

Scope of Program: 2 awards in 1990 (1 soloist, 1 ensemble)

Competition for Support: 425 applications in 1990

Application/Selection Process:
Deadline: Late December
Preferred Initial Contact: Call or write for application form
Application Procedure: Submit application form, $40 fee,
sample of work; semi-finals and finals held in New York in May
Selection Process: Jury of musicians from outside of organization
Notification Process: Letter (1st round), phone call (semi-final
and final rounds)

CONNECTICUT COMMISSION ON THE ARTS

227 Lawrence Street
Hartford, CT 06106
203-566-4770
CONTACT: LINDA DENTE, PROGRAM MANAGER

DIRECT SUPPORT PROGRAMS
➤ **ARTIST GRANTS**

Purpose: To provide financial support for artists to develop new work or to complete works-in-progress

Eligibility:
  Residency: Connecticut, 2 years
  Special Requirements: Originating artists only; no students; previous recipients ineligible for 3 years
  Art Forms: Visual arts (including performance art), poetry, playwriting, fiction, music composition, choreography, film, video, new genres (categories alternate each year between visual arts and other disciplines)

Type of Support: $5,000

Scope of Program: 20 awards in FY 1989-90

Competition for Support: 300 applications in 1989-90

Application/Selection Process:
  Deadline: January 29
  Preferred Initial Contact: Call or write for application/guidelines
  Application Procedure: Submit application form, samples of work, resumé, project budget
  Selection Process: Peer panel of artists
  Notification Process: Letter in June
  Formal Report of Grant Required: Yes

TECHNICAL ASSISTANCE PROGRAMS AND SERVICES
Programs of Special Interest: Connecticut-based writers, storytellers, poets, and performing groups of 2 or more may apply for inclusion in the annual CONNTOURS Directory; sponsors who present these artists are eligible for fee subsidies from the commission, and the artists receive consultative services regarding publicity and marketing. Artists selected for the CONNTOURS Program are also featured in various annual showcases. The commission maintains a list of presenters available to solo performers and ensembles. Artist residencies are available through the Arts-in-Education Program. Connecticut Volunteer Lawyers for the Arts provides a variety of free services for eligible artists and holds an annual Arts Law Conference.

CONTEMPORARY ARTS CENTER

900 Camp Street
P.O. Box 30498
New Orleans, LA 70190
504-523-1216
CONTACT: ELENA RONQUILLO

DIRECT SUPPORT PROGRAMS
➤ **REGIONAL ARTISTS PROJECTS (RAP)**

Purpose: To provide funding for experimental or multi-cultural projects that would not be considered in other arts discipline categories because they are new or nontraditional forms

Eligibility:
  Citizenship: U.S.
  Residency: Louisiana, Mississippi, Alabama, Arkansas
  Art Forms: Film, video, visual arts, dance, music, literature, interdisciplinary

Type of Support: $1,500-$6,500 project support

Scope of Program: $30,400 budget

Competition for Funding: 75 applications annually

Application/Selection Process:
  Deadline: December
  Preferred Initial Contact: Write for application/guidelines
  Application Procedure: Submit application form, project description, biographical information, samples of work
  Selection Process: Peer panel of artists
  Notification Process: Letter
  Formal Report of Grant Required: Yes

TECHNICAL ASSISTANCE PROGRAMS AND SERVICES
CONTACT: M. K. WEGMANN

Programs of Special Interest: The center offers information services in a wide range of areas, including employment, audition and touring opportunities, competitions, marketing, fellowships, and project support.

COUNCIL FOR INTERNATIONAL EXCHANGE OF SCHOLARS (CIES)

3007 Tilden Street, NW
Suite 5M
Washington, DC 20008-3009
202-686-7877

DIRECT SUPPORT PROGRAMS

➤ **FULBRIGHT AWARDS FOR FACULTY AND PROFESSIONALS**

Purpose: To support college and university lecturing or advanced research abroad; opportunities for professionals in the performing and visual arts are available depending upon the type of awards being offered in a given competition

Eligibility:

Citizenship: U.S.

Residency: Must not have lived outside of the U.S. in the past 10 years

Special Requirements: Terminal degree in field required for most awards; lecturing awards generally require previous college or university teaching experience; professional stature and experience may substitute for advanced degree in certain cases

Art Forms: Music (composition, musicology, performance), visual arts, theater/drama/playwriting, film/video, choreography/dance

Type of Support: Travel costs, maintenance stipend abroad, other benefits depending on country and type of award; opportunities for professionals in the performing and visual arts are frequently offered in the United Kingdom, Yugoslavia, Greece, Israel, and other select countries

Scope of Program: Approximately 1,000 award offerings in over 120 countries per year

Application/Selection Process:

Deadline: June 15 (Latin America, Australia, Soviet Union, South Asia/India), August 1 (Africa, Asia, Western and Eastern Europe, Middle East, Canada)

Preferred Initial Contact: Call for annual announcement of award opportunities and application

Selection Process: Peer review selection committees in the U.S. and abroad

Notification Process: Letter

Formal Report of Grant Required: Yes

CULTURAL ARTS COUNCIL OF HOUSTON (CACH)

1964 West Gray
Suite 224
Houston, TX 77019
713-527-9330
CONTACT: JEAN STORY, ADMINISTRATIVE DIRECTOR

DIRECT SUPPORT PROGRAMS
➤ CREATIVE ARTIST PROGRAM

Purpose: To support the development of Houston artists by enabling them to set aside time to create new works, complete works in progress, or pursue new avenues of artistic expression

Eligibility:
  Citizenship: U.S. (permanent residents also eligible)
  Residency: Houston, 2 years
  Special Requirements: Must be an originating, professional artist working in Houston; previous grantees ineligible for 3 years
  Art Forms: Visual arts, literature, choreography, music composition

Type of Support: $4,000; recipients required to provide some public service

Scope of Program: 10 awards for 1991 (1 choreography, 1 music composition)

Competition for Support: 255 applications in 1990

Application/Selection Process:
  Deadline: October 15
  Preferred Initial Contact: Request application/guidelines by phone or pick up at CACH office
  Application Procedure: Submit application form, samples of work, resumé, artist's statement (optional for composers), supporting materials (if available)
  Selection Process: Peer panel of artists
  Notification Process: Letter in May or June
  Formal Report of Grant Required: Yes

TECHNICAL ASSISTANCE PROGRAMS AND SERVICES

Programs of Special Interest: CACH's Cultural Resource Guide serves as an in-depth source of information about the arts in Houston; the weekly Arts Radio Show highlights current exhibitions and performances in the city. The arts council maintains a job bank and a library of reference materials on funding and other information for artists. (Individual memberships are $25.)

CUMMINGTON COMMUNITY OF THE ARTS

Rural Route #1
Box 145
Cummington, MA 01026
413-634-2172
CONTACT: LUCIUS PARSHALL, EXECUTIVE DIRECTOR

DIRECT SUPPORT PROGRAMS
➤ **ARTIST RESIDENCIES**

Purpose: To encourage artistic innovation and development, a commitment that favors emerging artists and writers, particularly those that offer alternative voices based on sex, race, age, or class

Eligibility:
  Special Requirements: Previous residents ineligible for up to 3 years
  Art Forms: Visual arts, fiction, playwriting, poetry, music composition, film/video, photography, performance art/choreography

Type of Support: 2-week to 3-month residency including room, studio; residents pay $400-$500 per month and maintain the community, but no one turned away for lack of money

Scope of Program: 120 residencies in 1990

Competition for Support: 1,500 applications in 1990

Application/Selection Process:
  Deadline: Multiple deadlines
  Preferred Initial Contact: Call or write for application/guidelines
  Application Procedure: Submit application form, $10 fee, samples of work, references, resumé, supporting materials (optional)
  Selection Process: Peer panel of artists
  Notification Process: Letter

DALLAS OFFICE OF CULTURAL AFFAIRS (OCA)

Majestic Theatre
Suite 500
1925 Elm Street
Dallas, TX 75201
214-670-3687

TECHNICAL ASSISTANCE PROGRAMS AND SERVICES

Programs of Special Interest: Ethnic and minority artists whose work reflects their cultural heritage may apply for inclusion on the Neighborhood Touring Program Roster. This pilot program is designed to give artists opportunities to teach, exhibit, and interact with community residents and to participate in neighborhood events throughout the city that showcase the community's unique history and cultural heritage. The Management Assistance Program (contact Hilary Anne Frost-Kumpf, Coordinator of Management Assistance) conducts free or low-cost workshops and seminars on subjects such as financial planning, marketing and public relations, school residencies, and grantwriting, and maintains information on funding sources for the arts and jobs in the arts. OCA maintains an artist/cultural organization registry.

DANCE THEATER WORKSHOP (DTW)

219 West 19th Street
New York, NY 10011
212-691-6500
CONTACT: TIA TIBBITTS, DIRECTOR OF SERVICES

PROFILE OF FINANCIAL SUPPORT TO ARTISTS
Total Funding/Value of In-Kind Support: $220,000 for FY 1990-91
Competition for Funding: Total applications, 250; total individuals funded/provided with in-kind support, 66
Grant Range: n/a

DIRECT SUPPORT PROGRAMS
➤ THE SUITCASE FUND
CONTACT: ANN ROSENTHAL, TOURING PROJECTS DIRECTOR
Phone: 212-645-6200

Purpose: To provide partial support for a select number of import, export, and cross-cultural projects; to assist independent American and foreign producers and writers in attending performing events, conferences, and colloquia around the world; and to assist producers and artists in conducting curatorial and research investigation in Latin America, Africa, and Asia

Eligibility:
Special Requirements: Additional funding from private and governmental sources required; emergency travel assistance and projects that duplicate well-established programmatic initiatives of other organizations and agencies are ineligible; geographic emphasis on Africa, Asia, and Latin America, in addition to Eastern and Western Europe; cross-cultural projects particularly encouraged
Art Forms: Performing arts

Type of Support: Cash grant
Scope of Program: 46 awards, totalling $200,000, in 1990-91

Application/Selection Process:
  Deadline: Ongoing (funding awarded on a first-come, first-served basis)
  Preferred Initial Contact: Call or write for application/guidelines
  Application Procedure: Submit project narrative, project budget, biography
  Selection Process: Staff review
  Notification Process: Letter
  Formal Report of Grant Required: Yes

➤ **NEW YORK DANCE AND PERFORMANCE AWARDS (THE BESSIES)**

Purpose: To award outstanding innovative artistic achievements of the New York performance season

Eligibility:
  Special Requirements: Must be nominated by a Bessie Committee member; unsolicited nominations not accepted; work must have been presented in New York City in the past year
  Art Forms: Performing arts (primarily dance)

Type of Support: $1,500 awards to choreographers/creators; $500 awards to dancers/performers, lighting designers, composers, visual designers

Scope of Program: 20-25 awards annually

Application/Selection Process:
  By nomination only; unsolicited nominations not accepted

TECHNICAL ASSISTANCE PROGRAMS AND SERVICES

Programs of Special Interest: DTW produces approximately 75 independent performing artists and companies in the fields of noninstitutional dance, theater, music, and interdisciplinary performance each year through a variety of full and assisted presentation programs. The National Performance Network (NPN) gives emerging, nonmainstream artists/companies with limited touring experience the opportunity to perform across the country in alternative spaces. Artists apply through NPN-designated Primary Sponsors (contact Ann Rosenthal, Touring Projects Director, 212-645-6200). DTW's Membership Services Program provides administrative, promotional, and technical support services to independent artists/companies. Available resources include mailing lists and services, a discount in-house advertising agency, a video documentation and archival project, access to the Artists Community Federal Credit Union, and consultation on issues such as promotion, management, and budgeting. ($60 membership fee; most services involve additional fees.)

DANE COUNTY CULTURAL AFFAIRS COMMISSION

City-County Building
Room 421
210 Martin Luther King, Jr. Boulevard
Madison, WI 53709
608-266-5915

PROFILE OF FINANCIAL SUPPORT TO ARTISTS

Total Funding/Value of In-Kind Support: n/a

Competition for Funding: Total applications, n/a; total individuals funded/provided with in-kind support, 22 in 1990

Grant Range: $500-$5,000

DIRECT SUPPORT PROGRAMS

➤ **CREATIVE ARTIST FELLOWSHIPS**

Purpose: To support artists of demonstrated ability whose current working situations do not otherwise offer unrestricted opportunities for professional development

Eligibility:

Residency: Dane County

Special Requirements: Originating artists only

Art Forms: Disciplines rotate on a 4-year cycle among literature (1988-89), visual arts (1989-90), choreography (1990-91), music composition (1991-92)

Type of Support: $5,000

Scope of Program: 2 awards per year

Application/Selection Process:

Deadline: September 1

Application Procedure: Submit application form, samples of work, resumé

Selection Process: Panel of arts professionals

Notification Process: December 1

Formal Report of Grant Required: Yes

➤ **ARTS PROJECT GRANTS/MINI GRANTS**

Purpose: Arts Project Grants support individuals and nonprofit groups seeking supplementary funds for arts projects such as performances, workshops, touring productions, commissioned art, and community art residencies; Mini Grants assist individuals and nonprofit organizations in emergency situations or with unique opportunities

Eligibility:

Residency: Dane County

Special Requirements: Project must take place in Dane County; grants must be matched in cash and in-kind support (part of match must be cash); applications for projects with 3 or more

participating individuals must be submitted by a nonprofit sponsor; degree credit students may not apply for projects directly related to their academic studies
Art Forms: Dance, theater, music, architecture, folk arts, literature, visual arts

Type of Support: Arts Project Grants, matching grant for up to 50% of project budget (up to $5,000 to individuals in 1990); Mini Grants, up to $500

Scope of Program: 10 grants to individuals in 1990

Application/Selection Process:
Deadline: February 1 (May 1-January 1 project period), June 1 (September 1-April 1), September 1 (December 1-July 1); no deadline for Mini Grants
Preferred Initial Contact: Discuss proposal with commission staff
Application Procedure: Submit application form, project narrative and budget, resumé, samples of work, letters of support (strongly recommended)
Selection Process: Advisory panel
Notification Process: Letter within 3 months

➤ **ARTS IN SCHOOLS GRANTS**

Purpose: To support cultural programs offering artistic experiences for students in Dane County schools; eligible programs include workshops, lecture-demonstrations, and residencies with an emphasis on the creative process

Eligibility:
Special Requirements: Grants must be matched in cash and in-kind support (at least 25% of cash must come from school, school district, parent-teacher organizations, or private underwriters)
Art Forms: Architecture, dance, music, theater, folk arts, literature, visual arts

Type of Support: Matching grant for up to 50% of project budget ($150-$2,890 grant range in 1990)

Scope of Program: 10 grants in 1990

Application/Selection Process:
Deadline: June 1
Application Procedure: Submit application form, project narrative and budget, samples of work, resumé, letters of support
Selection Process: Advisory panel
Notification Process: Letter
Formal Report of Grant Required: Yes

TECHNICAL ASSISTANCE PROGRAMS AND SERVICES

Programs of Special Interest: The Dane County Cultural Resources Directory profiles 260 local arts and historical organizations and lists local media contacts.

D'ANGELO SCHOOL OF MUSIC

Mercyhurst College
501 East 38th Street
Erie, PA 16546
814-825-0364
CONTACT: SAM ROTMAN, EXECUTIVE DIRECTOR, D'ANGELO YOUNG
ARTIST COMPETITION

DIRECT SUPPORT PROGRAMS

➤ **D'ANGELO YOUNG ARTIST COMPETITION**

Eligibility:
   Age: 18-30
   Special Requirements: Previous 1st place winners ineligible
   Art Forms: Music performance; competition rotates on 3-year cycle
   among piano, 1992; voice, 1993; strings (violin, viola, cello), 1994

Type of Support: 1st place, $10,000, season engagement with the
Erie Philharmonic, solo recital at D'Angelo School of Music Concert Series, guest appearance at Chautauqua Institution; 2nd place,
$5,000; 3rd place, $3,000; finalists, $1,000

Scope of Program: Annual competition

Competition for Support: 95 applications in 1991

Application/Selection Process:
   Deadline: January
   Preferred Initial Contact: Call or write for application/guidelines
   Application Procedure: Submit application form, $35 fee,
   samples of work; competition held in April
   Selection Process: Staff (preliminaries), panel of judges (competition)
   Notification Process: Artists selected for competition notified by
   letter by March 1

D.C. COMMISSION ON THE ARTS AND HUMANITIES

410 8th Street, NW
Fifth Floor
Washington, DC 20004
202-724-5613
CONTACT: JANN DARSIE, PROGRAM COORDINATOR

DIRECT SUPPORT PROGRAMS

➤ **ARTS-IN-EDUCATION GRANTS/COMPREHENSIVE ARTS
DEVELOPMENT GRANTS/GRANTS-IN-AID FELLOWSHIPS/
SPECIAL CONSTITUENCIES GRANTS**

Purpose: Arts-in-Education grants fund professional artists' residencies in District public schools; Comprehensive Arts Development

grants fund arts activities in traditionally underserved areas of the city; Grants-in-Aid provide fellowships and general operating support; Special Constituencies grants fund arts programming for populations such as senior citizens, the homeless, or the physically challenged

Eligibility:
  Residency: District of Columbia
  Age: 18 or older
  Art Forms: Dance, music, opera, theater, visual arts, design arts, crafts, media arts, literature, interdisciplinary, multi-disciplinary

Type of Support: For FY 1990 individual artists received up to $8,800 Arts-in-Education grants; $2,500 for Comprehensive Arts Development projects; $5,000 Grants-in-Aid fellowships; up to $3,700 for Special Constituency projects

Scope of Program: For FY 1990 individual artists received 13 Arts-in-Education grants; 8 Comprehensive Arts Development grants; 68 Grants-in-Aid fellowships; 4 Special Constituency grants

Competition for Support: 743 applications in 1990

Application/Selection Process:
  Preferred Initial Contact: Call or write for application/guidelines or call to explain project
  Application Procedure: Submit application form, samples of work, resumé, project budget
  Selection Process: Peer panel of artists
  Notification Process: Letter
  Formal Report of Grant Required: Yes

DEKALB COUNCIL FOR THE ARTS, INC. (DCA)

P.O. Box 875
Decatur, GA 30031
404-299-7910
CONTACT: SONDRA D. DANGELO, ACCOUNTING MANAGER

DIRECT SUPPORT PROGRAMS
➤ **INDIVIDUAL ARTISTS PROGRAM**

Purpose: To provide artists with financial assistance that will enable them to provide the citizens of DeKalb County with an arts service

Eligibility:
  Residency: DeKalb County, 1 year
  Art Forms: All disciplines

Type of Support: Up to $1,500

Scope of Program: 5 awards, totalling $3,550, in FY 1990

Competition for Support: 11 applications in 1990

Application/Selection Process:
    Deadline: December 8
    Preferred Initial Contact: Call or write for application/guidelines
    Application Procedure: Submit application form, samples of work, resumé, financial statement, project budget
    Selection Process: Peer panel of artists, organization staff, board of directors
    Notification Process: Letter 2-3 months after deadline
    Formal Report of Grant Required: Yes

TECHNICAL ASSISTANCE PROGRAMS AND SERVICES

Programs of Special Interest: The DeKalb Cultural Resources Directory lists area cultural and arts organizations, individual artists, and DCA members. Artists may make appointments for one-to-one consultations with staff for information about marketing, contracts, copyright, networking, tax matters, funding sources, and general professional development. DCA's bulletin board posts notices of competitions, grant opportunities, and events. Professional development workshops are conducted for individual artists. DCA sponsors an annual Community Cultural Awards Program, which recognizes the work of outstanding DeKalb County artists (submit accomplishments to DCA by August 1 for consideration). The De-Kalb Cultural Resources Booking Fair allows artists to present educational programs to representatives of schools and community organizations, and DCA hires performers for an annual Performing Arts Showcase. For some services members pay up to a $20 fee; nonmembers, up to $25.

DELAWARE STATE ARTS COUNCIL

Division of the Arts
820 North French Street
Wilmington, DE 19801
302-577-3540

CONTACT: BARBARA R. KING, VISUAL ARTS/INDIVIDUAL ARTIST FELLOWSHIP COORDINATOR

DIRECT SUPPORT PROGRAMS

➤ **INDIVIDUAL ARTIST FELLOWSHIPS**

Purpose: To enable artists to set aside time, purchase materials, and work in their fields with fewer financial constraints

Eligibility:
    Citizenship: U.S.
    Residency: Delaware

Special Requirements: No students; previous recipients in "established professional" category ineligible; previous recipients in "emerging professional" category ineligible for 3 years

Art Forms: All disciplines

Type of Support: $5,000 for established professional; $2,000 for emerging professional

Scope of Program: 6 established professional, 5 emerging professional awards in 1990

Competition for Support: 76 applications in 1990

Application/Selection Process:
   Deadline: March 22
   Preferred Initial Contact: Call or write for application/guidelines
   Application Procedure: Submit application form, samples of work, resumé, project proposal and budget, supporting materials
   Selection Process: Individuals from outside of organization
   Notification Process: Letter in July
   Formal Report of Grant Required: Yes

TECHNICAL ASSISTANCE PROGRAMS AND SERVICES
Programs of Special Interest: The Arts in Education Program publishes a directory of artists approved for school residencies.

EBEN DEMAREST TRUST

Mellon Bank, N.A.
1 Mellon Bank Center
Room 3845
Pittsburgh, PA 15258
412-234-5712
CONTACT: HELEN COLLINS, CONTROLLER, MELLON BANK

DIRECT SUPPORT PROGRAMS
➤ **EBEN DEMAREST TRUST**
Purpose: To allow a gifted artist or archeologist to pursue his or her work without dependence on public sale or approval of the work

Eligibility:
   Citizenship: Preference to U.S. citizens
   Age: Preference to mature artists
   Special Requirements: Artist's income must be less than income accruing from the trust; application must be sponsored by an arts organization; no students
   Art Forms: All arts disciplines and archeology

Type of Support: $9,100 grant in FY 1991-92

Scope of Program: 1 award per year

Competition for Support: 4 applications in 1991-92
Application/Selection Process:
  Deadline: June 1
  Preferred Initial Contact: Arts organization requests forms or writes letter on behalf of artist
  Application Procedure: Arts organization submits letter/forms, references, financial statement; unsolicited applications from individuals not accepted
  Selection Process: Board of directors
  Notification Process: Phone call or letter in mid-June

DENVER CENTER THEATRE COMPANY

1050 13th Street
Denver, CO 80204
303-893-4200

CONTACT: TOM SZENTGYORGYI, ASSOCIATE ARTISTIC DIRECTOR/
NEW PLAY DEVELOPMENT

DIRECT SUPPORT PROGRAMS
➤ **US WEST THEATRE FEST**

Purpose: To find unproduced scripts for development and production at Denver Center, and to publish produced plays in order to stimulate further productions
Eligibility:
  Special Requirements: Full-length, English-language plays only; no musicals or works for children
  Art Forms: Playwriting

Type of Support: 2 weeks of developmental readings with professional cast, director, and dramaturg (playwright receives $1,000 stipend, travel, room, and board); some works are published and receive full production the following year for a 3- to 6-week run (playwright receives royalties and support during rehearsal)
Scope of Program: Up to 8 developmental readings, up to 4 full productions per year
Competition for Support: 800 applications per year
Application/Selection Process:
  Deadline: December
  Preferred Initial Contact: Call or write for guidelines
  Application Procedure: Submit script
  Selection Process: Staff review, artistic director
  Notification Process: Letter

DENVER COMMISSION ON CULTURAL AFFAIRS (CCA)

303 West Colfax
Suite 1600
Denver, CO 80204
303-640-2678
CONTACT: GREGORY J. GEISSLER, DIRECTOR

DIRECT SUPPORT PROGRAMS
➤ **NEW WORKS PROGRAM**

Purpose: To provide opportunities for artists to work in the community and contribute to Denver's cultural vitality, and to encourage creative innovation across the broad spectrum of arts endeavors

Eligibility:
  Residency: City or County of Denver
  Special Requirements: Must apply through Denver nonprofit organization; must have matching funds; limit 1 application per artist or sponsor per year; project must take place in Denver and must include public presentation
  Art Forms: Music composition, choreography, visual arts, multidisciplinary/performance art, media arts, playwriting, poetry, prose, fiction

Type of Support: Up to $4,000 matching grant for project; 1:1 match may be cash or in-kind support

Scope of Program: 12 grants, totalling $25,000, for FY 1990

Application/Selection Process:
  Deadline: November
  Preferred Initial Contact: Call or write for application/guidelines
  Application Procedure: Sponsor submits application form, artist's resumé, samples of artist's work, project description and budget
  Selection Process: Individuals outside of organization
  Notification Process: Letter
  Formal Report of Grant Required: Yes

TECHNICAL ASSISTANCE PROGRAMS AND SERVICES

Programs of Special Interest: The Arts Education Collaborations Program funds collaborative efforts of schools and arts organizations to bring professional artists to Denver schools.

DIVERSE WORKS

1117 East Freeway
Houston, TX 77002
713-223-8346
CONTACT: DEBORAH GROTFELDT

DIRECT SUPPORT PROGRAMS
➤ **NEW FORMS REGIONAL INITIATIVE**

Purpose: To provide funds for works that challenge traditional art disciplines and explore new forms of art and culture

Eligibility:
  Residency: New Mexico, Texas, Arizona, Oklahoma
  Special Requirements: Individual artists and collaborating artists may apply; projects must challenge traditional definitions of art or culture; no students
  Art Forms: Projects may involve 1 or more of the following disciplines: visual arts, video, film, dance, music, theater, performance art, installations, text, sound art, environmental art

Type of Support: $2,000-$5,000 average

Scope of Program: 12 awards, totalling $30,000, in 1990

Competition for Support: 200 applications in 1990

Application/Selection Process:
  Deadline: May 1
  Preferred Initial Contact: Call or write for application/guidelines
  Application Procedure: Submit application form, resumé, samples of work
  Selection Process: Panel review
  Notification Process: Letter
  Formal Report of Grant Required: Yes

ALDEN B. DOW CREATIVITY CENTER

Northwood Institute
Midland, MI 48640-2398
517-832-4478
CONTACT: CAROL B. COPPAGE, DIRECTOR

DIRECT SUPPORT PROGRAMS
➤ **RESIDENT FELLOWSHIP PROGRAM**

Purpose: To provide individuals in all professions with an opportunity to pursue innovative ideas having the potential for impact in their fields

Eligibility:
    Special Requirements: Project must be new and innovative
    Art Forms: All arts and sciences
Type of Support: 10-week summer residency including round-trip travel to center, room, board, project expenses, stipend
Scope of Program: 4 residencies per year
Application/Selection Process:
    Deadline: December 31
    Preferred Initial Contact: Call or write for application/guidelines
    Application Procedure: Submit application form, samples of work, resumé, project budget; finalists make expenses-paid visit to Midland for interview
    Selection Process: Board of directors, professionals in applicant's field
    Notification Process: April 1
    Formal Report of Grant Required: Yes

DURHAM ARTS COUNCIL (DAC)

120 Morris Street
Durham, NC 27701
919-560-2720
CONTACT: MARGARET J. DEMOTT, DIRECTOR OF ARTIST SERVICES

DIRECT SUPPORT PROGRAMS
➤ **EMERGING ARTISTS PROGRAM**
CONTACT: ELLA FOUNTAIN PRATT, DIRECTOR AND GRANTS OFFICER
Phone: 919-560-2742

Purpose: To support developing professionals by funding projects pivotal to the advancement of their work and careers as artists
Eligibility:
    Residency: Chatham, Durham, Granville, Orange, or Person counties, 1 year
    Age: 18 or older
    Special Requirements: No degree-seeking students; previous grantees ineligible for 1 year
    Art Forms: All disciplines
Type of Support: Up to $1,000 for projects such as promotion/ presentation, travel, securing services, supplies, or training
Scope of Program: 21 awards, totalling $13,800, in FY 1990-91
Competition for Support: 61 applications in 1990-91
Application/Selection Process:
    Deadline: November 1
    Preferred Initial Contact: Call or write for application/guidelines

Application Procedure: Submit application form, samples of work, resumé, project budget, references (optional)
Selection Process: Anonymous judges, organizational committee
Notification Process: Phone or letter
Formal Report of Grant Required: Yes

TECHNICAL ASSISTANCE PROGRAMS AND SERVICES
Programs of Special Interest: Through the Creative Arts in Public Schools (CAPS) Program, DAC and Durham schools provide in-class arts residencies. CenterFest, an outdoor arts festival, exhibits the work of over 200 artists and performers. DAC also presents local, regional, and national musicians in various venues. The Artists Services Program offers artists workshops on topics such as marketing and project support.

DUTCHESS COUNTY ARTS COUNCIL (DCAC)

39 Market Street
Poughkeepsie, NY 12601
914-454-3222
CONTACT: SHERRE WESLEY, EXECUTIVE DIRECTOR

DIRECT SUPPORT PROGRAMS
➤ **INDIVIDUAL ARTISTS FELLOWSHIP PROGRAM**

Purpose: To provide support to individuals who are in the developmental phase of their careers as creative artists
Eligibility:
    Citizenship: U.S.
    Residency: Dutchess County, 2 years
    Age: 18 or older
    Special Requirements: No students enrolled in degree programs
    Art Forms: Eligible disciplines change yearly
Type of Support: $3,000; recipients perform a public service activity
Scope of Program: 3 awards in 1990
Application/Selection Process:
    Deadline: Mid-May
    Preferred Initial Contact: Call or write for application/guidelines
    Application Procedure: Submit application form, resumé, proof of residency, samples of work
    Selection Process: Peer panel of artists, board of directors
    Notification Process: Letter
    Formal Report of Grant Required: Yes

➤ **PROJECT GRANTS**

Purpose: To support art and cultural projects of Dutchess County nonprofit organizations

Eligibility:
    Citizenship: U.S.
    Special Requirements: Artists must be sponsored by a Dutchess County nonprofit organization; project must take place in Dutchess County and be open to the public
    Art Forms: Dance, music, opera/musical theater, theater, visual arts, design arts, crafts, photography, media arts, literature, folk arts, humanities, multi-disciplinary
Type of Support: Up to $5,000 for specific project
Scope of Program: $20,000 budgeted for 1991
Application/Selection Process:
    Deadline: Mid-September
    Preferred Initial Contact: Sponsor attends an application workshop or discusses project with DCAC staff
    Application Procedure: Sponsor submits application form, board list, financial statement, proof of nonprofit status, project budget, support documentation (e.g., samples of artist's work, reviews), artist's resumé
    Selection Process: Panel of community leaders, artists, and arts professionals, board of directors
    Notification Process: Letter
    Formal Report of Grant Required: Yes

TECHNICAL ASSISTANCE PROGRAMS AND SERVICES

Programs of Special Interest: DCAC provides artist referrals, maintains an arts resource library and an artist registry, and publishes several directories, including the Artist Skills Bank and the Arts-in-Education Registry. The annual Artscape Festival features music, theater, dance, workshops, exhibitions, and crafts. A telephone hotline publicizes arts events. Workshops address topics such as grantwriting and marketing. DCAC also offers group health insurance to members ($35 membership fee required).

EAST & WEST ARTISTS (EWA)

310 Riverside Drive, #313
New York, NY 10025
CONTACT: ADOLOVNI ACOSTA, EXECUTIVE DIRECTOR

DIRECT SUPPORT PROGRAMS

➤ **EAST & WEST ARTISTS INTERNATIONAL AUDITIONS FOR NEW YORK DEBUT**
Eligibility:
    Special Requirements: Artists must not have given a New York debut or be scheduled to give a New York debut in a major hall; 2-piano ensembles are ineligible; harpists, harpsichordists, and percussionists must provide their own instruments

Art Forms: Classical music (instrumental, vocal, ensemble)
Type of Support: Solo debut at Weill Recital Hall at Carnegie Hall
Scope of Program: 2 awards in 1991
Competition for Support: 125 applications in 1991
Application/Selection Process:
   Deadline: Late January
   Preferred Initial Contact: Write for application/guidelines; enclose SASE
   Application Procedure: Submit application form, application fee ($60 for soloists, $85 for chamber groups), biography, sample of work; preliminary, semi-final, and final auditions held in New York in March
   Selection Process: Jury
   Notification Process: Letter (applicants selected to audition are notified in February)

EL PASO ARTS RESOURCE DEPARTMENT (ARD)

2 Civic Center Plaza
El Paso, TX 79901-1196
915-541-4481
CONTACT: ALEJANDRINA DREW, DIRECTOR

DIRECT SUPPORT PROGRAMS
➤ **INDIVIDUAL PROJECT SUPPORT PROGRAM**
Purpose: To provide funds for community-based arts/cultural projects that have specific goals, objectives, and short-term time horizons
Eligibility:
   Residency: El Paso
   Special Requirements: Artist must apply with nonprofit, government, or educational umbrella organization; applicant must have matching funds (up to 50% may be in-kind support)
   Art Forms: All disciplines
Type of Support: Matching grant for specific project; grants ranged from $505-$3,178 in FY 1991
Scope of Program: 3 grants, totalling $5,767, in FY 1991
Competition for Support: 4 applications in 1991
Application/Selection Process:
   Deadline: January 15
   Preferred Initial Contact: Attend funding workshop
   Application Procedure: Submit application form, project budget, subcontract with sponsor, samples of artist's work (optional), references (optional), artist's resumé (optional)
   Selection Process: Organization staff, advisory board

Notification Process: Letter in March

Formal Report of Grant Required: Yes

➤ EMERGENCY FUNDING PROGRAM

Purpose: To provide limited funding to artists and groups in El Paso in the event of an emergency or an extraordinary opportunity that may arise outside of the regular funding cycle

Eligibility:

Residency: El Paso

Special Requirements: Artists must have a nonprofit sponsor and matching funds

Art Forms: All disciplines

Type of Support: Matching grant for a project emergency or extraordinary opportunity

Scope of Program: $8,700 granted to organizations in FY 1991

Application/Selection Process:

Deadline: 15th of each month

Application Procedure: Submit application form, project budget; applicants may be asked to appear at ARD Advisory Board meeting and to submit more detailed project budget or evidence of other forms of community support

Selection Process: Organization staff, advisory board

Formal Report of Grant Required: Yes

TECHNICAL ASSISTANCE PROGRAMS AND SERVICES

Programs of Special Interest: ARD's Discovery Series features new music, the Theatre and Dance Series presents companies from across the U.S., and the Art a la Carte Series presents local talent in noon-time concerts. ARD's local artist directory is distributed nationally to U.S. and Mexican presenters, and its bulletin board in City Hall provides information about auditions and competitions. Staff consultation regarding multi-cultural and international projects is available upon request.

FARGO-MOORHEAD SYMPHONY

810 Fourth Avenue South
Town Site Center
Moorhead, MN 56560
218-233-8397
CONTACT: EXECUTIVE DIRECTOR

DIRECT SUPPORT PROGRAMS

➤ SIGVALD THOMPSON COMPOSITION COMPETITION

Purpose: To select biennially an orchestral composition by an American composer to be premiered by the Fargo-Moorhead Symphony Orchestra

Eligibility:
    Citizenship: U.S.
    Special Requirements: Previous awardees ineligible; work must have been completed within the past 2 years and not have been performed publicly; work must be 8-15 minutes in duration
    Art Forms: Music composition (symphonic or chamber orchestra)
Type of Support: $2,500; orchestra reserves the right to perform work without fees for 1 year
Scope of Program: 1 biennial award
Competition for Support: 84 applications in 1990
Application/Selection Process:
    Deadline: September 30 (even-numbered years)
    Preferred Initial Contact: Call or write for application/guidelines
    Application Procedure: Submit cover letter, score of work
    Selection Process: Local panel, national judges, board
    Notification Process: Letter in February

FLORIDA DIVISION OF CULTURAL AFFAIRS/ FLORIDA ARTS COUNCIL

Department of State
The Capitol
Tallahassee, FL 32399-0250
904-487-2980
TDD: 904-488-5779
CONTACT: KATHY ENGERRAN

DIRECT SUPPORT PROGRAMS
➤ **FELLOWSHIP PROGRAM**

Purpose: To enable Florida artists to improve their artistic skills and enhance their careers
Eligibility:
    Residency: Florida, 1 year
    Age: 18 or older
    Special Requirements: Originating, professional artists only; no students pursuing degrees; previous grantees ineligible for 5 years
    Art Forms: Choreography, folk arts, literature, media arts, music composition, theater (design, playwriting, mime), visual arts, crafts
Type of Support: $5,000
Scope of Program: 39 awards in FY 1990-91
Competition for Support: 528 applications in 1990-91
Application/Selection Process:
    Deadline: May (visual arts), February (all other disciplines)

Application Procedure: Submit application form, samples of work, support materials (optional)
Selection Process: Panel of arts professionals, board
Formal Report of Grant Required: Yes

TECHNICAL ASSISTANCE PROGRAMS AND SERVICES

Programs of Special Interest: Performing artists may apply for inclusion in the State Touring Program; organizations presenting selected artists through the Florida Arts on Tour component are eligible for fee support from the Division of Cultural Affairs. The Florida Artists Roster lists artists interested in Arts in Education residencies (minimum residency, 10 days). The pilot Florida Visiting Artists Project supports 9- to 10-month artist residencies in community colleges (contact Mary Wadsworth) and is designed to provide artists with opportunities to travel throughout Florida. Artists on the division's mailing list receive a monthly informational memo regarding opportunities and competitions.

FROMM MUSIC FOUNDATION AT HARVARD

Music Department
Harvard University
Cambridge, MA 02138
617-495-2791
CONTACT: MARK KAGAN, ADMINISTRATOR

DIRECT SUPPORT PROGRAMS

➤ **FROMM MUSIC FOUNDATION AT HARVARD COMPOSER COMMISSIONS**

Purpose: To bring about meaningful interaction among composers, performers, and audiences by commissioning young and lesser-known composers as well as established composers
Eligibility:
  Art Forms: Music composition
Type of Support: Commission
Scope of Program: 10 commissions per year
Application/Selection Process:
  Deadline: June 1
  Preferred Initial Contact: Write for guidelines
  Application Procedure: Submit resumé, proposal, 2 letters of recommendation, sample of work
  Selection Process: Jury review, board of directors
  Notification Process: Letter in November
  Formal Report of Grant Required: No

GEORGIA COUNCIL FOR THE ARTS (GCA)

2082 E. Exchange Place
Suite 100
Tucker, GA 30084
404-493-5780
CONTACT: RICK GEORGE, GRANTS COORDINATOR

DIRECT SUPPORT PROGRAMS

➤ **INDIVIDUAL ARTIST GRANTS**

Purpose: To provide income for artists whose work demonstrates artistic merit and whose careers will potentially benefit from the completion of a particular project

Eligibility:
Residency: Georgia, 1 year
Special Requirements: Originating artists only; no full-time students; previous grantees ineligible for 2 years; matching funds encouraged but not required
Art Forms: Crafts, design arts, visual arts, literary arts, playwriting, media arts, performance art, choreography, music composition

Type of Support: Up to $5,000 for a specific project that includes a public service component

Scope of Program: 70 awards, totalling $158,105, in FY 1991

Competition for Support: 228 applications in 1991

Application/Selection Process:
Deadline: April 1
Preferred Initial Contact: Call or write for application/guidelines
Application Procedure: Submit application form, samples of work, resumé, project budget
Selection Process: Multi-disciplinary panels
Notification Process: Letter in June
Formal Report of Grant Required: Yes

TECHNICAL ASSISTANCE PROGRAMS AND SERVICES

Programs of Special Interest: The Artist-in-Education (AIE) Program (contact 404-493-5789) provides 3- to 18-week residencies in Georgia schools. The Georgia Touring Roster lists Georgia individual artists and incorporated groups approved for Georgia Touring Grants activities. The services of Georgia Volunteer Accountants and Georgia Volunteer Lawyers for the Arts are available to eligible artists.

GREATER COLUMBUS ARTS COUNCIL (GCAC)

55 East State Street
Columbus, OH 43215
614-224-2606

DIRECT SUPPORT PROGRAMS
➤ INDIVIDUAL ARTIST PROGRAM

Purpose: To support artists in creating new works or advancing their careers

Eligibility:
    Residency: Franklin County, 1 year
    Special Requirements: Must be registered voter; no students
    Art Forms: Disciplines change yearly

Type of Support: $5,000

Scope of Program: 6 awards in 1990

Competition for Support: 130 applications in 1990

Application/Selection Process:
    Deadline: July 15
    Application Procedure: Submit application form, other materials as requested
    Selection Process: Panel review
    Notification Process: Letter

TECHNICAL ASSISTANCE PROGRAMS AND SERVICES

Programs of Special Interest: The council maintains an Artists-in-Schools Roster (contact Diana Turner-Forte) and pays music, dance, and theater artists to perform at the annual Columbus Arts Festival (February 1 application deadline; contact Cleve Ricksecker, Arts Festival General Manager). Information is available on funding for emergency work-related needs, equipment, facilities, materials, and project support.

JOHN SIMON GUGGENHEIM MEMORIAL FOUNDATION

90 Park Avenue
New York, NY 10016
212-687-4470

DIRECT SUPPORT PROGRAMS
➤ FELLOWSHIPS TO ASSIST RESEARCH AND ARTISTIC CREATION

Purpose: To further the development of scholars and artists by assisting them to engage in research in any field of knowledge and creation in any of the arts

Eligibility:
Citizenship: U.S., Canada, Latin America, the Caribbean (permanent residents also eligible)
Special Requirements: Artists must have already demonstrated exceptional creative ability
Art Forms: All disciplines
Type of Support: $15,000-$30,000; $26,000 average grant for 1990
Scope of Program: Approximately 50 grants to artists in 1990
Competition for Support: 3,536 applications in 1990
Application/Selection Process:
Deadline: October 15 (U.S., Canada), December 1 (Latin America, the Caribbean)
Preferred Initial Contact: Write for application/guidelines
Application Procedure: Submit application form, samples of work, references, 3 supplementary statements regarding career and proposed use of funds
Selection Process: Juries of artists and arts professionals, Committee of Selection
Notification Process: 5-6 months after deadline
Formal Report of Grant Required: Yes

HARVESTWORKS, INC.

596 Broadway, 602
New York, NY 10012
212-431-1130
CONTACT: BRIAN KARL, ASSOCIATE DIRECTOR

DIRECT SUPPORT PROGRAMS
➤ **ARTIST-IN-RESIDENCE PROGRAM—PROJECT RESIDENCIES/PROGRAMMING RESIDENCIES**
Purpose: Project Residencies provide media artists and composers with studio production time to create new audio work for public presentation; Programming Residencies provide composers with studio time to receive instruction on and to experiment with computer music MIDI systems
Eligibility:
Special Requirements: Emerging and established artists in audio, film, dance, performance art, video, radio, music, and theater encouraged to apply for Project Residencies, regardless of technical skills; priority for Project Residencies to proposals for projects that can be presented in a public venue and that involve creative use of the facility and innovative use of sound; priority for Programming Residencies to composers of acoustic and

electronic music who wish to explore the capabilities of MIDI and computer music systems

Art Forms: Music composition, audio art, interdisciplinary projects involving sound as a creative medium

Type of Support: Project Residencies of 20-40 hours studio production time, including access to professional audio studio, full-time engineer, tape, and other materials; Programming Residencies of 40 hours studio time, including access to and instruction in computer music MIDI systems

Scope of Program: 12 Project Residencies, 8 Programming Residencies available for 1991

Application/Selection Process:
  Deadline: November 1
  Preferred Initial Contact: Call or write for application/guidelines
  Application Procedure: Submit application form, samples of work, resumé
  Selection Process: Panel review
  Notification Process: Letter by January
  Formal Report of Grant Required: No

TECHNICAL ASSISTANCE PROGRAMS AND SERVICES
Programs of Special Interest: Harvestworks offers seminars in new music technology by Artist-in-Residence recipients.

HAWAII STATE FOUNDATION ON CULTURE AND THE ARTS (SFCA)

335 Merchant Street
Room 202
Honolulu, HI 96813
808-548-4145
CONTACT: ESTELLE ENOKI, FIELD COORDINATOR

DIRECT SUPPORT PROGRAMS
➤ **FOLK ARTS APPRENTICESHIP AWARDS**
CONTACT: FOLK ARTS COORDINATOR

Purpose: To assist in the preservation of folk art in Hawaii by encouraging master folk artists to pass on their knowledge and skills to other individuals, particularly apprentices wishing to study within their own ethnic or cultural tradition

Eligibility:
  Residency: Hawaii
  Special Requirements: Master and apprentice must apply as a team

Art Forms: Folk arts from any cultural or ethnic group living in Hawaii

Type of Support: $1,500-$2,700 for 4- to 8-month apprenticeship involving minimum of 80-135 hours contact; 80% of award for master's fees, 20% for essential travel or supplies

Scope of Program: 12 awards, totalling $22,450, in FY 1988-89

Application/Selection Process:
    Deadline: April 30
    Preferred Initial Contact: Call or write for application/guidelines
    Application Procedure: Submit application form, project budget, references (optional), samples of work
    Selection Process: SFCA Folk Arts Advisory Committee, board of commissioners
    Notification Process: 2 months after deadline
    Formal Report of Grant Required: Yes

TECHNICAL ASSISTANCE PROGRAMS AND SERVICES

Programs of Special Interest: The SCFA administers an Arts in Education Program.

HEADLANDS CENTER FOR THE ARTS

944 Fort Barry
Sausalito, CA 94965
415-331-2787
CONTACT: JENNIFER DOWLEY, EXECUTIVE DIRECTOR

DIRECT SUPPORT PROGRAMS

➤ **REGIONAL RESIDENCIES/NATIONAL AND INTERNATIONAL RESIDENCY PROGRAM**

Purpose: To provide time for the incubation and investigation of new ideas and nurture exchange among artists of all mediums

Eligibility:
    Residency: San Francisco Bay Area (regional residencies), Ohio, North Carolina, Minnesota, Philadelphia, Italy
    Special Requirements: Originating artists only; no students; previous grantees ineligible for 5 years
    Art Forms: Visual arts, performance art, interdisciplinary, literary arts, music composition, choreography, film/video, arts professionals (critics, administrators)

Type of Support: Long-term regional residencies, 11-month residency including studio space and $2,500 stipend; short-term regional residencies, 2- to 4-week residency including studio space, housing, $200 weekly stipend; national and international residencies, 2- to

5-month residency including studio space, housing, $200 weekly stipend, travel expenses

Scope of Program: 5 long-term regional residencies, 3 short-term regional residencies, 7 national and international residencies in 1991

Application/Selection Process:
    Deadline: September
    Preferred Initial Contact: Call or write for application/guidelines
    Application Procedure: Submit application form, samples of work, resumé, references; prospective residents interviewed when possible
    Selection Process: Organization staff, board of directors, peer panel of artists
    Notification Process: Recipients by phone; nonrecipients by letter
Formal Report of Grant Required: No

HELENA PRESENTS

15 North Ewing
Helena, MT 59601
406-443-0287

DIRECT SUPPORT PROGRAMS
➤ **NEW FORMS REGIONAL INITIATIVE**

Purpose: To fund artists' projects that are innovative and adventurous, and that explore new definitions of art forms or culture

Eligibility:
    Residency: Colorado, Idaho, Montana, Nevada, Utah, Wyoming, 1 year
    Special Requirements: No students enrolled in degree programs; previous grantees ineligible for 1 cycle; projects that are solely traditional in intent are ineligible; intercultural projects must involve artists active in the ethnic traditions to be explored
    Art Forms: Dance, music/sound, theater, visual arts, video, film, text, performance art, installations, environmental art, environmental performance works, interdisciplinary, multi-disciplinary

Type of Support: $1,000-$5,000 (most grants $3,500 and under); public presentation of work required

Scope of Program: $23,000 budget for 1991 (approximately 10 awards per year)

Competition for Funding: 160 applications per year

Application/Selection Process:
    Deadline: February 1

Application Procedure: Submit application form, project description and budget, biographies or resumés for key artistic personnel, samples of work, 2 reviews or 2 letters of support
Selection Process: Interdisciplinary, culturally diverse panel of artists and arts professionals
Notification Process: 7 months after deadline
Formal Report of Grant Required: Yes

THE HOUSTON SYMPHONY

615 Louisiana
Houston, TX 77022
713-224-4240

DIRECT SUPPORT PROGRAMS
➤ IMA HOGG NATIONAL YOUNG ARTIST AUDITION
Purpose: To provide advanced students and beginning professional musicians with a cash award and a chance to perform with the Houston Symphony
Eligibility:
   Citizenship: U.S. (foreign students enrolled in a U.S. college, university, or conservatory also eligible)
   Age: 19-27
   Art Forms: Music performance (all standard orchestral instruments; no vocalists)
Type of Support: 1st prize, $5,000 and performance with Houston Symphony; 2nd prize, $2,500 and performance with Houston Symphony; 3rd prize, $1,000
Scope of Program: Annual audition
Competition for Support: 45 applications per year
Application/Selection Process:
   Deadline: February 1
   Preferred Initial Contact: Call or write for application/guidelines
   Application Procedure: Submit application form, $25 fee, sample of work; auditions required
   Selection Process: 2 panels of music experts
   Notification Process: Letter for preliminary round; winners of subsequent rounds announced at competitions

IDAHO COMMISSION ON THE ARTS (ICA)

304 West State Street
Boise, ID 83720
208-334-2119
CONTACT: JACQUELINE S. CRIST, ARTIST SERVICES DIRECTOR

DIRECT SUPPORT PROGRAMS

➤ **FELLOWSHIP AWARDS/WORKSITES AWARDS/SUDDEN OPPORTUNITY AWARDS**

Purpose: Fellowships recognize outstanding work of exceptionally talented individual artists; Worksites provide assistance for work with master artists, artist colony residencies, development of new work or work-in-progress, and travel to investigate ideas relevant to work; Sudden Opportunity Awards support a professional opportunity that is uniquely available during a limited time

Eligibility:
  Residency: Idaho, 1 year
  Age: 18 or older
  Special Requirements: No degree-seeking students; previous recipients ineligible for 5 years (Worksites)
  Art Forms: Disciplines for Fellowships and Worksites alternate between literature/dance/music/theater/media arts (odd-numbered years) and visual arts/crafts/design arts (even-numbered years); all disciplines eligible for Sudden Opportunity Awards

Type of Support: $5,000 Fellowships; up to $5,000 Worksites; up to $1,000 Sudden Opportunity Awards

Scope of Program: 18 awards, totalling $40,000, in FY 1991

Competition for Support: 110 applications in FY 1991

Application/Selection Process:
  Deadline: Mid-April (Fellowships, Worksites), quarterly (Sudden Opportunity Awards)
  Preferred Initial Contact: Call or write for application/guidelines
  Application Procedure: Submit application form, samples of work, resumé
  Selection Process: Peer panel of artists and arts professionals
  Notification Process: Phone call or letter

➤ **TRADITIONAL NATIVE ARTS APPRENTICESHIP PROGRAM (TNAAP)**

CONTACT: FOLK ARTS DIRECTOR

Purpose: To promote the work of Native American artists by supporting master/apprenticeship opportunities

Eligibility:
  Residency: Idaho, 1 year
  Age: 18 or older

Special Requirements: No degree-seeking students; must belong to an Idaho Native American community; master and apprentice apply together
Art Forms: Traditional Native American arts
Type of Support: Average $1,000 for apprenticeship ($10/hour master's fees for 100 hours plus travel and material expenses)
Scope of Program: n/a
Application/Selection Process:
Deadline: April, October
Preferred Initial Contact: Consult with Folk Arts Director or tribal representative before applying
Application Procedure: Submit application form, documentation of work (samples or letters), resumé or oral testimony, project budget
Selection Process: Panel composed of Idaho tribe members
Notification Process: Phone call or letter

ILLINOIS ARTS COUNCIL (IAC)

100 West Randolph
Suite 10-500
Chicago, IL 60601
800-237-6994 (in Illinois) or 312-814-6750
TDD: 312-814-4831
CONTACT: B. ROSE PARISI, ARTISTS SERVICES COORDINATOR

PROFILE OF FINANCIAL SUPPORT TO ARTISTS
Total Funding/Value of In-Kind Support: $525,077 for FY 1990
Competition for Funding: Total applications, 1,460; total individuals funded/provided with in-kind support, 227
Grant Range: $250-$10,000

DIRECT SUPPORT PROGRAMS
➤ ARTISTS FELLOWSHIP PROGRAM
Purpose: To enable Illinois artists of exceptional talent to pursue their artistic goals
Eligibility:
Citizenship: U.S. (permanent residents also eligible)
Residency: Illinois
Special Requirements: Originating artists only; no students; previous grantees ineligible for 1-3 years
Art Forms: Choreography, crafts, ethnic and folk arts, interdisciplinary/performance art, literature, media arts, music composition, photography, playwriting/screenwriting, visual arts
Type of Support: $5,000-$15,000 fellowships, $500 finalist awards

Scope of Program: 70 fellowship awards, 40 finalist awards in FY 1990
Application/Selection Process:
    Deadline: September 1
    Preferred Initial Contact: Call or write for application/guidelines
    Application Procedure: Submit application form, samples of work
    Selection Process: Panel of artists and arts professionals, IAC board
    Notification Process: Letter 3-4 months after deadline
    Formal Report of Grant Required: Yes

➤ **SPECIAL ASSISTANCE GRANTS**

Purpose: To assist artists with specific projects such as attendance at a conference, workshop, or seminar; consultant's fees for resolution of a specific artistic problem; exhibits, performances, or publications; materials, supplies, or services
Eligibility:
    Citizenship: U.S. (permanent residents also eligible)
    Residency: Illinois, 6 months
    Special Requirements: No students; low priority given to artists who have received Artists Fellowship or Special Assistance Grant in the same fiscal year
    Art Forms: All disciplines
Type of Support: Up to $1,500
Scope of Program: 81 grants in FY 1990
Application/Selection Process:
    Deadline: 8 weeks before beginning project
    Preferred Initial Contact: Consult IAC staff before applying
    Application Procedure: Submit application form, samples of work, resumé, project budget
    Selection Process: IAC staff and board
    Notification Process: 6-8 weeks after application
    Formal Report of Grant Required: Yes

➤ **ETHNIC AND FOLK ARTS APPRENTICESHIP**

CONTACT: ETHNIC AND FOLK ARTS PROGRAM STAFF

Purpose: To perpetuate ethnic and folk arts that generally are not learned in school but are handed down from generation to generation within a specific ethnic, regional, or occupational community
Eligibility:
    Citizenship: U.S. (permanent residents also eligible)
    Residency: Illinois, 6 months
    Art Forms: Ethnic and folk arts (includes visual arts, music, dance, other performers)
Type of Support: Applicant-designed apprenticeship funded with $1,800 honorarium for master and $700 stipend for apprentice
Scope of Program: 14 apprenticeships in FY 1991
Application/Selection Process:
    Deadline: June 1

Preferred Initial Contact: Consult program staff before applying
Application Procedure: Submit application form, samples of work
Selection Process: Panel of out-of-state jurors and non-voting in-state cultural specialists, IAC board
Notification Process: Letter 3-4 months after deadline
Formal Report of Grant Required: Yes

TECHNICAL ASSISTANCE PROGRAMS AND SERVICES

Programs of Special Interest: The Artstour Fee Support Program links Illinois performing artists and presenters; individual artists and companies selected for the biennial Illinois Artstour Roster are eligible to perform and conduct workshops, master classes, residencies, and lecture/demonstrations. IAC maintains the unjuried Illinois Artists Registry. The Special Projects and Services to the Field Program furnishes a wide variety of technical assistance to artists. The Arts-in-Education Residency Program administers 5-day to 8-month school and community residencies.

INDIANA ARTS COMMISSION (IAC)

402 West Washington
Room 072
Indianapolis, IN 46204
317-232-1268
TDD: 317-233-3001
CONTACT: PROGRAM SPECIALIST IN SPECIFIC DISCIPLINE

PROFILE OF FINANCIAL SUPPORT TO ARTISTS

Total Funding/Value of In-Kind Support: $102,000
Competition for Funding: n/a
Grant Range: $100-$5,000

DIRECT SUPPORT PROGRAMS

➤ **INDIVIDUAL ARTIST FELLOWSHIPS (IAF)**

Purpose: To assist artists with activities significant to their professional growth and recognition, or with the creation or completion of a project

Eligibility:
   Residency: Indiana, 1 year
   Special Requirements: High school and undergraduate students ineligible
   Art Forms: Visual arts and media arts eligible in odd-numbered years; performing arts (including dance, music, theater, folk arts) and literature eligible in even-numbered years

Type of Support: $2,000 Associate Fellowship, $5,000
Master Fellowship

Scope of Program: Approximately 25 fellowships per year

Application/Selection Process:
　Deadline: April 1
　Preferred Initial Contact: Call or write for application/guidelines
　Application Procedure: Submit application form, samples of work
　Selection Process: Panel of artists and arts professionals, board
　of directors
　Notification Process: Letter
　Formal Report of Grant Required: Yes

➤ **TECHNICAL ASSISTANCE (TA) GRANTS**

Purpose: To encourage the professional development of artists, arts
professionals, and administrators through funding consultant services and conference/workshop fees

Eligibility:
　Residency: Indiana, 1 year
　Special Requirements: High school and undergraduate students
　ineligible
　Art Forms: All disciplines

Type of Support: Up to $500 for professional development activity

Scope of Program: n/a

Application/Selection Process:
　Deadline: 6 weeks before beginning of activity
　Preferred Initial Contact: Call or write for application/guidelines
　Application Procedure: Submit application form, conference/
　workshop materials, resumé
　Selection Process: Staff and commission committees
　Notification Process: Letter
　Formal Report of Grant Required: Yes

TECHNICAL ASSISTANCE PROGRAMS AND SERVICES

Programs of Special Interest: The Arts in Education (AIE) Program
places professional artists in educational settings throughout Indiana for 1- to 8-month residencies; the Visiting Artist Program
(VAP) brings artists to educational settings to offer adults and
children introductory arts experiences (contact Education Program
Specialist). The Presenter Touring Program (PTP) brings Indiana artists to underfunded, underrepresented, urban, and rural areas of the
state to present performances, exhibitions, or readings. IAC maintains an unjuried Artists Registry and publishes an annual Fairs
and Festivals Directory. IAC Program Specialists are available to
consult with grant applicants.

INTAR

Box 788
New York, NY 10108
212-695-6134
CONTACT: LORENZO MANS, LITERARY MANAGER

DIRECT SUPPORT PROGRAMS

➤ **HISPANIC PLAYWRIGHTS-IN-RESIDENCE LABORATORY**

Purpose: To encourage and develop playwrights of Hispanic origin writing in English

Eligibility:
  Special Requirements: Must be Hispanic and write primarily in English
  Art Forms: Playwriting

Type of Support: 6-month residency including $3,000 stipend, staged reading of work by professional actors

Scope of Program: 6 awards per year

Competition for Support: 150 applications per year

Application/Selection Process:
  Deadline: June 30
  Preferred Initial Contact: Write for guidelines
  Application Procedure: Submit samples of work, biography
  Selection Process: Staff review
  Notification Process: Letter

INTERMEDIA ARTS

425 Ontario Street SE
Minneapolis, MN 55414
612-627-4444
CONTACT: AL KOSTERS, DIRECTOR OF ARTIST PROGRAMS

PROFILE OF FINANCIAL SUPPORT TO ARTISTS

Total Funding/Value of In-Kind Support: $94,000
Competition for Funding: n/a
Grant Range: $500-$12,000

DIRECT SUPPORT PROGRAMS

➤ **MCKNIGHT INTERDISCIPLINARY ARTISTS FELLOWSHIP**

Purpose: To provide support for artists who have a track record of pursuing personal interdisciplinary work

MONEY FOR PERFORMING ARTISTS

Eligibility:
    Citizenship: U.S.
    Residency: Iowa, Kansas, Minnesota, Nebraska, North Dakota, South Dakota, Wisconsin, 2 years
    Special Requirements: No full-time students or projects for a degree program; noncommercial work only
    Art Forms: All disciplines
Type of Support: $8,000-$12,000
Scope of Program: $70,000 available annually
Application/Selection Process:
    Deadline: Late fall or winter
    Preferred Initial Contact: Write for application/guidelines
    Application Procedure: Detailed in application workshops
    Selection Process: Independent panel review
    Notification Process: Letter
    Formal Report of Grant Required: Yes

➤ **DIVERSE VISIONS REGIONAL GRANTS PROGRAM**
Purpose: To support artists who are attempting to explore new definitions of, or boundaries between, cultures, arts disciplines, or traditions in their work
Eligibility:
    Citizenship: U.S.
    Residency: Iowa, Kansas, Minnesota, North Dakota, Nebraska, South Dakota, Wisconsin, 2 years
    Special Requirements: No full-time students or projects for a degree program; noncommercial work only
    Art Forms: Open
Type of Support: Up to $5,000 for established artists, up to $1,500 for emerging artists
Scope of Program: $24,000 available annually
Application/Selection Process:
    Deadline: Spring
    Preferred Initial Contact: Write for application/guidelines
    Application Procedure: Detailed in application workshops
    Selection Process: Panel review
    Notification Process: Letter 5 months after deadline
    Formal Report of Grant Required: Yes

TECHNICAL ASSISTANCE PROGRAMS AND SERVICES
Programs of Special Interest: Intermedia Arts serves as a fiscal sponsor for artists seeking funding from other sources.

IOWA ARTS COUNCIL (IAC)

Department of Cultural Affairs
Capitol Complex
Executive Hills
1223 E Court
Des Moines, IA 50319
515-281-4451

PROFILE OF FINANCIAL SUPPORT TO ARTISTS

Total Funding/Value of In-Kind Support: $53,949+ for FY 1990
Competition for Funding: n/a
Grant Range: $200-$1,500

DIRECT SUPPORT PROGRAMS

➤ **MINI-GRANTS**

CONTACT: JULIE BAILEY, DIRECTOR OF PARTNERSHIP PROGRAMS
Phone: 515-281-4018

Purpose: To provide grants for project support, training, or technical assistance to individual artists, and to support emergency or educational grants to organizations

Eligibility:
Citizenship: U.S.
Residency: Iowa
Special Requirements: Professional artists only
Art Forms: All disciplines

Type of Support: Up to $500 for project support or technical assistance; up to $200 for training (e.g., attendance at workshops, seminars)

Scope of Program: $18,000 total budget for FY 1991

Application/Selection Process:
Deadline: 6 weeks before project
Preferred Initial Contact: Call or write for application/guidelines
Application Procedure: Submit application, resumé, project budget, samples of work
Selection Process: Organization staff
Notification Process: Letter within 30 days of application
Formal Report of Grant Required: Yes

➤ **TOURING ARTS TEAMS**

CONTACT: KATHLEEN HILL, DIRECTOR OF EXPANSION ARTS
Phone: 515-281-8352

Purpose: To bring the arts to rural Iowa communities with populations of less than 2,000

Eligibility:
Special Requirements: Artists must be on an IAC roster
Art Forms: All disciplines

Type of Support: $1,100 plus transportation expenses, food, and lodging for 12-day tour of 5 towns; artists conduct workshops and give performances

Scope of Program: 21 artists funded in FY 1991

Application/Selection Process:
   Deadline: March 1
   Preferred Initial Contact: IAC mails application to all rostered artists 2-3 months before deadline
   Application Procedure: Submit application form, tentative workshop plans
   Selection Process: Organization staff
   Notification Process: Letter, follow-up phone call
   Formal Report of Grant Required: Yes

➤ **INDIVIDUAL ARTISTS GRANTS**

CONTACT: BRUCE WILLIAMS, DIRECTOR OF CREATIVE ARTISTS AND VISUAL ARTS
Phone: 515-281-4006

Purpose: To support the creation of new work by Iowa artists

Eligibility:
   Residency: Iowa or bordering towns, 1 year
   Age: 18 or older
   Special Requirements: No students; previous grantees ineligible for 1-2 years
   Art Forms: Dance, music, opera/musical theater, visual arts, design arts, crafts, photography/holography, media art, literature, interdisciplinary/collaborations, performance art

Type of Support: Grants of at least $500 (average $1,000-$2,000)

Scope of Program: n/a

Application/Selection Process:
   Deadline: January 10
   Preferred Initial Contact: Call or write for application/guidelines
   Application Procedure: Submit application form, samples of work, resumé, financial statement, project budget
   Selection Process: Individuals from outside of organization
   Notification Process: Letter
   Formal Report of Grant Required: Yes

➤ **FOLK ARTS APPRENTICESHIP**

CONTACT: DAVID BROSE, DIRECTOR, COMMUNITY ARTS AND CULTURAL HERITAGE
Phone: 515-281-4008

Purpose: To identify, document, honor, and perpetuate the diverse ethnic, community-based, occupational, and familial folk traditions of Iowa

Eligibility:
   Citizenship: U.S.
   Residency: Iowa (apprentice)
   Age: Applicants under 18 must have consent of guardian

Special Requirements: Apprentice and master apply as a team
Art Forms: Folk arts
Type of Support: Grant to cover master's fees, supplies, and travel costs; recipients may apply for up to $1,000 to showcase their skills in their local community or region of Iowa through the Community Folk Arts Residency Program
Scope of Program: 14 grants, averaging $1,100, in FY 1990
Application/Selection Process:
  Deadline: April
  Preferred Initial Contact: Call or write for application
  Application Procedure: Submit application form, samples of work, project budget, up to 3 references (optional), support documentation (optional)
  Selection Process: Peer panel of artists, individuals from outside IAC
  Notification Process: Letter 2 months after deadline
  Formal Report of Grant Required: Yes

TECHNICAL ASSISTANCE PROGRAMS AND SERVICES
Programs of Special Interest: Iowa performing artists may apply for inclusion in the biennial Arts to Go Touring Artist Roster; organizations that present these artists are eligible for IAC fee support (contact Julie Bailey, Director, Partnership Programs, 515-281-4018). Artists selected for the Residency Roster (priority to Iowa artists) are eligible for the Artists in Schools/Communities, Special Constituencies, and Arts to Share programs (contact Kay Swan, Director of Arts Education, 515-281-4100).

JEROME FOUNDATION

W-1050 First National Bank Building
332 Minnesota Street
St. Paul, MN 55101
612-224-9431
CONTACT: CYNTHIA A. GEHRIG, PRESIDENT

DIRECT SUPPORT PROGRAMS
➤ **TRAVEL AND STUDY GRANTS**
Purpose: To allow artists significant time for professional development through artist-to-artist communication on aesthetic issues, the experience of seeing artistic work outside of Minnesota, time for reflection and individualized study, a chance to develop future work and collaborations, and opportunities for the presentation or development of their work in other locations
Eligibility:
  Residency: Twin Cities 7-county metropolitan area of Minnesota, 1 year

Special Requirements: Professional artists or administrators only
Art Forms: All disciplines

Type of Support: $1,000-$5,000 for travel

Scope of Program: $90,000 available for FY 1990-91
  Preferred Initial Contact: Call or write for application/guidelines
  Application Procedure: Submit application form, travel
  proposal, resumé, samples of work
  Selection Process: Panel of arts professionals, board of directors
  Notification Process: Within 6 weeks of deadline
  Formal Report of Grant Required: Yes

JUNEAU ARTS AND HUMANITIES COUNCIL

P.O. Box 020562
Juneau, AK 99802-0562
907-586-2787
CONTACT: GINA SPARTZ, ADMINISTRATIVE ASSISTANT

DIRECT SUPPORT PROGRAMS

➤ **INDIVIDUAL ARTISTS ASSISTANCE PROGRAM**

Purpose: To enable experienced artists of exceptional talent to
produce works of art or advance their careers

Eligibility:
  Citizenship: U.S.
  Residency: Juneau, 1 year
  Special Requirements: Previous grantees ineligible for 2 years
  Art Forms: All disciplines

Type of Support: Up to $1,000 for a specific activity

Scope of Program: 10 awards, totalling $6,350, in 1990

Competition for Support: 21 applications in 1990

Application/Selection Process:
  Deadline: 2 deadlines per year
  Preferred Initial Contact: Call or write for application/guidelines
  Application Procedure: Submit application form, samples of
  work, resumé, financial statement, project budget, copies of
  other grant applications related to project
  Selection Process: Organization staff, board of directors,
  individuals outside of organization, peer panel of artists
  Notification Process: Phone and letter
  Formal Report of Grant Required: Yes

TECHNICAL ASSISTANCE PROGRAMS AND SERVICES

Programs of Special Interest: JAHC sponsors artists in schools,
maintains a resource library, and works with other arts organizations to closely monitor legislation regarding the arts.

KANSAS ARTS COMMISSION (KAC)

Jayhawk Tower
700 Jackson, Suite 1004
Topeka, KS 66603-3714
913-296-3335
CONTACT: CONCHITA REYES, ARTS PROGRAM COORDINATOR

PROFILE OF FINANCIAL SUPPORT TO ARTISTS

Total Funding/Value of In-Kind Support: $25,000 for FY 1990

Competition for Funding: Total applications, 111; total individuals funded/provided with in-kind support, 10

Grant Range: $385-$5,000

DIRECT SUPPORT PROGRAMS

➤ **ARTIST FELLOWSHIPS**

Purpose: To recognize outstanding Kansas artists and to assist them in furthering their careers

Eligibility:
Residency: Kansas
Special Requirements: No full-time students pursuing degrees; no previous recipients
Art Forms: Eligible disciplines rotate on a 3-year cycle among visual arts (1990-91), performing arts (1991-92), literature (1992-93)

Type of Support: $5,000

Scope of Program: 3 annual awards

Application/Selection Process:
Deadline: October 15
Preferred Initial Contact: Call or write for application/guidelines
Application Procedure: Submit application form, samples of work, resumé, artist's statement
Selection Process: Panels of arts professionals chaired by a KAC member
Notification Process: 4-5 months after deadline
Formal Report of Grant Required: Yes

➤ **PROFESSIONAL DEVELOPMENT GRANT**

Purpose: To encourage artists in the next step of their development as they create original works in any discipline

Eligibility:
Residency: Kansas
Special Requirements: Originating artists only; artists must match grant in cash or combination of cash and in-kind services; no students; no previous recipients
Art Forms: All disciplines

Type of Support: $100-$1,000 matching grant for specific project

Scope of Program: $5,000 available for FY 1990-91

Application/Selection Process:

Deadline: First-come, first-served basis (FY begins in July); request must be received 2 months before project begins

Preferred Initial Contact: Call or write to confirm availability of funds

Application Procedure: Submit application form, resumé, project description and budget, financial statement, samples of work, support materials (optional)

Selection Process: Staff, 2 experts in field, KAC commissioner

Notification Process: Letter; applications reviewed upon receipt

Formal Report of Grant Required: Yes

➤ **KANSAS FOLK ARTS APPRENTICESHIPS**

CONTACT: JENNIE CHINN, FOLKLORIST

Kansas Museum of History

6425 SW 6th Street

Topeka, KS 66615

913-272-8681

Purpose: To assist master artists in passing along their skills, particularly to individuals who share their ethnic or cultural background

Eligibility:

Residency: Kansas

Age: 18 or older

Art Forms: All folk arts

Type of Support: Funds to cover expenses of apprenticeship, average grant $1,092 in FY 1991

Scope of Program: 17 apprenticeships in 1991

Application/Selection Process:

Deadline: October 1

Preferred Initial Contact: Call or write for application/guidelines

Application Procedure: Submit application form, references

TECHNICAL ASSISTANCE PROGRAMS AND SERVICES

Programs of Special Interest: The Kansas Touring Program provides Kansas performing artists and groups with opportunities to tour communities across the state; organizations that present rostered artists may apply for KAC fee support. KAC administers an Arts in Education Artist in Residency Program and an Arts in Education Mentor/ Mentoree Program. A monthly bulletin and a quarterly newsletter supply information about arts events and opportunities.

KENNEDY CENTER FRIEDHEIM AWARDS

The John F. Kennedy Center for the Performing Arts
Washington, DC 20566-0001
202-416-8000

DIRECT SUPPORT PROGRAMS
➤ KENNEDY CENTER FRIEDHEIM AWARDS

CONTACT: COORDINATOR

Purpose: To pay tribute to living American composers for meritorious musical compositions in the fields of orchestral and chamber music

Eligibility:

Citizenship: U.S. (permanent residents also eligible)

Special Requirements: Work must be at least 15 minutes in duration and may not include voice except in the context of instrumental fabric and without text; work must have been given U.S. premiere in the past 2 years; works may be nominated by anyone, including the composer

Art Forms: Music composition (instrumental chamber music eligible in odd-numbered years; instrumental orchestral music eligible in even-numbered years)

Type of Support: 1st prize, $5,000; 2nd prize, $2,500; 3rd prize, $1,000; 4th prize, $500

Scope of Program: Annual program

Application/Selection Process:

Deadline: July 15

Preferred Initial Contact: Call or write for nomination form/guidelines

Application Procedure: Submit nomination form, $20 fee, score and recording of work, printed programs, composer's biography; works of 4 finalists performed at Kennedy Center in November

Selection Process: Jury of music authorities

Notification Process: Semi-finalists and finalists receive letter; prizes announced at Kennedy Center performance

KENTUCKY ARTS COUNCIL (KAC)

Berry Hill Mansion
Frankfort, KY 40601
502-564-3757

CONTACT: IRWIN PICKETT, DIRECTOR OF VISUAL ARTS AND ARTISTS' PROJECTS

DIRECT SUPPORT PROGRAMS
➤ AL SMITH FELLOWSHIPS

Purpose: To support individual Kentucky artists in developing their art forms

Eligibility:
  Citizenship: U.S.
  Residency: Kentucky
  Age: 18 or older
  Special Requirements: Originating artists only; previous grantees ineligible for 2 years
  Art Forms: Disciplines alternate on 2-year cycle between visual arts/media arts/new genres and writers/composers/choreographers
Type of Support: $5,000 fellowships, $1,000 assistance awards
Scope of Program: 22 fellowships, 20 assistance awards
Competition for Support: 150 applications in 1990
Application/Selection Process:
  Preferred Initial Contact: Call to explain project and need for funding
  Application Procedure: Submit application form, samples of work, resumé, project proposal
  Selection Process: Organization staff, board of directors, peer panel of artists
  Notification Process: Letter
  Formal Report of Grant Required: No

KING COUNTY ARTS COMMISSION (KCAC)

1115 Smith Tower
506 Second Avenue
Seattle, WA 98104
206-296-7580
CONTACT: MAYUMI TSUTUKAWA, MANAGER, CULTURAL RESOURCES DIVISION

DIRECT SUPPORT PROGRAMS
➤ **NEW WORKS PROJECTS**
CONTACT: VICKY LEE, PERFORMING ARTS COORDINATOR

Purpose: To encourage experimentation and to support the creation of new works
Eligibility:
  Residency: King County
  Special Requirements: Professional, originating artists only; previous recipients ineligible for 2 years
  Art Forms: Literature, visual arts, media arts, performing arts (choreography, music composition, playwriting, musical theater), interdisciplinary
Type of Support: $1,000-$5,000
Scope of Program: 8-10 awards per year ($40,500 awarded in 1990)
Competition for Support: 180 applications in 1990

Application/Selection Process:
  Deadline: Mid-January
  Preferred Initial Contact: Consult with staff before applying
  Application Procedure: Submit application form, samples of
  work, project narrative
  Selection Process: Peer panel of artists, commission members
  Formal Report of Grant Required: Yes

TECHNICAL ASSISTANCE PROGRAMS AND SERVICES

CONTACT: ROBERT ROTH, COMMUNITY ARTS COORDINATOR

Programs of Special Interest: Local and regional performing artists
and groups may apply for inclusion in the biennial Touring Arts
Booklet; sponsors presenting performances by these artists are
eligible for KCAC fee support. African-American, Latino, Asian-
American/Pacific Islander, and Native American artists may apply
for arts-in-education residencies through the Ethnic Artists-in-
Residence Program; the Disabled Artists-in-Residence places blind
and visually-impaired, deaf and hearing-impaired, deaf-blind, or
physically disabled artists in arts-in-education residencies.

KOUSSEVITSKY MUSIC FOUNDATION, INC.

200 Park Avenue
28th Floor
New York, NY 10166
212-351-3092
CONTACT: ELLIS J. FREEDMAN

➤ **SERGE KOUSSEVITSKY MUSIC FOUNDATION IN THE
LIBRARY OF CONGRESS**
Music Division
Library of Congress
Washington, DC 20540
202-707-5503

DIRECT SUPPORT PROGRAMS

➤ **KOUSSEVITSKY MUSIC FOUNDATION COMMISSIONS**
Purpose: To provide joint commissions to composers with
orchestras and chamber groups that have a record of excellence
in the performance of contemporary music
Eligibility:
  Special Requirements: Application must be sponsored by an
  orchestra or chamber group that will perform the commissioned
  work as part of its regular concert series within 2 years of receiving the complete score

Art Forms: Music composition (orchestral, chamber)
Type of Support: Symphonic commissions range from $20,000 to $30,000 (orchestra must pay 1/3 of commission); chamber commissions range from $12,500-$17,500 (no matching funds required)
Scope of Program: 8 commissions, totalling $119,000, in 1991
Competition for Support: 100+ applications annually
Application/Selection Process:
  Deadline: October 31
  Preferred Initial Contact: Call or write for application/guidelines
  Application Procedure: Sponsoring organization submits programs, brochures, financial statement, proposed instrumentation of work, samples of composer's work, composer's biography, composer's written consent
  Selection Process: Board of directors
  Notification Process: Letter
  Formal Report of Grant Required: No

LAKE REGION ARTS COUNCIL, INC. (LRAC)

112 W. Washington Avenue
P.O. Box 661
Fergus Falls, MN 56538-0661
218-739-5780
CONTACT: SONJA PETERSON, PROGRAM COORDINATOR

DIRECT SUPPORT PROGRAMS
➤ **LRAC/MCKNIGHT INDIVIDUAL ARTISTS GRANT PROGRAM**
Purpose: To provide small but critical grants to artists for specific projects that contribute directly to their growth and development as professionals
Eligibility:
  Citizenship: U.S.
  Residency: Minnesota (Becker, Clay, Douglas, Grant, Otter Tail, Pope, Stevens, Traverse, and Wilkin counties)
  Special Requirements: No students; previous recipients ineligible for 3 years
  Art Forms: All disciplines
Type of Support: Up to $500 for expenses such as production and presentation of work, training, supplies, or services
Scope of Program: 5 awards, totalling $2,000, in 1990
Competition for Support: 18 applications in 1990
Application/Selection Process:
  Deadline: February 5
  Preferred Initial Contact: Call or write for application/guidelines

Application Procedure: Submit application form, samples of work, references, resumé, project budget
Selection Process: LRAC board of directors
Notification Process: Letter in April
Formal Report of Grant Required: Yes

TECHNICAL ASSISTANCE PROGRAMS AND SERVICES
Programs of Special Interest: LRAC maintains an unjuried registry of artists and a file of touring arts performers, publishes a monthly newsletter, and holds grantwriting workshops.

LOCAL 802 (MUSICIANS UNION)

330 West 42nd Street
New York, NY 10036

DIRECT SUPPORT PROGRAMS
➤ **LOCAL 802 EMERGENCY RELIEF FUND**
CONTACT: MICHAEL MORIARITY, SECRETARY

Purpose: To assist musicians facing emergency situations such as eviction or disconnection of utilities (some emergency medical assistance available)
Eligibility:
    Residency: New York City, Nassau and Suffolk counties
    Special Requirements: Must have been member of Local 802 for at least past 2 years (annual dues, $136)
    Art Forms: Music
Type of Support: Up to $2,000
Scope of Program: $25,000-$30,000 available per year
Application/Selection Process:
    Deadline: Ongoing
    Preferred Initial Contact: Write for application/guidelines
    Application Procedure: Submit application form, documentation of emergency; interview often required
    Selection Process: Board of trustees
    Notification Process: Letter

TECHNICAL ASSISTANCE PROGRAMS AND SERVICES
CONTACT: MICHAEL CIPRESSI, DIRECTOR, MUSICIANS ASSISTANCE PROGRAM
Phone: 212-244-1802
Programs of Special Interest: The Musicians Assistance Program provides free consultations, social services, and financial advisory services.

LOS ANGELES CONTEMPORARY EXHIBITIONS (LACE)

1804 Industrial Street
Los Angeles, CA 90021
213-624-5650

DIRECT SUPPORT PROGRAMS
➤ ARTISTS' PROJECTS GRANTS

Purpose: To encourage innovative projects that push the boundaries of contemporary art and challenge traditional formats

Eligibility:
　　Residency: California (south of, but not including, Fresno), Hawaii
　　Special Requirements: No full-time students; artists of diverse backgrounds encouraged to apply; individual artists and collaborating artists are eligible
　　Art Forms: Single-disciplinary or interdisciplinary innovative projects

Type of Support: Cash grant

Scope of Program: 5-8 grants, totalling $30,250, available in 1991

Application/Selection Process:
　　Deadline: April 15
　　Application Procedure: Submit application form, samples of work, project description and budget, biographies of key artistic personnel
　　Selection Process: Independent panel of artists and arts professionals
　　Notification Process: August

LOS ANGELES CULTURAL AFFAIRS DEPARTMENT

433 South Spring Street
10th Floor
Los Angeles, CA 90013
213-485-2433
CONTACT: GRANTS DEPARTMENT, 213-620-9445

DIRECT SUPPORT PROGRAMS
➤ COMMUNITY ARTS PROGRAM—CULTURAL GRANTS
CONTACT: 213-620-8635

Purpose: To offer arts experiences within a community setting to nonprofessional artists and to bring professional artists in direct contact with the public

Eligibility:
　　Residency: City or County of Los Angeles

Special Requirements: Artist must submit a letter of agreement with proposed host venue to produce the project if funded; project must take place in the City of Los Angeles in a nontraditional community site with public access

Art Forms: Dance, interdisciplinary, multi-disciplinary, literature, media arts, music, theater, urban and design arts, traditional and folk arts, visual arts

Type of Support: $1,500-$15,000 for project

Scope of Program: n/a

Application/Selection Process:
  Deadline: Fall
  Preferred Initial Contact: Call or write for application/guidelines
  Application Procedure: Submit application form, materials as outlined in guidelines
  Selection Process: Peer panel of artists
  Notification Process: Letter 5-6 months after deadline
  Formal Report of Grant Required: Yes

TECHNICAL ASSISTANCE PROGRAMS AND SERVICES
CONTACT: JAMES BURKS
Phone: 213-485-2437

Programs of Special Interest: Retired composers who are ASCAP members, and musicians who belong to Musicians Union Local #47, may apply to the Cultural Affairs Department for performance opportunities; selected musicians and composers receive fees or honoraria.

LOUISIANA DIVISION OF THE ARTS (DOA)

900 Riverside North
Baton Rouge, LA 70802
504-342-8180
CONTACT: DEE WALLER, PERFORMING ARTS AND ARTS IN EDUCATION PROGRAMS

PROFILE OF FINANCIAL SUPPORT TO ARTISTS
Total Funding/Value of In-Kind Support: $74,000 for FY 1991
Competition for Funding: Total applications, 185; total individuals funded/provided with in-kind support, 16
Grant Range: $3,400-$5,000

DIRECT SUPPORT PROGRAMS
➤ ARTIST FELLOWSHIPS
Purpose: To enable artists of exceptional talent to pursue their artistic goals
Eligibility:
  Residency: Louisiana, 2 years

Special Requirements: Professional artists only; no students; previous grantees ineligible

Art Forms: Crafts, dance (performance, choreography), design arts, folk arts (visual, performing), literature, media arts, music (vocal or instrumental performance, composition), theater (acting, screenwriting, playwriting), visual arts

Type of Support: $5,000

Scope of Program: 10 awards in 1991

Application/Selection Process:

    Deadline: March 1

    Preferred Initial Contact: Write for application/guidelines

    Application Procedure: Submit application form, samples of work, resumé

    Selection Process: Individuals outside of organization

    Notification Process: Letter 5 months after deadline

    Formal Report of Grant Required: Yes

➤ **FOLKLIFE APPRENTICESHIPS**

CONTACT: MAIDA OWENS, PROGRAM DIRECTOR

Purpose: To enable master folk artists or craftspeople to pass on their skills within their communities

Eligibility:

    Residency: Louisiana, 2 years

    Special Requirements: No students; previous grantees ineligible

    Art Forms: Folk arts

Type of Support: Up to $5,000 for apprenticeship

Scope of Program: 6 apprenticeships in 1991

Application/Selection Process:

    Deadline: March 1

    Preferred Initial Contact: Write for application/guidelines

    Application Procedure: Submit application form, samples of work, resumé, project budget

    Selection Process: Individuals outside of organization

    Notification Process: Letter 5 months after deadline

    Formal Report of Grant Required: Yes

➤ **INDIVIDUAL ARTIST PROJECTS: FISCAL AGENTS**

Purpose: To support projects of exceptional merit initiated by individual artists

Eligibility:

    Residency: Louisiana, 2 years

    Special Requirements: Must be practicing artist; no students enrolled in arts-related degree or certificate-granting programs; must apply through a nonprofit organization; there should be a reasonable relationship between the project type and the primary purpose of the nonprofit, but the project must clearly be an individual artist project rather than an extension of the organization's programming

Art Forms: Visual arts, performing arts, folk arts, design arts, media arts
Type of Support: Up to $2,000
Scope of Program: n/a
Application/Selection Process:
  Deadline: March 1
  Preferred Initial Contact: Call or write for application/guidelines
  Application Procedure: Submit application form, other materials as requested
  Selection Process: Advisory panel, council
  Notification Process: Letter
  Formal Report of Grant Required: Yes

TECHNICAL ASSISTANCE PROGRAMS AND SERVICES

Programs of Special Interest: The Arts in Education Program supports Visiting Artists (1-10 days per site or school), Short-Term Residencies (11-40 days), and Long-Term Residencies (41+ days); to be eligible for residencies, artists must be selected to the Louisiana Artist Roster.

LOWER MANHATTAN CULTURAL COUNCIL (LMCC)

42 Broadway
New York, NY 10004
212-269-0320
CONTACT: GRETA GUNDERSON, ASSOCIATE DIRECTOR

DIRECT SUPPORT PROGRAMS
➤ **MANHATTAN COMMUNITY ARTS FUND**

Purpose: To support projects by small arts groups that have not yet received funding from traditional government sources
Eligibility:
  Special Requirements: Artists must apply under the aegis of a nonprofit sponsor not receiving DCA, NYSCA, or NEA support; previous grantees ineligible for 3 years
  Art Forms: Dance (ethnic, modern), music (new, ethnic, jazz, popular), theater (general), visual arts, design arts, media arts, literature, interdisciplinary, multi-disciplinary
Type of Support: Up to $3,000 for a specific project
Scope of Program: $64,940 awarded to organizations in FY 1988-89
Application/Selection Process:
  Preferred Initial Contact: Call or write for information
  Application Procedure: Sponsor submits letter of intent, project budget, artist's resumé, samples of work
  Notification Process: Letter or phone call within 6 weeks

125

MONEY FOR PERFORMING ARTISTS

TECHNICAL ASSISTANCE PROGRAMS AND SERVICES
Programs of Special Interest: The Performing Arts Program hires artists for mid-day public performance events in downtown Manhattan.

LYNDHURST FOUNDATION

Tallan Building
Suite 701
100 West M. L. King Boulevard
Chattanooga, TN 37402

DIRECT SUPPORT PROGRAMS
➤ **LYNDHURST PRIZE/YOUNG CAREER PRIZE**

Purpose: Lyndhurst Prize enables individuals who have made distinctive contributions in the arts, particularly writing and photography, and in community service and leadership to carry forth their interests over an extended period of time without financial pressure; Young Career Prize supports young adults whose work in public service and the arts shows passion and promise but is not likely to attract substantial financial award

Eligibility:
  Art Forms: All disciplines

Type of Support: 3-year stipend (Lyndhurst Prize); 2-year stipend (Young Career Prize)

Scope of Program: 24 individuals received $660,000 in FY 1989

Application/Selection Process:
  Awards granted solely at initiative of the board of trustees. No applications or nominations accepted.

JOHN D. AND CATHERINE T. MACARTHUR FOUNDATION

140 South Dearborn Street
Chicago, IL 60603
312-726-8000

DIRECT SUPPORT PROGRAMS
➤ **MACARTHUR FELLOWS PROGRAM**

Purpose: To support the work of extraordinarily creative and promising individuals at points in their careers when such an opportunity could make a marked difference

Eligibility:
  Residency: U.S.

Special Requirements: By nomination only by a designated nominator
Art Forms: Architecture, dance, media arts, music (performance, composition), photography, theater (acting, direction, stage art), visual arts, literature
Type of Support: $30,000-$75,000, depending on recipient's age
Scope of Program: n/a
Application/Selection Process:
By nomination only; unsolicited nominations not accepted

THE MACDOWELL COLONY

100 High Street
Peterborough, NH 03458
603-924-3886
CONTACT: SHIRLEY BEWLEY, ADMISSIONS COORDINATOR

DIRECT SUPPORT PROGRAMS
➤ **ARTIST RESIDENCY PROGRAM**
Purpose: To provide a place where creative artists can find freedom to concentrate on their work
Eligibility:
Special Requirements: Professional artists and emerging artists of recognized ability; previous applicants ineligible for 1 year
Art Forms: Music composition, literature, visual arts, architecture, film/video, mixed media, interdisciplinary
Type of Support: Residency including room, board, and studio for up to 2 months; funds available to defray travel costs to and from colony; artists who have financial resources pay on a voluntary basis
Scope of Program: 200+ residencies averaging 6 weeks
Competition for Support: 1,150 applications in 1989
Application/Selection Process:
Deadline: January 15 (Summer), April 15 (Fall-Winter), September 15 (Winter-Spring)
Preferred Initial Contact: Call or write for application/guidelines
Application Procedure: Submit application form, samples of work, references, resumé, $20 fee
Selection Process: Peer panel of artists
Notification Process: Letter 2 months after deadline
Formal Report of Grant Required: No

MAINE ARTS COMMISSION (MAC)

55 Capitol Street
Station 25
Augusta, ME 04333-0025
207-289-2724

CONTACT: KATHY ANN JONES, MUSEUM/VISUAL ARTS ASSOCIATE

DIRECT SUPPORT PROGRAMS

➤ **INDIVIDUAL ARTIST FELLOWSHIPS**

Purpose: To provide financial support for artists to advance their careers

Eligibility:
    Residency: Maine
    Age: 18 or older
    Special Requirements: No students
    Art Forms: Awards rotate on a 3-year basis among visual arts (1990), writing/design arts (1991), performing/traditional/media arts (1992)

Type of Support: $3,000

Scope of Program: 6 awards in 1991

Competition for Support: 109 applications in 1991

Application/Selection Process:
    Deadline: September 1
    Preferred Initial Contact: Call for application/guidelines
    Application Procedure: Submit application form, samples of work, resumé, statement of intent (optional)
    Selection Process: Individuals from outside of organization
    Notification Process: Phone call and follow-up letter to recipients in November; letter to nonrecipients
    Formal Report of Grant Required: Yes

➤ **TRADITIONAL ARTS APPRENTICESHIPS**

Purpose: To provide an opportunity for recognized master traditional artists to share skills and train qualified apprentices

Eligibility:
    Residency: Maine
    Special Requirements: Master and apprentice apply together and should belong to same ethnic, religious, occupational, or familial group
    Art Forms: Folk arts

Type of Support: $1,200 master's fees; up to $350 for supplies, materials, apprentice's travel

Scope of Program: Up to 7 apprenticeships for 1991

Application/Selection Process:
    Deadline: October 30
    Preferred Initial Contact: Call or write for application/guidelines
    Selection Process: MAC's Traditional Arts Panel

TECHNICAL ASSISTANCE PROGRAMS AND SERVICES

Programs of Special Interest: Artists may develop Arts in Education residency proposals with a school or nonprofit organization; MAC provides sponsoring organizations with matching funds to support 10-day to 1-year residencies (February 1 application deadline). The Maine Touring Artists Program provides organizations with a list of Maine artists who will travel throughout the state to present performances, workshops, residencies, and educational services (July 1 deadline for artists' applications).

MANITOBA ARTS COUNCIL (MAC)

525-93 Lombard Avenue
Winnipeg, Manitoba
Canada R3B 3B1
204-945-3033
CONTACT: T. PATRICK CARRABRE, PERFORMING ARTS CONSULTANT

PROFILE OF FINANCIAL SUPPORT TO ARTISTS

Total Funding/Value of In-Kind Support: $1,028,617 for FY 1988-89

Competition for Funding: Total applications, 800; total individuals funded/provided with in-kind support, n/a

Grant Range: n/a

DIRECT SUPPORT PROGRAMS

➤ **SHORT-TERM PROJECT GRANT IN THE PERFORMING ARTS**

Purpose: To assist performing artists with specific, short-term projects or with travel on occasions important to their careers

Eligibility:

    Citizenship: Canada (landed immigrants also eligible)

    Residency: Manitoba, 1 year

    Special Requirements: Professional artists only; performing artists, directors, technicians, and designers must have completed at least 1 full year of professional activity; creative artists must have had at least 1 work professionally performed in public; limit 1 award per year

    Art Forms: Performing arts

Type of Support: Up to $750

Scope of Program: 88 grants, totalling $53,516, in FY 1988-89

Application/Selection Process:

    Deadline: 4 weeks before project begins

    Preferred Initial Contact: Contact Performing Arts Consultant before applying

    Application Procedure: Submit application form, project budget, samples of work, references

Selection Process: Performing Arts Consultant
Notification Process: 1 month after application
Formal Report of Grant Required: Yes

➤ **CHOREOGRAPHER COMMISSION AND DEVELOPMENT GRANT**

Purpose: To support the creation of original works by Manitoba choreographers, as well as creative or production development projects

Eligibility:
Citizenship: Canada (landed immigrants also eligible)
Residency: Manitoba, 1 year
Special Requirements: Individuals, ensembles, and organizations are eligible; choreographers must have had at least 1 work professionally performed in public
Art Forms: Choreography

Type of Support: Up to $7,500

Scope of Program: 2 grants, totalling $8,000, to individuals in 1988-89

Application/Selection Process:
Deadline: March 1
Preferred Initial Contact: Contact Performing Arts Consultant before applying
Application Procedure: Submit application form, project budget, artistic statement, samples of work
Selection Process: Jury of independent performing arts professionals
Notification Process: 2 months after deadline
Formal Report of Grant Required: Yes

➤ **COMPOSER COMMISSION AND DEVELOPMENT GRANT**

Purpose: To support the creation of original musical compositions by Manitoba composers and to support creative or production development projects

Eligibility:
Citizenship: Canada (landed immigrants also eligible)
Residency: Manitoba, 1 year
Special Requirements: Professional artists only; must have had at least 1 work professionally performed in public; applicants may be individual performers, ensembles, or larger organizations committed to performance of commissioned work, or individual composers pursuing a creative development project; priority to projects with potential for multiple performances
Art Forms: Music composition

Type of Support: Up to $7,500 for costs such as commissioning fees, copying costs, studio expenses, workshop costs, or creative development project

Scope of Program: 9 grants, totalling $50,068, to individuals in FY 1988-89

Application/Selection Process:
Deadline: March 1, September 1

> **Preferred Initial Contact:** Contact Performing Arts Consultant before applying
> **Application Procedure:** Submit application form, project proposal and budget, artist's statement, samples of work
> **Selection Process:** Jury of independent professionals in the performing arts
> **Notification Process:** 2 months after deadline
> **Formal Report of Grant Required:** Yes

► **PLAYWRIGHT COMMISSION AND DEVELOPMENT GRANT**

Purpose: To support the creation of works by Manitoba playwrights and to support creative or production development projects

Eligibility:
> **Citizenship:** Playwrights must be Canadian citizens or landed immigrants
> **Residency:** Manitoba, 1 year (playwrights)
> **Special Requirements:** Applicants for commission grants must be professional theater companies, service organizations, or theater professionals; applicants for development grants may be individual playwrights; applicants for commission grants must be committed to a public presentation of commissioned work and must demonstrate ongoing commitment to the development of new works by Manitoba playwrights; playwrights must have had at least 1 work professionally performed in public
> **Art Forms:** Playwriting

Type of Support: Up to $7,500 to individual playwright per year

Scope of Program: $69,000 granted to organizations in FY 1988-89

Application/Selection Process:
> **Deadline:** March 1, September 1
> **Preferred Initial Contact:** Contact Performing Arts Consultant before applying
> **Application Procedure:** Submit application form, project budget, samples of work, artist's statement
> **Selection Procedure:** Independent jury of professionals in the performing arts
> **Notification Process:** 2 months after deadline
> **Formal Report of Grant Required:** Yes

► **CONCERT PRODUCTION GRANT/DANCE PRODUCTION GRANT/THEATRE PRODUCTION GRANT**

Purpose: To provide partial support toward the presentation of individual productions or series by professional Manitoba musicians, dance artists, and theater artists

Eligibility:
> **Special Requirements:** Individuals, ensembles, and organizations are eligible; majority of artists involved must be Canadian citizens or landed immigrants, have resided in Manitoba for at

least 1 year, and have completed at least 1 full year of professional activity

Art Forms: Music, dance, theater

Type of Support: Concert Production Grant, up to $5,000 per production; Dance and Theatre Production Grants, up to $10,000 per production

Scope of Program: Grants totalling $20,270 (music), $63,300 (theater), $13,000 (dance) in 1988-89

Application/Selection Process:
   Deadline: March 1 (all disciplines), September 1 (music only)
   Preferred Initial Contact: Contact Performing Arts Consultant before applying
   Application Procedure: Submit application form, project budget, program summary sheets, samples of artists' work, artists' resumés
   Selection Process: Jury of independent performing arts professionals
   Notification Process: 2 months after deadline
   Formal Report of Grant Required: Yes

➤ **ARTVENTURES "A" GRANTS**

CONTACT: JAMES HUTCHISON, WRITING AND PUBLISHING CONSULTANT
Phone: 204-945-5102

Purpose: To support developmental and innovative programs in the arts designed by artists or organizations

Eligibility:
   Residency: Manitoba, 1 year
   Art Forms: All disciplines

Type of Support: Up to $5,000

Scope of Program: 6 grants in the performing arts, totalling $27,234, in FY 1988-89

Application/Selection Process:
   Deadline: May 1, October 1
   Preferred Initial Contact: Call or write for application/guidelines
   Application Procedure: Submit application form, additional materials as requested
   Selection Process: Peer review panel, jury decision
   Notification Process: Letter
   Formal Report of Grant Required: Yes

TECHNICAL ASSISTANCE PROGRAMS AND SERVICES

Programs of Special Interest: The Performance Preparation Grant Program offers partial support to organizations that are committed to the public presentation of works by Manitoba composers (contact T. Patrick Carrabre, Performing Arts Consultant; deadline, March 1).

MARIN ARTS COUNCIL

251 North San Pedro Road
San Rafael, CA 94903
415-499-8350

DIRECT SUPPORT PROGRAMS

➤ INDIVIDUAL ARTISTS GRANTS PROGRAM

CONTACT: BECKY CARTER, ADMINISTRATOR, INDIVIDUAL ARTISTS GRANTS PROGRAM

Purpose: To support Marin's working artists by providing unrestricted fellowships

Eligibility:
Residency: Marin County, 1 year
Age: 18 or older
Special Requirements: Originating artists only; no under-graduate students; no graduate students enrolled in programs related to discipline of application; professional artists only; previous grantees ineligible for 3 years
Art Forms: Playwriting, literature, crafts, visual arts, photography, choreography, music composition, film/video, screenwriting, non-traditional media (performance art, conceptual, audio art, visionary architecture, artists' books, experimental, interdisciplinary)

Type of Support: Up to $10,000 in 1991

Scope of Program: $102,000 available in 1991

Competition for Support: 8 out of 32 applications in nontraditional media, choreography, and music composition funded in 1990

Application/Selection Process:
Deadline: January 30 (playwriting, poetry, fiction, creative prose), May 15 (all other disciplines)
Application Procedure: Submit application form, samples of work; finalists asked to submit additional materials
Selection Process: Jury of artists and arts professionals
Notification Process: 4 months after deadline

➤ COMMUNITY ARTS GRANTS PROGRAM

Purpose: To encourage artistic activities that provide excellent or unusual opportunities for the public to actively practice the arts with arts professionals in community settings

Eligibility:
Special Requirements: Arts organizations, groups, and in-dividuals are eligible; projects must take place in Marin County and actively involve the public in artistic activity; previous gran-tees ineligible for 1 year
Art Forms: All disciplines

Type of Support: Up to $5,000 in 1991-92

Scope of Program: $45,000 available in 1991-92

Application/Selection Process:
Deadline: June 1, December 1
Application Procedure: Submit application form, project budget, letter of support
Selection Process: Panel of arts professionals and community members, board of trustees
Notification Process: 2-3 months after deadline
Formal Report of Grant Required: Yes

TECHNICAL ASSISTANCE PROGRAMS AND SERVICES

Programs of Special Interest: The council provides assistance with financial management, marketing, and public relations through Business Volunteers for the Arts. The annual Arts Resource Directory profiles Marin-based arts organizations, businesses, arts educators, and individual artists. The council also offers group health insurance to members ($25 membership fee).

MARYLAND STATE ARTS COUNCIL (MSAC)

15 West Mulberry Street
Baltimore, MD 21201
301-333-8232
TDD: 301-333-6926
CONTACT: CHARLES CAMP, GRANTS OFFICER

DIRECT SUPPORT PROGRAMS

➤ **INDIVIDUAL ARTIST AWARDS**
Purpose: To identify, develop, and sustain artistic excellence in Maryland
Eligibility:
Citizenship: U.S.
Residency: Maryland, 6 months
Age: 18 or older
Special Requirements: Originating artists only; no students; previous grantees ineligible for 1 year
Art Forms: Choreography (ballet, ethnic, jazz, modern), fiction, media arts, music composition (chamber, choral, electronic, jazz, new/experimental, orchestral, solo recital), new genres (collaborations, installations, interdisciplinary, multi-media, performance art), playwriting, poetry, crafts, visual arts, photography
Type of Support: $2,500-$6,000
Scope of Program: 25 awards in 1991
Application/Selection Process:
Deadline: November 9

Preferred Initial Contact: Call or write for application/guidelines
Application Procedure: Submit application form, samples of work
Selection Process: Peer panel of artists, MSAC board
Notification Process: Letter in May or June
Formal Report of Grant Required: Yes

TECHNICAL ASSISTANCE PROGRAMS AND SERVICES
Programs of Special Interest: MSAC matches Meet the Composer
grants for events featuring composers and their music (contact
Robert E. Benson, Program Coordinator). MSAC sponsors an Arts-
in-Education Program.

MEET THE COMPOSER (MTC)

2112 Broadway
Suite 505
New York, NY 10023
212-787-3601

PROFILE OF FINANCIAL SUPPORT TO ARTISTS
Total Funding/Value of In-Kind Support: $1,802,705 for FY 1990
Competition for Funding: Total applications, 1,670+; total indi-
viduals funded/provided with in-kind support, 979
Grant Range: $150-$70,000

DIRECT SUPPORT PROGRAMS
➤ COMPOSER/CHOREOGRAPHER PROJECT
CONTACT: TRACY WILLIAMS, COMPOSER/CHOREOGRAPHER PROJECT MANAGER
Purpose: To award commission fees and related music costs to
emerging and established composers and choreographers in order
to foster collaborations that bring quality music to dance
Eligibility:
Citizenship: U.S. (permanent residents also eligible)
Age: 18 or older
Special Requirements: Composers and choreographers must
apply through a nonprofit dance company that has been in exis-
tence at least 2 years (nonprofit umbrella organizations may be
used as fiscal agents); dance companies may commission guest
choreographers or their own artistic director; commissioned
work must be completed and performed 6 times within 3 years
of grant notification; repeat collaborations between previously
funded composers and choreographers are ineligible; no students
Art Forms: Collaborative music composition/choreography

Type of Support: Commission fees for composer and choreographer of $5,000-$30,000 each; grant requests may also include funding for music copying costs, assisting musicians (during creation of score), musicians for live performance, audiotape and videotape

Scope of Program: 42 commissioned artists received $399,000 in FY 1990

Application/Selection Process:
   Deadline: February 15
   Preferred Initial Contact: Call or write for application/guidelines
   Application Procedure: Dance company submits application form, project budget, description of company's history, composer's and choreographer's resumés, samples of work (choreographer, composer, and dance company)
   Selection Process: Peer panel of artists
   Notification Process: Letter 3 months after deadline
   Formal Report of Grant Required: Yes

➤ **MEET THE COMPOSER/READER'S DIGEST COMMISSIONING PROGRAM**

CONTACT: TRACY WILLIAMS, COMMISSIONING PROGRAM MANAGER

Purpose: To foster and support the creation and performance of new American works by awarding composer commissions in concert music, opera, music theater, jazz, and radio

Eligibility:
   Citizenship: U.S. (permanent residents also eligible)
   Age: 18 or older
   Special Requirements: Composers must apply through a consortium of nonprofit, tax-exempt organizations located in different areas of the country; consortium members may be symphony and chamber orchestras, chamber and new music ensembles, jazz ensembles, jazz orchestras, soloists, opera companies, musical theater companies, theater companies, choruses, vocal ensembles, festivals, presenting organizations, public radio and television stations; commissioned work must receive at least 6 performances, shared by consortium members
   Art Forms: Music composition

Type of Support: $5,000-$100,000 for composer's fees, copying costs, and librettist's fees

Scope of Program: 31 composers received $381,000 in FY 1990

Application/Selection Process:
   Deadline: April 15
   Preferred Initial Contact: Call or write for application/guidelines
   Application Procedure: 1 consortium member submits application form, letter of consent form and description of each consortium member, resumé for each composer and librettist, samples of work (composer and consortium members)
   Selection Process: Peer panel of artists

Notification Process: Letter 4 months after deadline
Formal Report of Grant Required: Yes

➤ **MEET THE COMPOSER/ROCKEFELLER FOUNDATION/AT&T JAZZ PROGRAM**

CONTACT: LIZ BERSETH, JAZZ PROGRAM MANAGER

Purpose: To provide financial support for residencies and commissions that create new opportunities for jazz composers to write for all forms of musical expression and to encourage producing and presenting organizations in all disciplines to commission and perform works by jazz composers

Eligibility:
    Citizenship: U.S. (permanent residents also eligible)
    Age: 18 or older
    Special Requirements: Composers must apply through a professional, nonprofit arts organization (symphony and chamber orchestras; choruses; chamber ensembles; theater, dance, music theater, and opera companies; and presenting organizations are eligible to apply); jazz ensembles are ineligible to apply, but presenting organizations may apply for a composer to write for his/her ensemble, providing the work is substantial in size and requires additional musicians; composer's own ensemble may be used for theater, dance, or musical theater works; jazz musicians may be used in works for chamber ensemble and symphony or chamber orchestra; commissioned jazz work must be publicly performed at least twice; all residencies must include audience or community-related activities
    Art Forms: Music composition (jazz)

Type of Support: $10,000-$100,000 for commission, residency, and copying costs; grants are usually for less than amount requested, and sponsoring organization must fund the difference in copying and residency costs; residency may be divided into 2 or more periods over 1-3 years and must conclude with public performances of the commissioned work

Scope of Program: 18 composers received $283,000 in FY 1990

Application/Selection Process:
    Deadline: October 15
    Preferred Initial Contact: Call or write for application/guidelines; applicant should also discuss proposal with staff
    Application Procedure: Sponsoring organization submits application form, project budget, resumés for composer and key artistic personnel, sample of composer's work
    Selection Process: Peer panel of artists
    Notification Process: Letter 3 months after deadline
    Formal Report of Grant Required: Yes

TECHNICAL ASSISTANCE PROGRAMS AND SERVICES

Programs of Special Interest: Meet the Composer's Commissioning Music Handbook offers information on fees, copyrights, performance, royalties, and residual rights; the Composers in the Marketplace handbook addresses career-related legal and financial issues. The Education Program offers financial assistance to composers for residencies in primary and secondary schools located in New York, New Jersey, Pennsylvania, Maryland, Delaware, Virginia, West Virginia, and Washington, D.C. (contact Theodore Wiprud, Education Program Manager). The Composers Performance Fund provides financial assistance to composers participating in events featuring their music that take place in this 8-state region (contact Monika Morris, Composers Performance Fund Manager). Meet the Composer's Affiliate Network distributes Composer Performance Fund grants nationally through 7 regional affiliates. Artists interested in participating in this program through presenting organizations located outside of the Mid-Atlantic region should consult the following entries: Meet the Composer/California (CA), New England Arts Foundation (CT, ME, MA, NH, RI, VT), Southern Arts Federation (AL, FL, GA, KY, LA, NC, SC, MS, TN), Mid-America Arts Alliance (AR, KS, MO, NE, OK, TX), Arizona Commission on the Arts (AZ), Arts Midwest (IL, IN, IA, MI, MN, ND, OH, SD, WI), Western States Arts Federation (AK, CO, ID, MT, NV, NM, OR, UT, WA, WY).

MEET THE COMPOSER/CALIFORNIA

P.O. Box 38176
Los Angeles, CA 90038
213-623-1122
CONTACT: CARL STONE, DIRECTOR

TECHNICAL ASSISTANCE PROGRAMS AND SERVICES

Programs of Special Interest: Meet the Composer/California offers financial assistance to composers participating in California events featuring their music (deadlines, September 1, January 3, May 1; apply to deadline that falls at least 6-8 weeks before project begins).

MEMPHIS STATE UNIVERSITY

Music Department
Memphis, TN 38152
901-678-3784
CONTACT: ANGELINE CASE-NEWPORT, DIRECTOR, IMPCF

DIRECT SUPPORT PROGRAMS
➤ **INTERNATIONAL MASTERS PIANO COMPETITION AND FESTIVAL (IMPCF)**
Eligibility:
  Age: 20-35
  Special Requirements: Previous 1st prize winners ineligible
  Art Forms: Music performance (piano)
Type of Support: 1st prize, $5,000 and solo recital in Memphis State University Visiting Artist Series; 2nd prize, $3,000; 3rd prize, $2,000
Scope of Program: Annual competition
Competition for Support: 40 applications in 1989
Application/Selection Process:
  Deadline: July
  Preferred Initial Contact: Call or write for application/guidelines
  Application Procedure: Submit application form, $50 fee, samples of work, repertoire list, resumé; 12-15 semi-finalists are invited to October competition (semi-finalists provide their own transportation; every effort is made to accommodate contestants in private housing)
  Selection Process: Peer panel of artists

METROPOLITAN REGIONAL ARTS COUNCIL (MRAC)

413 Wacouta Street
Suite 300
St. Paul, MN 55102
612-292-8010

DIRECT SUPPORT PROGRAMS
➤ **ARTS PROJECT SUPPORT/MANAGEMENT ASSISTANCE**
Purpose: To support nonprofit organizations or groups of 3 or more artists to undertake time-specific activities that produce art or provide services; Management Assistance grants fund projects intended to lead to the development of a formal arts organization
Eligibility:
  Special Requirements: Individual artists must apply in groups of 3 or more; project must take place in St. Paul metropolitan area;

applicants must have matching funds; projects must not be exclusively for or by student organizations or schools

Art Forms: All disciplines

Type of Support: Maximum $7,500 for up to 50% of project or program (match may include in-kind support)

Scope of Program: $260,000 budget for 1991

Application/Selection Process:
Deadline: January 31
Preferred Initial Contact: Call or write for information

MICHIANA ARTS AND SCIENCES COUNCIL, INC. (MASC)

P.O. Box 1543
South Bend, IN 46634
219-284-9160
CONTACT: LESLIE J. CHOITZ, ARTS PROGRAM DIRECTOR

DIRECT SUPPORT PROGRAMS

➤ **INDIVIDUAL ARTIST FELLOWSHIP PROGRAM**

Purpose: To foster the development of individual artists by funding the creation or completion of a project or activities significant to the artist's professional growth and recognition

Eligibility:
Residency: St. Joseph, Elkhart, LaPorte, Kosciusko counties, 1 year
Special Requirements: Must be emerging artist with less than 3 years professional stature; no high school or undergraduate students; Indiana Arts Commission fellowship recipients ineligible for 1 year

Art Forms: All disciplines

Type of Support: $1,000

Scope of Program: 2 awards in FY 1990-91

Competition for Support: 10 applications in 1990-91

Application/Selection Process:
Deadline: Fall
Preferred Initial Contact: Call or write for application/guidelines
Application Procedure: Submit application form, samples of work, resumé, supporting materials (e.g., catalogs, reviews)
Selection Process: Peer panel of artists, board of directors
Notification Process: Letter 6-8 weeks after deadline
Formal Report of Grant Required: Yes

TECHNICAL ASSISTANCE PROGRAMS AND SERVICES
Programs of Special Interest: MASC maintains a resource library for the arts, a job bank, and a computerized file of performing and visual artists. The Encore Performances Program gives local performing artists an opportunity to present their work.

MICHIGAN COUNCIL FOR THE ARTS (MCA)

1200 Sixth Street
Detroit, MI 48226-2461
313-256-3731
TDD: 313-256-3734
CONTACT: BETTY BOONE, PROGRAM MANAGER

DIRECT SUPPORT PROGRAMS
➤ **CREATIVE ARTIST GRANTS**

Purpose: To enable Michigan artists to create new work or complete works-in-progress by providing funds that may be used for living expenses, materials, rent, presentation and documentation costs, and other expenses involved in producing original art

Eligibility:
  Residency: Michigan
  Special Requirements: Originating artists only; no students; previous grantees ineligible for 2 years
  Art Forms: All disciplines

Type of Support: Up to $10,000

Scope of Program: 88 awards, averaging $6,761, in FY 1991

Competition for Support: 631 applications in 1991

Application/Selection Process:
  Deadline: April 5
  Preferred Initial Contact: Call or write for application/guidelines
  Application Procedure: Submit application form, samples of work, resumé, project budget
  Selection Process: Peer panel of artists, board of directors
  Notification Process: Letter
  Formal Report of Grant Required: Yes

TECHNICAL ASSISTANCE PROGRAMS AND SERVICES
Programs of Special Interest: The council maintains a listing of Michigan artists and operates an Artists-in-Schools Program. The Touring Arts Program provides support to organizations and nonprofit groups that present performances or exhibitions by juried Michigan artists (contact the Touring Arts Agency, Midland Center for the Arts, 1801 West St., Andrews, Midland, MI 48640-2695; 517-631-5930).

MID-AMERICA ARTS ALLIANCE (M-AAA)

912 Baltimore Avenue
Suite 700
Kansas City, MO 64105
816-421-1388
CONTACT: CINDY DENMARK, DIRECTOR OF PERFORMING ARTS

TECHNICAL ASSISTANCE PROGRAMS AND SERVICES

Programs of Special Interest: Professional performing artists from
Arkansas, Kansas, Missouri, Oklahoma, Nebraska, and Texas may be
nominated by their state arts agency for inclusion in the Regional Touring
Program Roster; M-AAA supplies fee support to selected organizations
who present rostered artists. M-AAA also administers and provides
fee support for Meet the Composer (contact David Pinson), Dance
on Tour, and American Originals/National Touring programs.

MID ATLANTIC ARTS FOUNDATION

11 East Chase Street
Suite 2A
Baltimore, MD 21202
301-539-6656
TDD: 301-539-4241

TECHNICAL ASSISTANCE PROGRAMS AND SERVICES

Programs of Special Interest: The Dance on Tour Program provides
fee support to nonprofit organizations presenting out-of-state professional dance artists; preference is given to presentations involving
artists from outside the region. The Music and Theatre Presenting
Program furnishes fee support to nonprofit organizations presenting
professional musicians, ensembles, theater companies, and individual
artists based within the Mid-Atlantic region but outside of the
presenter's state. Mid Atlantic Arts Foundation maintains a regional
Performing Arts Presenter Directory and a regional Performing Artists
Directory, and develops periodic technical assistance projects and
schedules focus groups and networking sessions in conjunction
with regional conferences, showcases, festivals, and exhibitions.

THE MILLAY COLONY FOR THE ARTS

Steepletop
P.O. Box 3
Austerlitz, NY 12017-0003
518-392-3103
CONTACT: ANN-ELLEN LESSER, EXECUTIVE DIRECTOR

DIRECT SUPPORT PROGRAMS
➤ ARTIST RESIDENCIES

Purpose: To provide residencies for visual artists, writers, and composers, regardless of their financial resources

Eligibility:

Art Forms: Music composition, visual arts, photography, literature, some media and interdisciplinary arts

Type of Support: 1-month residency at the colony including living and work space and meals

Scope of Program: 60 residencies per year

Competition for Support: 300 applications per year

Application/Selection Process:

Deadline: February 1 (June-September), May 1 (October-January), September 1 (February-May)

Preferred Initial Contact: Call or write for application/guidelines

Application Procedure: Submit application form, samples of work, 1 reference

Selection Process: Peer panel of artists

Notification Process: Letter

Formal Report of Grant Required: No

MILWAUKEE ARTS BOARD (MAB)

809 North Broadway
P.O. Box 324
Milwaukee, WI 53202
414-223-5790

DIRECT SUPPORT PROGRAMS
➤ NEIGHBORHOOD ARTS PROGRAM

Purpose: To assist nonprofit, neighborhood-based organizations in Milwaukee to strengthen their capacity to work with local artists and to provide local arts programming

Eligibility:

Residency: Preference given to Milwaukee artists

Special Requirements: Artists must apply with nonprofit sponsor organization that serves a particular Milwaukee neighborhood and whose governing board is composed primarily of community residents; project must serve a Milwaukee neighborhood; grant must be matched 1:1 (in-kind matches acceptable for first-time applicants)
Art Forms: All disciplines
Type of Support: Up to $7,000 matching grant
Scope of Program: n/a
Application/Selection Process:
  Deadline: May 1
  Preferred Initial Contact: Call or write for application/guidelines
  Application Procedure: Sponsor submits application form, project budget, financial statement, artist's resumé
  Selection Process: Peer panel of artists, individuals outside of organization, board of directors
  Notification Process: Letter
  Formal Report of Grant Required: Yes

TECHNICAL ASSISTANCE PROGRAMS AND SERVICES
Programs of Special Interest: MAB is developing a technical assistance workshop series.

MINNESOTA STATE ARTS BOARD

432 Summit Avenue
St. Paul, MN 55102
612-297-2603
CONTACT: KAREN MUELLER, ARTIST ASSISTANCE PROGRAM ASSOCIATE

PROFILE OF FINANCIAL SUPPORT TO ARTISTS
Total Funding/Value of In-Kind Support: $274,395 for FY 1990
Competition for Funding: Total applications, 730; total individuals funded/provided with in-kind support, 72
Grant Range: $400-$6,000

DIRECT SUPPORT PROGRAMS
➤ **ARTIST ASSISTANCE PROGRAM—FELLOWSHIPS/CAREER OPPORTUNITY GRANTS**
Purpose: Fellowships support artists by providing time, materials, or living expenses; Career Opportunity Grants help artists take advantage of impending, concrete opportunities that will significantly advance their work or careers
Eligibility:
  Citizenship: U.S.
  Residency: Minnesota, 6 months

Age: 18 or older

Special Requirements: Professional artists only; previous fellowship recipients ineligible for 2 years; previous Career Opportunity Grant recipients ineligible for 1 year

Art Forms: Visual arts, dance (performance, choreography), music (performance, composition, conducting), theater (acting, directing, playwriting, screenwriting), literature

Type of Support: $6,000 fellowships; $100-$1,000 Career Opportunity Grants for specific project

Scope of Program: 34 fellowships for FY 1991; $20,000 a year available for Career Opportunity Grants

Application/Selection Process:

Preferred Initial Contact: Call or write for application/guidelines

Application Procedure: Submit application form, samples of work, resumé, project proposal, project budget (Career Opportunity Grants only)

Selection Process: Organization staff, board of directors, individuals outside of organization, peer panel of artists

Notification Process: Letter 2 weeks after board or committee meeting

Formal Report of Grant Required: Yes

➤ **FOLK ARTS APPRENTICESHIPS**

CONTACT: PHILIP NUSBAUM, FOLK ARTS PROGRAM ASSOCIATE

Purpose: To help promising apprentices to study a traditional art form with an outstanding master folk artist

Eligibility:

Residency: Minnesota (apprentice)

Art Forms: Minnesota-based folk arts

Type of Support: $100-$4,000 for master artist fees, travel expenses, and materials

Scope of Program: $20,000 awarded in 1990

Application/Selection Process:

Deadline: December 1

Preferred Initial Contact: Call for information

TECHNICAL ASSISTANCE PROGRAMS AND SERVICES

Programs of Special Interest: Minnesota artists may apply through the arts board for 5-month residencies at the Headlands Center for the Arts in Sausalito, California. Artists with school residency experience may apply for inclusion in the Artists in Education Roster of Artists. The Folk Artists Directory is a juried list of Minnesota folk artists interested in performing or demonstrating their skills for live audiences.

MISSISSIPPI ARTS COMMISSION

239 North Lamar Street
Suite 207
Jackson, MS 39201
601-359-6030
CONTACT: CINDY JETTER, PROGRAM ADMINISTRATOR

DIRECT SUPPORT PROGRAMS
➤ **ARTIST FELLOWSHIPS**

Purpose: To encourage and support the creation of new art and to recognize the contributions of artists of exceptional talent

Eligibility:
  Citizenship: U.S.
  Residency: Mississippi
  Age: 18 or older
  Special Requirements: No students; professional artists and folk artists only; previous grantees ineligible for 5 years
  Art Forms: Disciplines rotate on 3-year cycle among creative writing/music composition/folk arts (1990-91); visual arts/choreography/film/video/media installations (1991-92); and crafts/new genres (includes performances and interdisciplinary)/playwriting/screenwriting (1992-93)

Type of Support: Up to $5,000

Scope of Program: 5 awards, totalling $25,000, in 1991

Competition for Support: 20 applications in 1990

Application/Selection Process:
  Deadline: March 1
  Preferred Initial Contact: Call or write for application/guidelines
  Application Procedure: Submit application form, samples of work, resumé
  Selection Process: Peer panel of artists, board of directors
  Notification Process: Letter in early July
  Formal Report of Grant Required: Yes

TECHNICAL ASSISTANCE PROGRAMS AND SERVICES

Programs of Special Interest: The Mississippi Arts Commission maintains an Arts in Education Residency Program Artist Roster and a Touring Arts Artist Roster (application deadline, March 1); nonprofit organizations contracting with rostered artists may apply to the commission for fee support. The commission's Arts Management Library holds books and periodicals covering a broad range of subjects relating to the arts and arts management and is open to the public.

MISSOURI ARTS COUNCIL

Wainwright Office Complex
111 North 7th Street
Suite 105
St. Louis, MO 63101-2188
314-340-6845

DIRECT SUPPORT PROGRAMS
➤ **CREATIVE ARTISTS' PROJECT**

CONTACT: PROGRAM ADMINISTRATOR

Purpose: To foster the creation of significant original work and to foster meaningful collaborations between creative artists and organizations interested in the development of such work

Eligibility:
Residency: Missouri, 2 years
Special Requirements: Originating artists only; no students in degree-granting programs; project must include a public component; artist must apply through a nonprofit sponsor; sponsors may submit only 1 application per year
Art Forms: Music composition, choreography, literature, visual arts, film/video

Type of Support: Up to $5,000 matching grant for artists' fees not to exceed 50% of project cost (match may be any combination of cash and in-kind support)

Scope of Program: n/a

Application/Selection Process:
Deadline: January
Application Procedure: Sponsor submits application form, financial statement, project budget, artist's statement, samples of artist's work, artist's resumé
Selection Process: Organization staff, board of directors, advisory panel
Notification Process: After July 1
Formal Report of Grant Required: Yes

TECHNICAL ASSISTANCE PROGRAMS AND SERVICES

Programs of Special Interest: Artists selected for the Missouri Touring Program Roster are eligible to tour Missouri communities to present arts-related activities including exhibitions, lecture-demonstrations, and residencies. The arts council administers an Artists-in-Education Program that provides residencies (2-week minimum), sponsors a Traditional Arts Apprenticeship Program (contact TAAP Project Specialist, 314-882-6296), and hosts the annual Missouri Arts Conference, which includes a variety of technical assistance workshops for artists and arts organizations.

MONTANA ARTS COUNCIL (MAC)

48 North Last Chance Gulch
Helena, MT 59620
406-444-6430
CONTACT: JULIE SMITH, DIRECTOR OF ARTISTS SERVICES

DIRECT SUPPORT PROGRAMS
➤ INDIVIDUAL ARTIST FELLOWSHIP PROGRAM

Purpose: To recognize, reward, and encourage outstanding professional artists in Montana

Eligibility:
  Residency: Montana
  Age: 18 or older
  Special Requirements: No students; previous grantees ineligible
  Art Forms: Dance, music, opera/musical theater, theater, visual arts, crafts, photography, media arts, literature (alternate years only)

Type of Support: $2,000

Scope of Program: 8 awards in 1990

Competition for Support: 107 applications in 1990

Application/Selection Process:
  Deadline: May 1
  Preferred Initial Contact: Call or write for application/guidelines
  Application Procedure: Submit application form, samples of work, resumé, support materials (optional)
  Selection Process: Peer panel of artists, board of directors
  Notification Process: Phone call to recipients in early July; letter to nonrecipients
  Formal Report of Grant Required: Yes

TECHNICAL ASSISTANCE PROGRAMS AND SERVICES

Programs of Special Interest: MAC provides technical assistance through telephone consultation and office visits, maintains a database of individual artists, and publishes *ArtistSearch*, a monthly bulletin describing competitions, job openings, and workshops. The Artists in Schools/Communities Program offers 1-week to 10-month residencies.

MUSICAL THEATRE WORKS

440 Lafayette Street
New York, NY 10003
212-677-0040
CONTACT: GARY LITTMAN

DIRECT SUPPORT PROGRAMS

Purpose: To help young and emerging playwrights, composers, librettists, and lyricists in creating and developing new works for musical theater

Eligibility:
　Art Forms: Musical theater

Type of Support: Opportunity to work with professionals to develop work through series of readings and productions

Scope of Program: Average 25 informal readings, 12-15 staged readings, 8 showcase productions, 3-4 main stage productions per year

Competition for Support: 300 applications per year

Application/Selection Process:
　Deadline: Ongoing
　Preferred Initial Contact: Write for guidelines
　Application Procedure: Submit tapes, script
　Selection Process: Staff and committee review
　Notification Process: Letter 3 months after application

MUSICIAN'S CLUB OF NEW YORK

165 West 66th Street
Suite 11C
New York, NY 10023
CONTACT: CONSTANCE MENSCH, COMMITTEE CHAIR

DIRECT SUPPORT PROGRAMS

➤ OLGA KOUSSEVITZKY YOUNG ARTIST AWARDS

Purpose: To further young artists' opportunities for advancement

Eligibility:
　Age: 16-26
　Special Requirements: Competitors must perform major American work
　Art Forms: Categories rotate on 4-year cycle among piano (1992), voice (1993), strings (1994), woodwind (1995)

Type of Support: 1st prize, $2,000; 2nd prize, $1,000; 3rd prize, $500; additional cash awards sometimes available

Scope of Program: Annual competition

Competition for Support: 80 applications in 1991

Application/Selection Process:
Deadline: March 1
Preferred Initial Contact: Write for application/guidelines; enclose SASE
Application Procedure: Submit application form, $30 fee, biography; audition required
Selection Process: Panel of judges
Notification Process: Letter after 1st round, phone call for later rounds

MUSICIANS FOUNDATION, INC.

200 West 55th Street
New York, NY 10019-5218
CONTACT: EXECUTIVE DIRECTOR

DIRECT SUPPORT PROGRAMS
➤ **EMERGENCY ASSISTANCE GRANTS**
Purpose: To provide emergency assistance to professional musicians
Eligibility:
Citizenship: U.S.
Age: Preference to older musicians
Special Requirements: No students; professional musicians only; must require emergency assistance
Art Forms: Music
Type of Support: Emergency assistance grant
Scope of Program: n/a
Application/Selection Process:
Deadline: None
Preferred Initial Contact: Write for application/guidelines
Application Procedure: Submit application form
Selection Process: Board of directors
Notification Process: Letter

MUSIC IN THE MOUNTAINS FESTIVAL

State University of New York
The College at New Paltz
New Paltz, NY 12561
914-257-3860
CONTACT: DEAN OF FINE AND PERFORMING ARTS

DIRECT SUPPORT PROGRAMS
➤ **MUSIC IN THE MOUNTAINS NATIONAL ORCHESTRAL COMPOSITION COMPETITION**
Purpose: To foster the composition and performance of new American works for chamber or symphony orchestra

Eligibility:
  Citizenship: U.S. (permanent residents also eligible)
  Age: 21 or older
  Special Requirements: Work must have been written in the past 10 years and not have won any other national awards; works requiring chorus, solo vocals, or electronic tape are ineligible; works should be 10-20 minutes in duration
  Art Forms: Music composition (symphony or chamber orchestra)
Type of Support: $1,500 and performance of composition by the Music in the Mountains Orchestra
Scope of Program: 1 award per year
Competition for Support: 25 applications per year
Application/Selection Process:
  Deadline: March 31
  Preferred Initial Contact: Write for application/guidelines
  Application Procedure: Submit cover letter, $25 fee, score of work
  Selection Process: Panel of independent composers and conductors
  Notification Process: Letter

NATIONAL ENDOWMENT FOR THE ARTS, DANCE PROGRAM

Nancy Hanks Center
1100 Pennsylvania Avenue, NW
Room 620
Washington, DC 20506
202-682-5435
CONTACT: SUZANNE CALLAHAN, PROGRAM SPECIALIST

DIRECT SUPPORT PROGRAMS
➤ **CHOREOGRAPHERS' FELLOWSHIPS**

Purpose: To assist the artistic development of professional choreographers whose work has attained a level of national excellence
Eligibility:
  Citizenship: U.S. (permanent residents also eligible)
  Special Requirements: Must have choreographed at least 5 works during professional career; must have shown work professionally in public for at least 5 years at the time of application; artists from diverse aesthetic, cultural, and ethnic backgrounds are encouraged to apply
  Art Forms: Choreography
Type of Support: Most grants are $20,000 for a 2-year period; a few 1-year $7,000 and 3-year $45,000 grants are also available

Scope of Program: 92 grants, totalling $816,000, in FY 1990 Competition for Support: 572 applications in 1990

Application/Selection Process:

    Deadline: Early December

    Preferred Initial Contact: Call or write for application/guidelines

    Application Procedure: Submit application form, resumé; program panelists and consultants make "site visits" to evaluate live performances of applicant's work

    Selection Process: Panel of artists and nonartists

    Notification Process: Letter in October

    Formal Report of Grant Required: Yes

➤ **DANCE/FILM/VIDEO**

Purpose: To support film or video projects of the highest quality that creatively extend, enhance, or preserve the art of dance

Eligibility:

    Citizenship: U.S.

    Special Requirements: Individuals and organizations are eligible; collaborative or documentary projects that encompass a wide spectrum of aesthetic, cultural, and racial perspectives are encouraged; priority to projects where dance takes priority over the film or video art form; projects involving the use of film/video in live performance are ineligible; filmmaker/videomaker should have prior experience working with dance

    Art Forms: Dance and film/video

Type of Support: Up to $15,000 to individuals (most grants are substantially less)

Scope of Program: 2 grants to individuals, totalling $18,500, for FY 1989

Application/Selection Process:

    Deadline: Early January

    Preferred Initial Contact: Call or write for application/guidelines

    Application Procedure: Submit application form, project budget, samples of work, financial statement, resumés for key artistic personnel

    Selection Process: Panel of artists and nonartists

    Notification Process: Letter in October

    Formal Report of Grant Required: Yes

TECHNICAL ASSISTANCE PROGRAMS AND SERVICES

Programs of Special Interest: Dance on Tour grants are available to state arts agencies for projects that present out-of-state dance companies/artists, and to regional arts organizations for fee support to presenters to encourage multi-state touring of dance companies/artists. Choreographers and dancers should contact their state or regional arts agency for details. Grants to Dance Presenters provide artists' fee support to organizations sponsoring 3 or more dance companies/artists, or a long-term engagement of at least 2 weeks.

NATIONAL ENDOWMENT FOR THE ARTS, INTER-ARTS PROGRAM

Nancy Hanks Center
1100 Pennsylvania Avenue, N.W.
Room 710
Washington, D.C. 20506
202-682-5444

DIRECT SUPPORT PROGRAMS

➤ **ARTISTS' PROJECTS: NEW FORMS**

Purpose: To encourage experimental art projects that explore the boundaries between arts disciplines, traditions, or cultures, and to support the creation and production of original work that reflects the cultural and aesthetic diversity of the U.S.

Eligibility:

Citizenship: U.S. (permanent residents also eligible)

Special Requirements: Must apply through a nonprofit sponsoring organization; artists of diverse backgrounds encouraged to apply; projects best reviewed by a single-discipline panel (e.g., visual arts, design arts) ineligible; projects supported by New Forms Regional Initiative ineligible

Art Forms: Interdisciplinary, multi-disciplinary

Type of Support: $7,000-$15,000 for specific project; part of project budget must reflect artist's fees

Scope of Program: 60 grants, totalling $772,825, in 1989

Application/Selection Process:

Deadline: January

Preferred Initial Contact: Call or write for application/guidelines

Application Procedure: Sponsoring nonprofit submits an intent to apply card, then submits application form, project budget, artist's project description, samples of artist's work, artist's resume

Selection Process: Panel of artists and arts professionals, National Council on the Arts review panel, NEA chairman

Notification Process: 7 months after deadline

Formal Report of Grant Required: Yes

NATIONAL ENDOWMENT FOR THE ARTS, INTERNATIONAL ACTIVITIES OFFICE

Nancy Hanks Center
1100 Pennsylvania Avenue, NW
Washington, DC 20506
202-682-5422
CONTACT: MARIANNE GLICKMAN, 202-682-5505

DIRECT SUPPORT PROGRAMS

➤ UNITED STATES/JAPAN ARTIST EXCHANGE FELLOWSHIP PROGRAM
CONTACT: GARY O. LARSON, PROGRAM OFFICER
Phone: 202-682-5562
Purpose: To enable American artists to enrich their art by living and working in Japan, to observe Japanese artistic developments in their fields of interest, and to meet with their professional counterparts and pursue opportunities for artistic growth
Eligibility:
  Citizenship: U.S. (permanent residents also eligible)
  Special Requirements: No students; artists who have previously spent more than a total of 3 months in Japan are generally ineligible; artists may not earn additional income in Japan for lectures or demonstrations of their work
  Art Forms: All disciplines
Type of Support: 6-month residency in Japan including 400,000 yen monthly living stipend, 100,000 yen monthly housing supplement, up to 100,000 yen monthly for professional support services, roundtrip travel for artist, spouse, and children; stipend for Japanese language study in U.S. available if necessary
Scope of Program: 5 residencies per year
Application/Selection Process:
  Deadline: January-March (exact date depends on discipline/media)
  Preferred Initial Contact: Contact appropriate discipline program for application/guidelines (Dance, Suzanne Callahan, 202-682-5435; Folk Arts, Pat Sanders, 202-682-5449; Inter-Arts, Loris Bradley, 202-682-5444; Opera-Musical Theater, Jillian Miller, 202-682-5447; Music, Emery Lewis (Composers Program), Jeff Watson (Jazz Program), Georgia Jones (Solo Recitalists Program), 202-682-5445; Theater, Alane Marco, 202-682-5448)
  Application Procedure: Submit application form, samples of work, references, resumé, financial statement, project budget to appropriate discipline program
  Selection Process: Discipline panels, American Selection Committee of artists and arts managers, Japanese Agency for Cultural Affairs
  Notification Process: Letter
  Formal Report of Grant Required: Yes

NATIONAL ENDOWMENT FOR THE ARTS, MUSIC PROGRAM

Nancy Hanks Center
1100 Pennsylvania Avenue, NW
Room 702
Washington, DC 20506
202-682-5445

PROFILE OF FINANCIAL SUPPORT TO ARTISTS

Total Funding/Value of In-Kind Support: $875,000 for FY 1990

Competition for Funding: Total applications, 786; total individuals funded/provided with in-kind support, 104

Grant Range: $1,700-$25,000

DIRECT SUPPORT PROGRAMS

➤ **COMPOSERS AND COLLABORATIVE FELLOWSHIPS**

CONTACT: EMERY LEWIS, COMPOSERS PROGRAM SPECIALIST

Purpose: To encourage the creation or completion of musical works by composers and other creative artists working with composers

Eligibility:

Citizenship: U.S. (permanent residents also eligible)

Special Requirements: Applications for collaborations with librettists, video artists, filmmakers, poets, or choreographers must be made by composer; previous grantees ineligible for 1 year; projects funded by the New American Works/Organizations and New American Works/Individuals as Producers categories of the NEA's Opera/Musical-Theater Program are ineligible for fellowship grants during same year

Art Forms: Music composition (except jazz)

Type of Support: $5,000-$25,000 Composers Fellowship, $5,000-$35,000 Collaborative Fellowship (all fellowships are awarded on a 2-year basis)

Scope of Program: 17 grants, totalling $275,000, in 1989

Application/Selection Process:

Deadline: Early January

Preferred Initial Contact: Call or write for application/guidelines

Application Procedure: Submit application form, samples of work, project budget

Selection Process: Peer panel of artists

Notification Process: Letter in September

Formal Report of Grant Required: Yes

➤ **JAZZ PERFORMANCE FELLOWSHIPS**

CONTACT: JEFF WATSON, JAZZ PROGRAM SPECIALIST

Purpose: To encourage the creative development of individual, professional musicians who perform traditional, innovative, or extended forms of jazz through funding specific projects such as preparing or presenting performances, master classes, lecture/ demonstrations, or workshops

Eligibility:
   Citizenship: U.S. (permanent residents also eligible)
   Special Requirements: Previous grantees ineligible for 1 year; collaborative performances, performances at commercial clubs or festivals, and study at commercial schools or studios are ineligible
   Art Forms: Music performance (jazz)

Type of Support: $5,000-$15,000

Scope of Program: 30 grants in 1989

Application/Selection Process:
   Deadline: Early January
   Preferred Initial Contact: Call or write for application/guidelines
   Application Procedure: Submit application form, samples of work, project budget
   Selection Process: Peer panel of artists
   Notification Process: Letter in October
   Formal Report of Grant Required: Yes

➤ **JAZZ COMPOSITION FELLOWSHIPS**

CONTACT: JEFF WATSON, JAZZ PROGRAM SPECIALIST

Purpose: To encourage the creative development of professional jazz composers working in traditional, innovative, or extended forms of the art by supporting the creation of new works, the completion of works-in-progress, and the reproduction of scores or parts of completed works

Eligibility:
   Citizenship: U.S. (permanent residents also eligible)
   Special Requirements: Previous grantees ineligible for 1 year; funds may not be used for rehearsals, performances, collaborations, or demonstration tapes
   Art Forms: Music composition (jazz)

Type of Support: $5,000-$10,000

Scope of Program: 5 grants in 1989

Application/Selection Process:
   Deadline: Early January
   Preferred Initial Contact: Call or write for application/guidelines
   Application Procedure: Submit application form, samples of work, project budget
   Selection Process: Peer panel of artists
   Notification Process: Letter in October
   Formal Report of Grant Required: Yes

MONEY FOR PERFORMING ARTISTS

➤ **JAZZ STUDY FELLOWSHIPS**

CONTACT: JEFF WATSON, JAZZ PROGRAM SPECIALIST

Purpose: To enable jazz composers and performers to undertake intensive one-on-one study in a non-institutional setting

Eligibility:

Citizenship: U.S.

Special Requirements: Must be accepted as a student by a professional jazz artist before applying; must display a high level of musicianship and be actively engaged in, or demonstrate the potential for, a professional career in jazz; projects involving master classes, commercial studios, or studies leading to a degree are ineligible; individuals may not receive study grants for more than 3 consecutive years

Art Forms: Music performance and composition (jazz)

Type of Support: $2,000-$5,000

Scope of Program: 37 grants in 1989

Application/Selection Process:

Deadline: Early January

Preferred Initial Contact: Call or write for application/guidelines

Application Procedure: Submit application form, formal letter of agreement from teacher, teacher's biography, samples of work, project budget

Selection Process: Peer panel of artists

Notification Process: Letter in October

Formal Report of Grant Required: Yes

➤ **AMERICAN JAZZ MASTERS FELLOWSHIPS**

CONTACT: JEFF WATSON

Purpose: To provide one-time fellowships to distinguished jazz masters who have made a significant contribution to the art form in the African-American tradition

Eligibility:

Citizenship: U.S. (permanent residents also eligible)

Special Requirements: Must be nominated by a member of the jazz community or the public

Art Forms: Music (jazz)

Type of Support: $20,000

Scope of Program: Up to 5 awards per year

Application/Selection Process:

Deadline: Early January

Preferred Initial Contact: Call or write for guidelines

Application Procedure: Nominator submits letter of recommendation

Selection Process: Peer panel of artists

Notification Process: Letter in October

➤ **SOLO RECITALISTS FELLOWSHIPS**
CONTACT: GEORGIA JONES, SOLO RECITALISTS PROGRAM SPECIALIST
Purpose: To support individuals of outstanding talent who have the potential for major careers as solo or duo recitalists
Eligibility:
  Citizenship: U.S. (permanent residents also eligible)
  Special Requirements: Must be a professional artist who performs as a solo recitalist, a recitalist with an accompanist, or a member of a duo; must have given at least 5 different public performances, each with substantially different repertoire, for a contracted fee; artists whose solo or duo careers are already well established are ineligible
  Art Forms: Music performance (vocal and keyboard recitalists may apply in odd-numbered years; all other recitalists may apply in even-numbered years)
Type of Support: $7,500-$15,000 for soloists, $10,000-$15,000 for duos
Scope of Program: 12 grants, totalling $150,000, in 1989
Application/Selection Process:
  Deadline: Early January
  Preferred Initial Contact: Call or write for application/guidelines
  Application Procedure: Submit application form, resumé, samples of work, project budget
  Selection Process: Peer panel of artists
  Notification Process: Letter in September
  Formal Report of Grant Required: Yes

TECHNICAL ASSISTANCE PROGRAMS AND SERVICES
Programs of Special Interest: The Music Program makes grants to organizations and to solo and duo performers to record and distribute American music. Support is also available to a music performing organization that wishes to sponsor a composer-in-residence.

NATIONAL ENDOWMENT FOR THE ARTS, OPERA/MUSICAL-THEATER PROGRAM

Nancy Hanks Center
1100 Pennsylvania Avenue, NW
Room 703
Washington, DC 20506
202-682-5447
TDD: 202-682-5496
CONTACT: JILLIAN MILLER, PROGRAM SPECIALIST

PROFILE OF FINANCIAL SUPPORT TO ARTISTS
Total Funding/Value of In-Kind Support: $102,500 for FY 1989

Competition for Funding: Total applications, 37; total individuals funded/provided with in-kind support, 6

Grant Range: $7,500-$35,000

DIRECT SUPPORT PROGRAMS

➤ NEW AMERICAN WORKS—INDIVIDUALS AS PRODUCERS

Purpose: To develop skilled producers and encourage new work by assisting independent producers who produce the works of others and creative artists who work as their own producers

Eligibility:

Citizenship: U.S.

Special Requirements: Artist-producers may not apply for Phase I grants only; producers should generally work outside of established producing organizations, but producers affiliated with an organization may apply; projects funded under New Works—Organizations cannot be funded under this program in the same fiscal year

Art Forms: Opera, musical theater

Type of Support: $5,000-$45,000 1:1 matching grant (Phase I grants up to $15,000 to be used for creative artists only; Phase II grants up to $30,000 for producer's fees and expenses, and for creative artists and activities involved in the project)

Scope of Program: 5 grants, totalling $95,000, in 1989

Application/Selection Process:

Deadline: Early September

Preferred Initial Contact: Call or write for application/guidelines

Application Procedure: Submit application form, resumés for producer and artistic personnel, project budget, references, artist's statement, fundraising proposal, samples of work

Selection Process: Peer panel of artists

Notification Process: Letter in March

Formal Report of Grant Required: Yes

➤ SPECIAL PROJECTS—PRODUCING/ARTISTIC APPRENTICES

Purpose: To provide grants to individuals to apprentice with established independent producers, dramaturgs, stage directors, designers, choreographers, composers, librettists, dramatists, or conductors

Eligibility:

Citizenship: U.S. (permanent residents also eligible)

Special Requirements: Must have some background in opera/musical theater; must identify proposed sponsor at time of application; sponsor must have an established reputation; already existing associations are ineligible for support unless grant will enable a substantive change in the nature of the association; projects that focus on the development of new work are encouraged

Art Forms: Opera, musical theater

Type of Support: $5,000-$20,000 for apprentice's salary, fringe benefits, initial relocation, and travel costs

Scope of Program: 1 grant, totalling $7,500, in 1991

Application/Selection Process:

Deadline: Early September

Preferred Initial Contact: Call or write for application/guidelines; consult with staff before applying

Application Procedure: Submit application form, project budget, sponsor's and apprentice's resumés

Selection Process: Peer panel of artists

Notification Process: Letter in March

Formal Report of Grant Required: Yes

TECHNICAL ASSISTANCE PROGRAMS AND SERVICES

Programs of Special Interest: The New American Works—Organizations category offers matching grants to professional producing organizations for the creation, completion, or adaptation of a single new American work through commissions to creative artists, and for the development or rehearsal and production of a new work or a second production of a recently premiered work.

NATIONAL ENDOWMENT FOR THE ARTS, THEATER PROGRAM

Nancy Hanks Center
1100 Pennsylvania Avenue, NW
Room 608
Washington, DC 20506
202-682-5425
CONTACT: ELEANOR D. MONCURE, SENIOR PROGRAM SPECIALIST

PROFILE OF FINANCIAL SUPPORT TO ARTISTS

Total Funding/Value of In-Kind Support: $475,000 for FY 1989

Competition for Funding: Total applications, 307; total individuals funded/provided with in-kind support, 35

Grant Range: $5,000-$25,000

DIRECT SUPPORT PROGRAMS

➤ **FELLOWSHIPS FOR PLAYWRIGHTS**

Purpose: To encourage the development of professional playwrights of exceptional talent by enabling them to set aside time for writing, research, travel, and other activities that will enhance their artistic vision

Eligibility:

Citizenship: U.S. (permanent residents also eligible)

Special Requirements: No students; must have had a script presented by a professional theater company in the last 5 years; playwrights participating in an NEA-supported commission are ineligible to hold a fellowship at the same time

Art Forms: Playwriting

Type of Support: $10,000-$17,500 1-year awards; a limited number of $35,000 2-year awards may be granted; additional $2,500 grant available for residency at a professional U.S. theater of the playwright's choice

Scope of Program: 19 grants, totalling $300,000, in 1989

Application/Selection Process:
  Deadline: Late June
  Preferred Initial Contact: Call or write for application/guidelines
  Application Procedure: Submit application form, samples of work, references, resumé, artist's statement
  Selection Process: Peer panel of artists
  Notification Process: Letter in February or March
  Formal Report of Grant Required: Yes

➤ **FELLOWSHIPS FOR SOLO PERFORMANCE THEATER ARTISTS AND MIMES**

Purpose: To assist the work of professional solo performance theater artists exploring new styles and forms of theater, and to assist mimes working as solo performers independent of professional mime companies

Eligibility:
  Citizenship: U.S. (permanent residents also eligible)
  Special Requirements: Activities that normally might be accomplished under the auspices of mime or theater companies eligible for NEA support are generally not funded; members of mime or theater companies are eligible only if activities during the grant period would be undertaken outside the company association; performance of touring or solo plays is generally ineligible
  Art Forms: Solo theater performance

Type of Support: $5,000-$12,000

Scope of Program: 12 grants, totalling $75,000, in 1989

Application/Selection Process:
  Deadline: Early November (letter of intent), early December (formal application)
  Preferred Initial Contact: Call or write for application/guidelines
  Application Procedure: Submit application form, resumé, references, artistic statement; program panelists and consultants make "site visits" to evaluate live performances of applicant's work
  Selection Process: Peer panel of artists
  Notification Process: Letter in June
  Formal Report of Grant Required: Yes

NATIONAL ENDOWMENT FOR THE ARTS, VISUAL ARTS PROGRAM

Nancy Hanks Center
1100 Pennsylvania Avenue, NW
Room 729
Washington, DC 20506
202-682-5448
CONTACT: SILVIO LIM, PROGRAM SPECIALIST

DIRECT SUPPORT PROGRAMS
➤ **VISUAL ARTS FELLOWSHIPS**

Purpose: To encourage the creative development of professional artists, enabling them to pursue their work

Eligibility:

Citizenship: U.S. (permanent residents also eligible)

Special Requirements: Professional artists only; no students pursuing undergraduate or graduate degrees; previous recipients who received $15,000 or more ineligible for 2 cycles; artists may apply in only 1 fellowship area per cycle

Art Forms: Eligible media rotate on 2-year cycle; new genres (includes conceptual, performance, video), painting, works on paper eligible in odd-numbered years; photography, sculpture, crafts eligible in even-numbered years

Type of Support: $15,000 fellowships in 1991-92

Scope of Program: $2,130,000 awarded to 177 artists in FY 1990

Competition for Support: 5,353 applications in 1990

Application/Selection Process:

Deadline: January-March (exact date depends on media)

Preferred Initial Contact: Call or write for application/guidelines

Application Procedure: Submit application form, samples of work, resumé

Selection Process: Peer panel of artists, National Council on the Arts, NEA chair

Notification Process: Letter in September

Formal Report of Grant Required: Yes

NATIONAL ORCHESTRAL ASSOCIATION

475 Riverside Drive
Suite 249
New York, NY 10115
212-870-2009

DIRECT SUPPORT PROGRAMS

➤ NEW MUSIC ORCHESTRAL PROJECT—FIRST READINGS/
SECOND PRESENTATIONS

Purpose: To read, tape, and perform new orchestral works by living American composers, and to make second presentations to provide works that have already premiered with additional public and professional exposure

Eligibility:
  Citizenship: U.S.
  Art Forms: Music composition (orchestra; works may include electronic components, soloists, solo ensemble, and chorus)

Type of Support: Reading, taping, possibility of premiere performance at Carnegie Hall (First Readings); performance of work at Carnegie Hall (Second Presentations)

Scope of Program: 10 awards in 1990-91 (each year either First Readings or Second Presentations awards are made)

Competition for Support: 450 applications in 1990-91

Application/Selection Process:
  Deadline: June 15
  Preferred Initial Contact: Call or write for guidelines
  Application Procedure: Submit samples of work, resumé or biography, documentation of world premiere (Second Readings)
  Selection Process: New York-based jury, national jury, artistic director
  Notification Process: Letter

NEBRASKA ARTS COUNCIL (NAC)

1313 Farnam on-the-Mall
Omaha, NE 68102-1873
402-595-2122 (dial 471-2211 free of charge from Lincoln)
CONTACT: SUZANNE T. WISE, VISUAL ARTS COORDINATOR

DIRECT SUPPORT PROGRAMS

➤ INDIVIDUAL ARTIST FELLOWSHIP PROGRAM

Purpose: To recognize exemplary achievements by originating artists in Nebraska

Eligibility:
  Citizenship: U.S.
  Residency: Nebraska, 2 years
  Age: 18 or older
  Special Requirements: Originating, professional artists only; no students enrolled in degree- or certificate-granting program in artistic field for which application is being made
  Art Forms: Visual arts, literature, performing arts (choreography, music composition, playwriting), interdisciplinary arts; visual arts awards given every year, literature and performing arts awards in alternate years
Type of Support: $3,500 master awards; $1,000 merit awards
Scope of Program: 10 awards per year (1 master award and 4 merit awards in visual arts; 1 master award and 4 merit awards in performing arts or literature)
Competition for Support: 150 applications per year
Application/Selection Process:
  Deadline: November 1
  Preferred Initial Contact: Call or write for application/guidelines
  Application Procedure: Submit application form, samples of work, resumé, artist's statement
  Selection Process: Panel of out-of-state artists and arts professionals
  Notification Process: Letter
  Formal Report of Grant Required: No

TECHNICAL ASSISTANCE PROGRAMS AND SERVICES

Programs of Special Interest: NAC offers grants workshops and operates the Arts Information Referral Service, an unpublished, unjuried directory of Nebraska artists. NAC approves Nebraska artists for 1-week to 12-month Artists-in-Schools/Communities residencies (February 1 deadline) and for participation in the Nebraska Touring Program (March 15 deadline).

NEVADA STATE COUNCIL ON THE ARTS (NSCA)

329 Flint Street
Reno, NV 89501
702-688-1225
CONTACT: KIRK ROBERTSON, PROGRAM DIRECTOR

PROFILE OF FINANCIAL SUPPORT TO ARTISTS

Total Funding/Value of In-Kind Support: $73,145 for FY 1990 (includes Artist-in-Residence program)
Competition for Funding: Total applications, 80; total individuals funded/provided with in-kind support, 43
Grant Range: $250-$5,000

DIRECT SUPPORT PROGRAMS

➤ **FELLOWSHIPS/MINI-GRANTS**

Purpose: Fellowships assist artists' efforts to advance their careers by supporting the creation of new works; mini-grants provide short-term project support to meet immediate needs

Eligibility:
    Citizenship: U.S. (permanent residents also eligible)
    Residency: Nevada, 1 year
    Special Requirements: No students
    Art Forms: All disciplines

Type of Support: $2,000-$10,000 fellowships; up to $1,000 mini-grants

Scope of Program: $20,000 in fellowships, $20,000 in mini-grants awarded annually

Application/Selection Process:
    Deadline: May 15 (fellowships), 90 days before project (mini-grants)
    Preferred Initial Contact: Call or write for application/guidelines
    Application Procedure: Submit application form, samples of work, references, resumé, project budget
    Selection Process: Peer panel of artists, board of directors (fellowship); executive director, chairman (mini-grants)
    Notification Process: Letter
    Formal Report of Grant Required: Yes

➤ **FOLK ARTS APPRENTICESHIPS**

CONTACT: ANDREA GRAHAM, FOLK ARTS PROGRAM DIRECTOR

Purpose: To support master traditional artists who wish to teach experienced apprentices
    Citizenship: U.S. (permanent residents also eligible)
    Residency: Either master or apprentice must be Nevada resident
    Special Requirements: Master and apprentice must apply together
    Art Forms: Traditional and folk arts

Type of Support: $2,500 for master's fees, supplies, and travel

Scope of Program: 4 apprenticeships per year

Application/Selection Process:
    Deadline: June 15
    Preferred Initial Contact: Call for application/guidelines
    Application Procedure: Submit application form, support materials
    Selection Process: Panel and council review
    Notification Process: Letter
    Formal Report of Grant Required: No

TECHNICAL ASSISTANCE PROGRAMS AND SERVICES

Programs of Special Interest: The Artist-in-Residence Program provides residencies for practicing, professional artists in a variety of settings.

NEW BRUNSWICK DEPARTMENT OF TOURISM, RECREATION AND HERITAGE—ARTS BRANCH

P.O. Box 12345
Fredericton, New Brunswick
Canada E3B 5C3
506-453-2555
CONTACT: ARTS BRANCH STAFF

PROFILE OF FINANCIAL SUPPORT TO ARTISTS
Total Funding/Value of In-Kind Support: $363,700 for 1991
Competition for Funding: n/a
Grant Range: Up to $10,000

DIRECT SUPPORT PROGRAMS
➤ **TRAVEL PROGRAM**

Purpose: To increase participation in regional, national, and international festivals, fairs, and competitions, and to increase exposure of New Brunswick arts products
Eligibility:
  Citizenship: Canada (landed immigrants also eligible)
  Residency: New Brunswick, 2 of past 4 years
  Age: 18 or older
  Special Requirements: Must have received recognized honor at the provincial level or provide a letter of invitation
  Art Forms: All disciplines
Type of Support: Maximum $5,000 for up to 30% of costs
Scope of Program: $25,000 annual budget
Application/Selection Process:
  Deadline: March 15, September 15 (at least 60 days before event)
  Application Procedure: Submit application form, supporting materials as specified
  Selection Procedure: Multi-disciplinary jury of professional artists
  Notification Process: Letter 2 months after deadline
  Formal Report of Grant Required: Yes

➤ **PRODUCTION AND CREATION GRANTS**

Purpose: To support research and development or approved projects by artists or curators
Eligibility:
  Citizenship: Canada (landed immigrants also eligible)
  Residency: New Brunswick, 2 of past 4 years
  Art Forms: All disciplines
Type of Support: $1,000-$6,000 grants
Scope of Program: $182,000 annual budget

Application/Selection Process:
Deadline: January 15, July 15
Application Procedure: Submit application form, supporting materials as specified
Selection Process: Multi-disciplinary jury of professional artists
Notification Process: Letter 2 months after deadline
Formal Report of Grant Required: Yes

➤ EXCELLENCE AWARDS

Purpose: To reward and honor excellence in the arts
Citizenship: Canada (landed immigrants also eligible)
Residency: New Brunswick, 2 of past 4 years
Special Requirements: Must be nominated by an individual or group
Art Forms: Visual arts, literature, crafts, performing arts, cinematic arts

Type of Support: Cash prize

Scope of Program: $35,000 distributed according to jury's discretion

Application/Selection Process:
Deadline: September 15 for nominations
Application Procedure: Nominator submits nomination form, supporting materials as specified
Selection Process: Multi-disciplinary jury of professional artists
Notification Process: Letter 2 months after deadline
Formal Report of Grant Required: No

TECHNICAL ASSISTANCE PROGRAMS AND SERVICES

Programs of Special Interest: The Artist-in-Residence Program grants matching funds to educational institutions and organizations that wish to sponsor 1- to 12-month residencies by senior professional artists. The Artists-in-Schools Program supplies matching funds to schools for workshops and demonstrations by professional artists.

NEW ENGLAND FOUNDATION FOR THE ARTS (NEFA)

678 Massachusetts Avenue
Suite 801
Cambridge, MA 02139
617-492-2914
CONTACT: BJ LARSON-BREWER, PROGRAM COORDINATOR

DIRECT SUPPORT PROGRAMS

➤ NEW FORMS REGIONAL INITIATIVE

Purpose: To support projects by lesser-known artists whose work explores new definitions of cultures, artistic disciplines, or traditions and is not easily defined by historical Western-European fine arts traditions

Eligibility:

Citizenship: U.S. (permanent residents also eligible)

Residency: Connecticut, Maine, Massachusetts, New Hampshire, Rhode Island, Vermont

Special Requirements: No students

Art Forms: Experimental work that is innovative in form or content, collaborative or traditional work that explores new forms or contexts (eligible projects include performance art, multi-media, installations, dance, environmental work, textiles, theater work)

Type of Support: $2,000-$5,000 for project support

Scope of Program: 6-12 awards available in FY 1990-91

Competition for Support: 232 applications in 1990-91

Application/Selection Process:

Deadline: January 31

Preferred Initial Contact: Call or write for application/guidelines

Application Procedure: Submit application form, samples of work, resumé, project budget and description

Selection Process: Peer panel of artists

Notification Process: Letter

TECHNICAL ASSISTANCE PROGRAMS AND SERVICES

Programs of Special Interest: NEFA provides fee support to organizations presenting artists on the New England Touring Program Roster (artist application deadline, September 15; contact Rebecca Blunk, Director of Performing Arts). EARNEST (Exchange of Arts Resources among the New England States) funds presenters who engage New England artist groups based outside the presenter's state. The artists and companies must be members of their own state's touring roster but not members of the New England Touring Program Roster. Meet the Composer/New England offers grants to organizations that create opportunities for interaction between composers and audiences in conjunction with performances of the composer's work; commissions of new work may also be supported. The Dance on Tour initiative provides fee support to nonprofit presenters engaging out-of-state professional dance companies or artists. Dancers should contact presenters outside of their state or region to develop touring plans. Each regional arts organization maintains a database of presenters in its region. Other regional organizations participating in Dance on Tour are Arts Midwest, Mid-America Arts Alliance, Mid Atlantic Arts Foundation, Southern Arts Federation, and Western States Arts Federation. The Jazz/New England program maintains a database of artists, presenters, and other jazz resources; provides technical assistance through workshops, consultations, and publications; and supports New England tours of outstanding jazz performances (contact Stephanie Ancona).

NEW HAMPSHIRE STATE COUNCIL ON THE ARTS (NHSCA)

40 North Main Street
Concord, NH 03301
603-271-2789
TDD: 603-225-4033
CONTACT: AUDREY SYLVESTER, ARTIST SERVICES COORDINATOR

DIRECT SUPPORT PROGRAMS

➤ **INDIVIDUAL ARTIST FELLOWSHIPS**

Purpose: To recognize artistic excellence and professional commitment

Eligibility:
  Residency: New Hampshire, 1 year
  Age: 19 or older
  Special Requirements: Must demonstrate professional commitment; no full-time students; previous recipients ineligible for 1 year
  Art Forms: All disciplines

Type of Support: $1,000-$2,000 Fellowships; finalists eligible to apply for up to $500 matching cash Artist Opportunity Grant for professional development project; Fellowship winners asked to make public presentation of their work

Scope of Program: 10 Fellowships and 6 Artist Opportunity Grants, totalling $23,000, in FY 1991

Competition for Support: 125 applications in 1991

Application/Selection Process:
  Deadline: May 1
  Preferred Initial Contact: Call or write for application/guidelines
  Application Procedure: Submit application form, samples of work, resumé
  Selection Process: Peer panel of artists
  Notification Process: Letter or phone call in October
  Formal Report of Grant Required: Yes

TECHNICAL ASSISTANCE PROGRAMS AND SERVICES

Programs of Special Interest: NHSCA maintains a roster of professional artists eligible for Arts in Education residencies (artist application deadline, May 1; contact Arts in Education Coordinator). The Touring Program offers grants to organizations that present New Hampshire performing artists included on the council's Touring Roster (artist application deadline, May 1; contact Touring Program Coordinator). The Rural Arts Program provides funds for short-term community residencies by performing and literary artists from the Rural Artist Roster (contact Rural Arts Coordinator).

THE NEW HARMONY PROJECT

4040 Vincennes Circle
Suite 600
Indianapolis, IN 46268
317-879-4057
CONTACT: JEFFREY L. SPARKS

DIRECT SUPPORT PROGRAMS
➤ THE NEW HARMONY PROJECT CONFERENCE/LABORATORY

Purpose: To support playwrights and screenwriters in developing new scripts in a conference/laboratory setting

Eligibility:
  Special Requirements: Scripts selected based on sensitivity and truthfulness in exploring values and on marketability; participants must attend expenses-paid pre-conference week-end in April
  Art Forms: Playwriting, screenwriting

Type of Support: 2-week May script development conference with professional actors, directors, and staff (room, board, and travel to conference paid)

Scope of Program: 4-6 recipients per year

Application/Selection Process:
  Deadline: December 1
  Preferred Initial Contact: Write for guidelines
  Application Procedure: Submit script, biography
  Selection Process: Staff, committee
  Notification Process: Phone call to recipients, letter to nonrecipients

NEW JERSEY STATE COUNCIL ON THE ARTS (NJSCA)

4 North Broad Street
CN 306
Trenton, NJ 08625
609-292-6130
CONTACT: KATHI R. LEVIN, DIRECTOR OF FUNDING AND ARTS MANAGEMENT SERVICES

DIRECT SUPPORT PROGRAMS
➤ FELLOWSHIP AWARDS

Purpose: To enable experienced, professional artists to set aside time and purchase materials to create original works of art

Eligibility:
  Residency: New Jersey
  Special Requirements: No students; previous grantees ineligible for 3 years

Art Forms: Choreography, crafts, design arts, experimental art, film, interdisciplinary, music composition, photography, playwriting, literature, visual arts, video

Type of Support: $5,000 to $15,000

Scope of Program: 68 awards, averaging $7,000, in 1991

Competition for Support: 1,072 applications in 1991

Application/Selection Process:
  Deadline: March
  Preferred Initial Contact: Call or write for application/guidelines
  Application Procedure: Submit application form, samples of work, resumé
  Selection Process: Peer panel of artists
  Notification Process: Letter 6 months after deadline
  Formal Report of Grant Required: Yes

TECHNICAL ASSISTANCE PROGRAMS AND SERVICES

Programs of Special Interest: The Artists-in-Education (AIE) Program recommends artists for 4-day to 4-month residencies in schools, communities, and correctional facilities (April 15 deadline). The Performing Arts Program holds in-depth seminars on subjects such as marketing and touring readiness, and maintains a Performing Arts Registry of New Jersey artists and organizations. The council also sponsors performing arts showcases.

NEW LANGTON ARTS

1246 Folsom
San Francisco, CA 94103
415-626-5416

DIRECT SUPPORT PROGRAMS
➤ NEW FORMS REGIONAL INITIATIVE

Purpose: To support individual artists working on interdisciplinary or collaborative projects

Eligibility:
  Residency: Northern California, Oregon, Washington State, Alaska
  Art Forms: Dance, literature, performance art, film, video, visual arts

Type of Support: $3,000-$5,000

Scope of Program: 9-13 awards per year

Competition for Support: 225 applications per year

Application/Selection Process:
  Deadline: Early Spring
  Preferred Initial Contact: Write for application after November 1 (include SASE)

Application Procedure: Submit application form, samples of work, project budget, supporting documentation
Selection Process: Independent review panel of artists
Notification Process: Letter
Formal Report of Grant Required: Yes

NEW MEXICO ARTS DIVISION

224 East Palace Avenue
Santa Fe, NM 87501
505-827-6490

DIRECT SUPPORT PROGRAMS

➤ ARTS PROJECTS—FOLK ARTS PROJECTS/CULTURALLY DIVERSE ARTS PROJECTS/OTHER ARTS PROJECTS

CONTACT: GRANTS AND SERVICES OFFICE STAFF

Purpose: Folk Arts Projects recognize the wide variety of distinctive folk arts in New Mexico by purchasing short-term arts services from folk artists; Culturally Diverse Arts Projects recognize culturally specific and multi-cultural arts in New Mexico by procuring short-term arts services from those who practice such arts; Other Arts Projects support projects in all disciplines that do not meet eligibility requirements for Folk Arts or Culturally Diverse Arts

Eligibility:
  Residency: Projects involving New Mexico artists encouraged
  Special Requirements: Artists must apply with a nonprofit organization that agrees to act as a fiscal agent; project must be publicly presented in New Mexico; Other Arts Project applicants must provide 1:1 cash match of grant; Folk Arts Projects and Culturally Diverse Arts Projects applicants must provide cash matches after 2 years of funding; Folk Arts Projects artists must be members of same cultural group to which art form belongs; Culturally Diverse Arts Projects must be by and for culturally specific groups (Hispanic, American Indian, African-American, Asian-American artists encouraged to apply)
  Art Forms: All disciplines
Type of Support: Up to $5,000
Scope of Program: n/a
Application/Selection Process:
  Deadline: March 1
  Preferred Initial Contact: Consult with Grants and Services Office staff
  Application Procedure: Fiscal agent submits application forms, samples of artist's work, artist's resumé, project budget
  Selection Process: Peer panel of artists, commission
  Notification Process: July
  Formal Report of Grant Required: Yes

➤ **FOLK ARTS MASTER/APPRENTICE TEAMS**
CONTACT: STATE FOLK ARTS COORDINATOR
Purpose: To encourage the survival of New Mexico's diverse folk arts by supporting their transmission within the home community
Eligibility:
Residency: New Mexico (apprentice)
Special Requirements: Preference given to masters and apprentices who belong to same cultural group as the art form; master should have reached high level of expertise in art form; apprentice should have some experience in art form
Art Forms: Folk arts
Type of Support: Up to $1,750 for short-term apprenticeship lasting up to 4 months; up to $3,500 for long-term apprenticeship lasting up to 8 months
Scope of Program: n/a
Application/Selection Process:
Deadline: April 1
Preferred Initial Contact: Call or write for application/guidelines

TECHNICAL ASSISTANCE PROGRAMS AND SERVICES
Programs of Special Interest: The Incentives to Present New Mexico Touring Artists program provides fee support to organizations presenting artists listed in *A Resource Directory for Presenters and Artists*. Artists listed in the directory are also eligible for Arts in Education (AIE) residencies in community, rural, and institutional settings (contact AIE staff). The Southwest Arts Conference, which takes place in Scottsdale, Arizona each March, offers workshops for artists.

NEW YORK CITY DEPARTMENT OF CULTURAL AFFAIRS (DCA)

2 Columbus Circle
New York, NY 10019
212-974-1150

DIRECT SUPPORT PROGRAMS
➤ **MATERIALS FOR THE ARTS (MFA)**
CONTACT: SUSAN GLASS, DIRECTOR, MATERIALS FOR THE ARTS, 410 WEST 16TH STREET, FOURTH FLOOR, NEW YORK, NY 10011
Phone: 212-255-5924
Purpose: To link materials donations from both private and governmental sources to nonprofit cultural organizations and individual artists involved in public projects

Eligibility:
Special Requirements: Must be working with a registered, non-profit cultural organization on a specific project in a public setting in New York City
Art Forms: All disciplines
Type of Support: Donated equipment, furniture, and supplies
Scope of Program: Over $1,000,000 in goods distributed to 819 organizations in FY 1989
Application/Selection Process:
Application Procedure: Submit resumé, proposal, letter from 1 sponsoring organization

TECHNICAL ASSISTANCE PROGRAMS AND SERVICES

Programs of Special Interest: The Arts Apprenticeship Program (AAP) assists young artists, students, and arts administrators to bridge the gap between their education and careers by promoting professional experience through training with artists and nonprofit cultural organizations. The Arts Partners arts-in-education program identifies and works with arts organizations to enhance the curriculum of New York City public schools by providing access to professional artists; programming includes classroom workshops, artist residencies, and performances. The Community Arts Developmental Program provides grants to nonprofit arts groups and organizations that provide cultural services in low- or moderate-income areas of the city. DCA maintains an artists' housing mailing list to keep the community informed of live/work space opportunities.

NEW YORK FOUNDATION FOR THE ARTS (NYFA)

5 Beekman Street, #600
New York, NY 10038
212-233-3900
CONTACT: DAVID GREEN, DIRECTOR, COMMUNICATIONS

DIRECT SUPPORT PROGRAMS

➤ **ARTISTS' FELLOWSHIPS**

Purpose: To support individual, originating artists from diverse cultures and at all stages of professional development
Eligibility:
Residency: New York State, 2 years
Age: 18 or older
Special Requirements: Originating artists only; no students; previous grantees ineligible for 3 years
Art Forms: Literature, playwriting/screenwriting, crafts, film, photography, visual arts, music composition, architecture, choreography, performance art/emergent forms, video

Type of Support: $7,000
Scope of Program: 241 awards in FY 1990
Competition for Support: 7,000 applications in 1990
Application/Selection Process:
  Deadline: September-October, depending on discipline
  Preferred Initial Contact: Call or write for application/guidelines
  Application Procedure: Submit application form, samples of
  work, resumé
  Selection Process: Peer panel of artists
  Notification Process: Letter in early April
  Formal Report of Grant Required: Yes

TECHNICAL ASSISTANCE PROGRAMS AND SERVICES

Programs of Special Interest: The foundation's Communications
Program holds workshops, conferences, and seminars to educate artists about advocacy and lobbying efforts and opportunities for
fellowships, project support, residencies in schools, sponsorship,
and emergency financial assistance for personal needs. The Artists'
New Works Program helps individual artists find funding for
projects (emphasis on film and video). The Artists in Residence
Program awards matching grants to organizations to support school
and community residencies. The annual Common Ground conference addresses the concerns of arts councils, individual artists,
and educators. The free quarterly newsletter *FYI* contains information on career opportunities and grants deadlines.

NEW YORK STATE COUNCIL ON THE ARTS (NYSCA)

915 Broadway
New York, NY 10010
212-614-2900 (general)/212-614-3988 (Individual Artists Program)

DIRECT SUPPORT PROGRAMS

➤ INDIVIDUAL ARTISTS PROGRAM

Purpose: To provide financial support that allows artists to create,
develop, and present new work
Eligibility:
  Residency: New York State
  Age: 18 or older
  Special Requirements: No students; request for theater commissions may be made by theater companies or unaffiliated artists
  and unincorporated ensembles under the aegis of a nonprofit organization; requests for full support for composers' fees may be
  initiated by musical organizations and artists/companies under
  the aegis of a nonprofit organization

Art Forms: Visual arts, music composition commissions (orchestral, chamber, solo instrumental, choral, opera eligible in odd-numbered years; jazz, electronic, scores for dance, incidental theater eligible in even-numbered years), theater commissions (directing, playwriting, design), film, electronic media

Type of Support: Up to $25,000 for music commission, up to $10,000 for theater commission

Scope of Program: 146 awards in FY 1990 (17 theater commissions, totalling $74,000; 35 music composition commissions, totalling $200,000)

Competition for Support: 1,021 applications in 1990

Application/Selection Process:
  Deadline: March 1 (for sponsor's application)
  Preferred Initial Contact: Call for guidelines
  Application Procedure: Sponsor submits application form (artist provides project description for application); artist later submits supplemental application form, expanded project description, artist's statement (optional), resumé, itemized budget, samples of work
  Selection Process: Peer panel of artists, council committee, and board of directors
  Notification Process: Letter
  Formal Report of Grant Required: Yes

NEW YORK YOUTH SYMPHONY

Carnegie Hall 504
881 Seventh Avenue
New York, NY 10019
212-581-5933

DIRECT SUPPORT PROGRAMS
➤ FIRST MUSIC

Purpose: To enable young composers to write for a large orchestra with the assurance of abundant rehearsals, high quality performances, and a prestigious premiere

Eligibility:
  Citizenship: U.S.
  Age: 29 or younger
  Special Requirements: Must be available for rehearsals in New York City for 5 successive Sundays prior to premiere; commissioned work must be previously unpublished and unperformed
  Art Forms: Music composition (chamber or symphony orchestra)

Type of Support: $1,500 commission, production costs of score and parts, premiere at Carnegie Hall

Scope of Program: 3 commissions per year

Competition for Support: 100+ applications per year

Application/Selection Process:

    Deadline: December 31

    Preferred Initial Contact: Call or write for guidelines

    Application Procedure: Submit resumé, samples of work

    Selection Process: Panel of composers, New York Youth Symphony Music Director

    Notification Process: Letter 1 month after deadline

NORTH CAROLINA ARTS COUNCIL

Department of Cultural Resources
Raleigh, NC 27611
919-733-2111
CONTACT: NANCY TROVILLION, ASSISTANT DIRECTOR

DIRECT SUPPORT PROGRAMS

➤ **FELLOWSHIPS/PROJECT GRANTS**

CONTACT: DIRECTOR OF APPROPRIATE DISCIPLINE PROGRAM (DANCE, MUSIC, THEATER ARTS)

Purpose: Fellowships recognize exemplary originating artists who have made career commitments to their art; Project grants support the realization of specific artistic projects by professional artists

Eligibility:

    Residency: North Carolina, 1 year

    Special Requirements: No students in degree-granting programs; previous grantees ineligible for 3-5 years; jazz musicians who have demonstrated their creativity through improvisation are eligible for jazz composition fellowships; composers must have made substantial contributions, for at least 5 years, through the creation of their art; playwrights must demonstrate significant career commitment

    Art Forms: Fellowships for music composition, jazz composition, playwriting, visual arts, choreography (offered in odd-numbered years only), literature; Project grants for visual arts, crafts, film, video, dance, folk arts

Type of Support: $5,000-$8,000 fellowships in 1990; up to $5,000 project grants

Scope of Program: 41 grants, totalling $200,000 (estimate), in 1988-89

Competition for Support: 497 applications in 1988-89

Application/Selection Process:

    Deadline: February 1

    Preferred Initial Contact: Call or write for application

    Application Procedure: Submit application form, samples of work, references (optional), resumé, project budget (project grants only)

Selection Process: Individuals from outside of organization
Notification Process: Letter within 5 months of deadline
Formal Report of Grant Required: Yes

TECHNICAL ASSISTANCE PROGRAMS AND SERVICES

Programs of Special Interest: Artists may submit applications for placement on the North Carolina Arts Council Resident Artists Roster; rostered artists may be considered for residencies in the council's Artists-in-Schools and Visiting Artist programs (contact Artists-in-Residence Coordinator, Community Development Section; deadline, February 1). North Carolina playwrights may contact the council for information about 8-week residencies available at the Headlands Center for the Arts in Sausalito, California. Out-of-state performing artists may apply for inclusion on the National Touring Theater Roster; dance, music, and theater artists based in North Carolina may apply to be listed in the North Carolina Touring Roster. The council gives fee support to organizations presenting rostered artists (contact Touring Director; deadline, January 15). North Carolina emerging artists may apply to participating local arts councils for small grants to assist them in furthering their careers (contact Community Development Section).

THE NORTH CAROLINA SYMPHONY

P.O. Box 28026
Raleigh, NC 27611
919-733-2750
CONTACT: CAROL WENBERG, MUSIC SECRETARY

DIRECT SUPPORT PROGRAMS

➤ **BRYAN INTERNATIONAL STRING COMPETITION**

Purpose: To encourage young violinists, violists, and cellists from around the world

Eligibility:
    Age: 18-30
    Art Forms: Music performance (violin, viola, cello)

Type of Support: 1st prize, $12,000, appearance with North Carolina Symphony (winner agrees to rehearse and perform with symphony during following season with no additional renumeration); 2nd prize, $6,000; 3rd prize, $3,000

Scope of Program: Quadrennial competition

Competition for Support: 91 applications in 1988

Application/Selection Process:
    Deadline: January 1 (1992, 1996)
    Preferred Initial Contact: Write for application/guidelines

Application Procedure: Submit application form, audition tape, 3 letters of reference, programs and reviews; up to 16 applicants are invited to May competition in Raleigh

Selection Process: 2 panels of music professionals

Notification Process: Letter by March 1 (acceptance or rejection as competitor); winners announced at competition

NORTH DAKOTA COUNCIL ON THE ARTS (NDCA)

Black Building, Suite 606
Fargo, ND 58102
701-237-8962
CONTACT: LILA HAUGE, ARTISTS AND EDUCATION SERVICES COORDINATOR

PROFILE OF FINANCIAL SUPPORT TO ARTISTS

Total Funding/Value of In-Kind Support: $25,000 for FY 1991 (includes Professional Development Grants to arts professionals)

Competition for Funding: Total applications, 21; total individuals funded/provided with in-kind support, 9

Grant Range: Up to $5,000

DIRECT SUPPORT PROGRAMS

➤ **ARTIST FELLOWSHIPS**

Purpose: To assist North Dakota artists in furthering their careers

Eligibility:
  Citizenship: U.S.
  Residency: North Dakota
  Age: 18 or older
  Special Requirements: No students pursuing college degrees
  Art Forms: Dance, music, opera/musical theater, theater, visual arts, crafts, photography, media arts, literature

Type of Support: $5,000 in FY 1991

Scope of Program: 3 awards in FY 1991

Application/Selection Process:
  Preferred Initial Contact: Call or write for application/guidelines
  Application Procedure: Submit application form, samples of work, resumé
  Selection Process: Panel of artists and arts professionals
  Notification Process: 6 weeks after deadline
  Formal Report of Grant Required: Yes

➤ **PROFESSIONAL DEVELOPMENT GRANTS**

CONTACT: BRAD STEPHENSON OR LILA HAUGE

Purpose: To provide artists and nonartists with funds for informational/educational opportunities related to the arts and arts development, or for consultants and technical or artistic advice

Eligibility:
  Residency: North Dakota
  Special Requirements: No students
  Art Forms: All disciplines
Type of Support: Up to $300 for professional development project
Scope of Program: $10,000 awarded to individuals and organizations
in FY 1991
Application/Selection Process:
  Deadline: None
  Preferred Initial Contact: Call or write for application/guidelines
  Application Procedure: Submit application form, resumé, 2 letters
  of recommendation
  Selection Process: NCDA Community Programs Committee
  Notification Process: Letter
  Formal Report of Grant Required: Yes

TECHNICAL ASSISTANCE PROGRAMS AND SERVICES

Programs of Special Interest: The NDCA, in conjunction with the
South Dakota Arts Council, sponsors the biennial Dakota Arts Congress for artists and arts professionals. The Artists-In-Residence
Program maintains a roster of artists qualified to work in schools.
The Touring Arts Program provides a roster of touring events and
makes grants to nonprofit sponsors of these events (artist application deadline, October 1). The "Opportunities" section of the NDCA's
bimonthly newsletter describes other available programs.

NORTHWEST TERRITORIES DEPARTMENT OF CULTURE AND COMMUNICATIONS

Government of the Northwest Territories
Box 1320
Yellowknife, Northwest Territories
Canada X1A 2L9
403-920-3103
CONTACT: PETER CULLEN, ARTS LIAISON COORDINATOR

DIRECT SUPPORT PROGRAMS

➤ NWT ARTS COUNCIL PROGRAM

Purpose: To promote the arts in the Northwest Territories by ap-
proving funding for artistic work on a project-specific basis
Eligibility:
  Residency: Northwest Territories, 2 years
  Art Forms: Visual arts, performing arts, literature
Type of Support: Up to $21,900 for specific project in FY 1990
Scope of Program: 21 awards in 1990

Competition for Support: 41 applications in 1990

Application/Selection Process:

Deadline: January 31, April 30 (1 other deadline if funds available)

Preferred Initial Contact: Call or write for application/guidelines

Application Procedure: Submit application form, samples of work, 2 letters of support for project

Selection Process: Members of NWT Arts Council

Notification Process: Letter within 12 weeks of deadline

Formal Report of Grant Required: Yes

➤ SUPPORT TO NORTHERN PERFORMERS

Purpose: To provide financial contributions and professional assistance towards the performance of northern performing artists at local, regional, national, and international festivals and events

Eligibility:

Residency: Northwest Territories, 2 years

Special Requirements: Performing artists, groups and organizations, and festivals and events that intend to contract performers from the NWT are eligible

Art Forms: Theater, music, dance

Type of Support: Project support grant

Scope of Program: 8 grants, totalling $152,000, in FY 1991-92

Competition for Support: 15 applications in 1991-92

Application/Selection Process:

Deadline: None (while funds are available)

Preferred Initial Contact: Call or write for guidelines

Application Procedure: Submit proposal, project budget, 2 letters of support

Selection Process: Staff

Notification Process: Letter or phone call

Formal Report of Grant Required: Yes

OHIO ARTS COUNCIL (OAC)

727 East Main Street
Columbus, OH 43205-1796
614-466-2613
TDD: 614-466-4541
CONTACT: SUSAN DICKSON, COORDINATOR, INDIVIDUAL ARTISTS PROGRAM

PROFILE OF FINANCIAL SUPPORT TO ARTISTS

Total Funding/Value of In-Kind Support: $799,172 for FY 1990

Competition for Funding: Total applications, 1,000+; total individuals funded/provided with in-kind support, 148

Grant Range: $228-$25,000

DIRECT SUPPORT PROGRAMS

➤ **INDIVIDUAL ARTIST FELLOWSHIP PROGRAM**

Purpose: To recognize and support originating artists who have created excellent work

Eligibility:

Residency: Ohio, 1 year

Age: 18 or older

Special Requirements: No students; practicing, professional, originating artists only; previous grantees ineligible for 1 year

Art Forms: Choreography, crafts, creative writing (including playwriting), design arts, interdisciplinary and performance art, media arts, music composition, photography, visual arts

Type of Support: $5,000-$10,000 award and opportunity to apply to residency program at the Headlands Center for the Arts

Scope of Program: 96 awards in FY 1991

Application/Selection Process:

Deadline: January 15

Preferred Initial Contact: Call or write for application/guidelines

Application Procedure: Submit application form, samples of work

Selection Process: Peer panel of artists

Notification Process: Letter within 2 weeks of panel meeting

Formal Report of Grant Required: Yes

➤ **INDIVIDUAL ARTISTS MAJOR FELLOWSHIP PROGRAM**

Purpose: To support Ohio artists of extraordinary talent and achievement who have contributed substantially to Ohio's artistic vitality

Eligibility:

Residency: Ohio, 5 years

Special Requirements: Must have 10- to 15-year record of professional achievement; grantees ineligible for Individual Artists funding for 5 years

Art Forms: Choreography, crafts, creative writing (including playwriting), design arts, interdisciplinary and performance art, media arts, music composition, photography, visual arts

Type of Support: 2-year, $50,000 award; recipients must fulfill public service requirement

Scope of Program: 2 or 3 awards per year

Application/Selection Process:

Deadline: September 1

Preferred Initial Contact: Call or write for application/guidelines

Application Procedure: Submit application form, samples of work, resumé

Selection Process: Peer panel of artists

Notification Process: Letter within 2 weeks of panel meeting

Formal Report of Grant Required: Yes

➤ **PROFESSIONAL DEVELOPMENT ASSISTANCE AWARDS (PDAA)**

Purpose: To provide assistance for artists to attend programs or events that will further their professional development

Eligibility:

Residency: Ohio, 1 year

Special Requirements: No students; professional, originating artists only; current Fellowship or Major Fellowship recipients ineligible

Art Forms: Choreography, crafts, creative writing (including playwriting), design arts, interdisciplinary and performance art, media arts, music composition, photography, visual arts

Type of Support: Up to $1,000 to participate in such activities or programs as workshops, conferences, colonies, seminars, symposia, and rental of studio facilities

Scope of Program: 20 awards, averaging $750, in 1990

Application/Selection Process:

Deadline: 60 days before intended use of funds; awards given on first-come, first-served basis (fiscal year begins July 1)

Preferred Initial Contact: Consult with staff about availability of funds and application process

Application Procedure: Submit samples of work, resumé, financial statement, project budget, information on and letter of acceptance from program or event

Selection Process: Organization staff

Notification Process: Letter within 3 weeks of application

Formal Report of Grant Required: Yes

➤ **TRADITIONAL AND ETHNIC ARTS APPRENTICESHIP PROGRAM**

CONTACT: JOHN H. SETO, COORDINATOR OF TRADITIONAL AND ETHNIC ARTS

Purpose: To assist traditional master artists in passing on their skills and their tradition, one-on-one, to new apprentice artists

Eligibility:

Residency: Ohio (apprentice)

Special Requirements: Master artist and apprentice must apply as a team; preference given to apprentices who wish to study in their own cultural or ethnic tradition

Art Forms: Folk arts

Type of Support: Up to $2,000 for master artist's fees and supplies and travel

Scope of Program: 24 apprenticeships, averaging $1,233, in 1990

Application/Selection Process:

Deadline: September 1

Preferred Initial Contact: Call or write for application/guidelines

Application Procedure: Submit application form, samples of work, project budget

Selection Process: Panel that includes artists

Notification Process: Letter 8 weeks after deadline

Formal Report of Grant Required: Yes

TECHNICAL ASSISTANCE PROGRAMS AND SERVICES

Programs of Special Interest: The Arts in Education Program publishes a directory of artists eligible for residencies in educational, arts, and community settings (contact Vonnie Sanford, Arts in Education Coordinator; February 1 deadline). Ohio performing artists may apply for inclusion in the Ohio Artists on Tour Roster; the Presenting/Touring Program offers fee support to organizations presenting performances by rostered artists (contact Ira S. Weiss, Presenting/Touring Coordinator; April 1 deadline). Support is available to organizations for the commissioning and production of performing arts works.

EUGENE O'NEILL THEATER CENTER

305 Greatneck Road
Waterford, CT 06385
203-443-5378

234 West 44th Street
New York, NY 10036
212-382-2790

DIRECT SUPPORT PROGRAMS

➤ NATIONAL PLAYWRIGHTS CONFERENCE

CONTACT: PEGGY VERNIEU, ADMINISTRATOR

Phone: 212-382-2790

Purpose: To develop talented writers for the theater by offering them the opportunity to work on their plays together with other talented professional theater and media artists in a noncompetitive atmosphere

Eligibility:

Citizenship: U.S. (permanent residents also eligible)

Special Requirements: Submitted works must be unproduced and not under option; adaptations are ineligible

Art Forms: Playwriting

Type of Support: 1-month summer residency in Waterford, Connecticut, including transportation, room, board, $1,000 stipend; stage plays are given 2 professional, staged readings in front of an audience

Scope of Program: 10-15 residencies per year

Competition for Support: 1,400 applications per year

Application/Selection Process:

Deadline: December 1

Preferred Initial Contact: Write for guidelines in the fall

Application Procedure: Submit $5 fee, script, biography

Selection Process: Panel of theater and television professionals, artistic director

Notification Process: Letter by mid-April

➤ **NATIONAL MUSIC THEATER CONFERENCE**

CONTACT: PAULETTE HAUPT, ARTISTIC DIRECTOR

Phone: 212-382-2790

Purpose: To offer composers, lyricists, and playwrights the opportunity to collaborate in the development of new musical theater works of all styles

Eligibility:

Special Requirements: Works that have received a full production or that are under option are ineligible; singing must play dominant role in work; works need not be complete

Art Forms: Musical theater (composers, lyricists, and playwrights are eligible)

Type of Support: 2-3 week summer residency in Waterford, Connecticut, including round-trip surface transportation, room, board, $500 stipend; minimally staged and unstaged readings presented publicly and privately with script in hand

Scope of Program: 3-8 residents per year

Competition for Support: 100 applications per year

Application/Selection Process:

Deadline: February 1

Preferred Initial Contact: Write for application/guidelines in the fall

Application Procedure: Submit application form, $10 fee, samples of work, synopsis of script, biography

Selection Process: Committee, artistic director

Notification Process: May

ONTARIO ARTS COUNCIL (OAC)

151 Bloor Street West
Suite 500
Toronto, Ontario
Canada M5S 1T6
800-387-0058 (toll-free in Ontario) or 416-961-1660

CONTACT: MARGARET DRYDEN, VISUAL ARTS OFFICER

PROFILE OF FINANCIAL SUPPORT TO ARTISTS

Total Funding/Value of In-Kind Support: $4,547,849 for FY 1989-90

Competition for Funding: Total applications, n/a; total individuals funded/provided with in-kind support, 2,207

Grant Range: n/a

DIRECT SUPPORT PROGRAMS

➤ INDEPENDENT CHOREOGRAPHERS GRANTS

CONTACT: SUSAN COHEN, DANCE OFFICER

Purpose: To encourage talented professional choreographers by enabling them to create dances for the stage that develop their art

Eligibility:

Citizenship: Canada (landed immigrants also eligible)

Residency: Ontario, 1 year

Special Requirements: Category A applicants must have more than 5 years of documented professional experience and at least 5 choreographies to their credit; Category B applicants must have 1-5 years of documented professional experience and at least 2 professional choreographies to their credit

Art Forms: Choreography

Type of Support: Category A, up to $10,000; Category B, up to $3,000

Scope of Program: 20 grants in 1988-89

Application/Selection Process:

Deadline: April 15, August 15, December 1, February 1

Preferred Initial Contact: Call or write for application/guidelines; first-time applicants should make an appointment to discuss the program and their project

Application Procedure: Submit application form, samples of work, project budget, references, resumé

Selection Process: Peer panel of artists

Notification Process: Letter 3 months after deadline

Formal Report of Grant Required: Yes

➤ THE CHALMERS FUND PERFORMING ARTS TRAINING GRANTS

CONTACT: SUSAN COHEN, DANCE OFFICER

Purpose: To assist young professional performing artists to undertake intensive study or professional upgrading, either privately with outstanding master teachers or at highly regarded institutions

Eligibility:

Citizenship: Canada (landed immigrants also eligible)

Residency: Ontario, 1 year

Special Requirements: Must have completed basic training; undergraduate students ineligible; must have been accepted by master teacher or approved institution

Art Forms: Theater (acting, directing, design), dance (choreography, performance), music theater (performance, directing, choreography), music (performing, conducting, opera direction)

Type of Support: Up to $18,000 for training-related costs and travel

Scope of Program: 20 grants, totalling $183,958, in 1988-89

Application/Selection Process:

Deadline: February 15

Preferred Initial Contact: Call or write for application/guidelines

Application Procedure: Submit application form, project budget, appropriate support material (samples of work, references, reviews)
Selection Process: Jury
Notification Process: Letter 4 months after deadline

➤ **CULTURE-SPECIFIC DANCE PROJECT GRANTS**

CONTACT: SUSAN COHEN, DANCE OFFICER

Purpose: To support projects that raise the performance standard of culture-specific artists and groups, expand their artistic program, or contribute to the understanding and sharing of culture-specific dance movements and ideas

Eligibility:
Citizenship: Canada (landed immigrants also eligible)
Residency: Ontario
Special Requirements: Individuals and nonprofit, Ontario-based organizations that produce or perform culture-specific dance forms are eligible; individuals must be involved in special projects sponsored by eligible organizations; matching funds required; competitions, costume and set costs, and performing arts' groups travel to competitions and festivals are ineligible
Art Forms: Dance

Type of Support: Up to $10,000 for partial project support

Scope of Program: n/a

Application/Selection Process:
Deadline: March 1, October 15
Preferred Initial Contact: Call or write for application/guidelines
Application Procedure: Submit application form, samples of work, project budget, references (optional), reviews (optional)
Selection Process: Independent jury
Notification Process: Letter within 2 months of deadline

➤ **MUSIC COMMISSIONING PROGRAM**

CONTACT: MUSIC OFFICER

Purpose: To encourage the creation of new works by Canadian composers having the skill, training, and talent to make a significant contribution to musical composition, and to give Canadians a greater opportunity to hear Canadian music

Eligibility:
Citizenship: Composers and librettists must be Canadian citizens or landed immigrants
Residency: Ontario
Special Requirements: Ontario-based musical performing ensembles, organizations, and professional musical performing artists are eligible to commission works; opera and dance companies also eligible to commission work; commissioner must premiere work in Ontario
Art Forms: Music, musical theater/opera

Type of Support: Up to $7,000 for composer's fees (up to $10,000 for extended musical theater, opera, or ballet); up to $5,000 for librettist's fees; copying costs

Scope of Program: 50 commissions in 1988-89

Application/Selection Process:
Deadline: May 1, October 1
Preferred Initial Contact: Call or write for application/guidelines
Application Procedure: Submit application form, resumé/repertoire (commissioner, composer, librettist), samples of work (composer), project budget
Selection Process: Jury
Notification Process: Letter

➤ **PLAYWRIGHT RECOMMENDOR PROGRAM**

CONTACT: TIM LEARY, THEATER OFFICER

Purpose: To enable playwrights to write and to create opportunities to improve their art through association with theater companies

Eligibility:
Citizenship: Canada (landed immigrants also eligible)
Residency: Ontario
Special Requirements: Must be recommended by the artistic director of an Ontario-based professional theater company designated as a recommendor company by the OAC; Category II applicants must have had work previously published or previously produced by a professional theater company; recommendor companies may not recommend their own artistic directors, managers, or board members
Art Forms: Playwriting

Type of Support: Category I grants, up to $3,000; Category II grants, up to $6,000

Scope of Program: 81 grants in 1990-91

Application/Selection Process:
Preferred Initial Contact: Call or write for list of recommendor companies
Application Procedure: Apply to recommendor company for recommendation; submit application/recommendation form, resumé to OAC
Selection Process: Recommendor companies
Formal Report of Grant Required: Yes

➤ **PLAYWRIGHT RESIDENCY PROGRAM**

CONTACT: TIM LEARY, THEATER OFFICER

Purpose: To permit playwrights to take advantage of the creative environment of the theater in order to write and to create new works

Eligibility:
Citizenship: Canada (landed immigrants also eligible)
Residency: Ontario

Special Requirements: Must apply with the artistic director of an Ontario-based professional theater; playwrights in attendance during the production of their own work are ineligible; previous grantees ineligible for 1 year

Art Forms: Playwriting

Type of Support: 6- to 20-week residency including $400 weekly stipend

Scope of Program: 7 residencies in 1990-91

Application/Selection Process:
  Deadline: July 1
  Preferred Initial Contact: Call or write for guidelines; consult with staff before applying
  Application Procedure: Submit project proposal, resumé, samples of work
  Selection Process: Jury of theater professionals
  Notification Process: Letter in August
  Formal Report of Grant Required: Yes

➤ **MULTI-DISCIPLINARY PROJECT GRANTS**

CONTACT: SUSAN COHEN, DANCE OFFICER

Purpose: To support the development and presentation of unique multi-disciplinary works, including workshops and studio presentations

Eligibility:
  Citizenship: Canada (landed immigrants also eligible)
  Residency: Ontario
  Special Requirements: Professional artists only; projects must begin 8-10 weeks after deadline and result in live art event whose format transcends any single artistic discipline; projects whose end product is a video, painting, film, book, or recording are ineligible
  Art Forms: Multi-disciplinary

Type of Support: Up to $12,500 for project

Scope of Program: 3 grants to individual artists in FY 1988-89

Application/Selection Process:
  Deadline: August 15, February 1
  Preferred Initial Contact: Call or write for application/guidelines
  Application Procedure: Submit application form, references, samples of work, project budget
  Selection Process: Peer panel of artists
  Notification Process: 8-10 weeks after deadline
  Formal Report of Grant Required: Yes

➤ **CREATIVE ARTISTS IN SCHOOLS (CAIS) PROJECTS**

CONTACT: STEVEN J. T. CAMPBELL

Purpose: To place professional creative artists of all artistic disciplines in schools to work with students and educators

Eligibility:
  Citizenship: Canada (landed immigrants also eligible)

Residency: Ontario, 1 year

Special Requirements: Professional, originating artists only; project must be developed with school that will pay 30% of artist's fees; projects must fill at least 5 full school days

Art Forms: Visual arts, crafts, literature, theater, music, film, photography, video, dance, mixed media

Type of Support: Up to $2,625 for 70% of artist's fees (recommended fee $185 per day), travel expenses up to $750 if artist must travel more than 100 km roundtrip, up to $235 for materials

Scope of Program: 238 grants in FY 1990-91

Application/Selection Process:

Deadline: June 1 (for projects after September 1), October 1 (for projects after January 1), January 15 (for projects after April 1)

Preferred Initial Contact: Call or write for application/guidelines

Application Procedure: Submit application form (signed by school), resumé, samples of work, project budget, letter of support from school (optional)

Selection Process: Jury of artists and educators

Notification Process: Letter 8 weeks after deadline

Formal Report of Grant Required: Yes

TECHNICAL ASSISTANCE PROGRAMS AND SERVICES

Programs of Special Interest: The Theater Projects Program provides subsidies to emerging theater companies to assist with the creative costs of new work development through production or workshop activity by independent artists or groups. Ontario non-profit performing organizations and groups may apply for funding to develop new Canadian opera or musical theater works that have never had a major production. Community choirs may apply for assistance with the professional artistic costs of engaging Canadian artists (guest soloists, conductors, instrumentalists). The Touring Arts Fund provides fee support to community organizations outside the metropolitan Toronto area that present full touring performances by professional Canadian artists in theater, music, dance, or mime (contact Jean-Paul Gagnon, Touring Officer). Touring performing artists may apply to showcase their work at the annual Contact Ontario Conference. The juried Artists and the Workplace Program assists professional artists in all fields to work in residence with the trade union movement on projects initiated by the trade union movement to make the arts more accessible to their membership (contact Naomi Lightbourn, Community Arts Development Officer).

OPERA AMERICA

777 14th Street, NW
Suite 520
Washington, DC 20005
202-347-9262
CONTACT: AUDITIONS COORDINATOR

DIRECT SUPPORT PROGRAMS
➤ **OPERA AMERICA AUDITIONS**
Purpose: To identify outstanding emerging singers and to award grants that assist them in developing their operatic careers
Eligibility:
   Citizenship: U.S., Canada
   Special Requirements: Must be nominated by designated nominator; must have performed at least 2 professional solo roles (opera productions only) during the past 2 years and a maximum of 15 professional solo roles (operatic and symphonic) in the past 3 years
   Art Forms: Vocal performance (opera)
Type of Support: $5,000 Sullivan Award for vocal study; eligibility for $500 Sullivan Role Preparation grants
Scope of Program: 14 awards available in 1991
Competition for Support: 250 applications in 1991
Application/Selection Process:
   Deadline: June (nomination form), August (application form)
   Preferred Initial Contact: Nominees are sent application forms
   Application Procedure: Nominator submits nomination form; nominee submits application form, 2 letters of endorsement from opera professionals; auditions held in New York, Chicago, and San Francisco in November
   Notification Process: Letter

OREGON ARTS COMMISSION (OAC)

835 Summer Street, NE
Salem, OR 97301
503-378-3625
CONTACT: VINCENT DUNN, ASSISTANT DIRECTOR

DIRECT SUPPORT PROGRAMS
➤ **INDIVIDUAL ARTIST FELLOWSHIPS**
Purpose: To assist the development of Oregon's professional artists working in all media

Eligibility:
　Residency: Oregon
　Age: 18 or older
　Special Requirements: No students; professional artists only; previous Masters Fellowship grantees ineligible; previous Fellowship grantees eligible only for Masters Fellowships
　Art Forms: All disciplines; film/video awards given every year, visual arts awards in odd-numbered years, literature and performing arts in even-numbered years
Type of Support: $3,000 Fellowships, $10,000 Masters Fellowships; Masters Fellowship winners expected to undertake major project that includes public component
Scope of Program: Budget for film/video awards, $10,000; total awards for other disciplines, 8 Fellowships and 2 Masters Fellowships
Competition for Support: 296 applications in 1990
Application/Selection Process:
　Deadline: Early September
　Preferred Initial Contact: Call or write for application/guidelines
　Application Procedure: Submit application form, samples of work, resumé
　Selection Process: Peer panel of artists, board of directors
　Notification Process: Letter 3 months after deadline
　Formal Report of Grant Required: Yes

➤ **TRADITIONAL ARTS APPRENTICESHIP PROGRAM**
Purpose: To provide apprenticeship funds and technical assistance, particularly with marketing skills, to traditional artists from refugee communities in the Willamette Valley and from Native American tribes throughout the state
Application/Selection Process:
　Call or write for information

TECHNICAL ASSISTANCE PROGRAMS AND SERVICES
Programs of Special Interest: OAC cooperates with local arts agencies to present workshops and seminars for artists, and publishes an annual sponsor directory for touring artists. Oregon performing artists and ensembles may apply for inclusion on the Touring Program's biennial Oregon on Tour Roster. Fee support is available to organizations presenting rostered and nonrostered artists (artist application deadline, May 1 of even-numbered years). OAC's annual Northwest Booking Conference offers workshops, showcasing, and exhibit hall opportunities. Artists accepted in the Arts in Education Program receive special training for educational residencies.

PALENVILLE INTERARTS COLONY

2 Bond Street
New York, NY 10012
212-254-4614

Summer Address (June-Sept):
P.O. Box 59
Palenville, NY 12463
518-678-3332
CONTACT: JOANNA SHERMAN, COLONY DIRECTOR

DIRECT SUPPORT PROGRAMS
➤ **SUMMER ARTIST RESIDENCIES**

Purpose: To encourage new works and new insights by encouraging interdisciplinary and intercultural communication among recognized and emerging artists, collaborating artists, and groups of artists of the highest caliber

Eligibility:
  Special Requirements: Minimum 3 years' experience as professional artist
  Art Forms: All disciplines

Type of Support: 1- to 8-week residencies include housing, meals, and studio space as required; residents are asked to pay $175 per week but stipends and full or partial fee waivers available to artists in need

Scope of Program: 97 residencies in 1990; 19 artists received full fee waivers, 10 received $50-$125 weekly stipends

Competition for Support: 467 applications in 1990

Application/Selection Process:
  Deadline: April 1
  Preferred Initial Contact: Call or write for application/guidelines
  Application Procedure: Submit application form, $10 fee, samples of work, references, resumé, supporting documentation (if available); accepted artists requesting financial aid submit financial statement
  Selection Process: Peer panel of artists, individuals outside of organization
  Notification Process: Phone call or letter within 4 weeks of deadline
  Formal Report of Grant Required: No

PENNSYLVANIA COUNCIL ON THE ARTS

216 Finance Building
Harrisburg, PA 17120
717-787-6883

DIRECT SUPPORT PROGRAMS
➤ FELLOWSHIP PROGRAM

Purpose: To support the development of Pennsylvania artists
Eligibility:
  Citizenship: U.S.
  Residency: Pennsylvania, 2 years
  Special Requirements: No students; professional artists only; previous grantees ineligible for 2 years; dancers in career transition may apply for dance fellowships
  Art Forms: Dance (choreography, criticism, history), music (composition, jazz composition and performance, solo recital), visual arts, crafts, photography, poetry, fiction, interdisciplinary
Type of Support: Up to $10,000 (most awards are $5,000)
Scope of Program: 106 awards, totalling $713,628, in FY 1990-91
Application/Selection Process:
  Deadline: October 1
  Preferred Initial Contact: Call or write for application/guidelines
  Application Procedure: Submit application form, samples of work, resumé, project budget
  Selection Process: Peer panel of artists, board of directors
  Notification Process: Letter in December
  Formal Report of Grant Required: Yes

➤ THEATER PROGRAM INDIVIDUAL ARTISTIC DEVELOPMENT GRANTS

CONTACT: THEATER PROGRAM DIRECTOR

Purpose: To assist established professional theater artists in activities that will provide artistic stimulation and enable them to refresh their approach to their art
Eligibility:
  Residency: Pennsylvania, 3 years
  Special Requirements: Must have been a full-time professional for at least 7 years; previous grantees ineligible for 3 years
  Art Forms: Theater (acting, directing, design, playwriting)
Type of Support: Up to $5,000
Scope of Program: 6 grants, totalling $30,000, in FY 1990-91
Application/Selection Process:
  Deadline: April 1
  Preferred Initial Contact: Call or write for application/guidelines

Application Procedure: Submit application form, project budget, resumé, letters of interest (if project includes other theaters or artists)
Selection Process: Peer panel of artists, board of directors
Notification Process: Letter
Formal Report of Grant Required: Yes

➤ **CONDUIT GRANTS**

CONTACT: DISCIPLINE PROGRAM DIRECTORS

Purpose: To support the creation of new work or the presentation of performances
Eligibility:
    Residency: Pennsylvania, 2 years
    Special Requirements: No students; professional artists only; artists must apply through a Pennsylvania nonprofit organization
    Art Forms: Performing and visual arts
Type of Support: Matching grant
Scope of Program: n/a
Application/Selection Process:
    Deadline: April 1
    Preferred Initial Contact: Call or write for application/guidelines
    Application Procedure: Sponsor submits application form, project budget, financial statement, artist's resumé
    Selection Process: Peer panel of artists, board of directors
    Notification Process: Letter
    Formal Report of Grant Required: Yes

➤ **MINORITY ARTS PROGRAM TECHNICAL ASSISTANCE FOR THE INDIVIDUAL ARTIST GRANTS**

CONTACT: MINORITY ARTS DIRECTOR

Purpose: To provide partial funding for individual artists to attend conferences and other noncredit career advancement sessions
Eligibility:
    Residency: Pennsylvania
    Special Requirements: Must not be on staff of an organization; must be member of ethnic minority
    Art Forms: All disciplines
Type of Support: Up to $200
Scope of Program: n/a
Application/Selection Process:
    Deadline: 8 weeks before event
    Preferred Initial Contact: Call or write for application/guidelines
    Application Procedure: Submit application form, project budget, resumé
    Selection Process: Executive director
    Notification Process: Letter
    Formal Report of Grant Required: Yes

TECHNICAL ASSISTANCE PROGRAMS AND SERVICES

Programs of Special Interest: The Arts in Education Program places professional artists in school and community residencies lasting 10-180 days (priority to Pennsylvania artists). Resident artists spend 50% of the residency period working with the site population and the other 50% working on their own creative projects (deadline February 15). The Dance Program provides up to 100% fee support for dance companies commissioning guest choreographers and up to 50% salary support to dance companies hiring new artistic personnel. The Theater Program makes grants to organizations for the commissioning and production of new work, and for the hiring of guest directors, actors, and choreographers. Support is available to organizations for composer residencies and to presenters for commissions and the presentation of touring artists/ensembles.

PERFORMERS OF CONNECTICUT

17 Morningside Drive South
Westport, CT 06880
203-227-8998

DIRECT SUPPORT PROGRAMS

➤ YOUNG ARTISTS COMPETITION

Eligibility:
  Age: 19-33 (vocalists), 18-28 (instrumentalists)
  Special Requirements: Must not be under professional management
  Art Forms: Music performance (vocal, strings eligible in odd-numbered years; brass, piano, woodwinds eligible in even-numbered years)
Type of Support: 1st place, $2,000; 2nd place, $1,000; 3rd place, $500
Scope of Program: Annual competition
Application/Selection Process:
  Deadline: October 10
  Preferred Initial Contact: Call or write for application/guidelines
  Application Procedure: Submit application form, $35 fee, samples of work; auditions held in December; finalists appear in concert in December
  Selection Process: Panel of judges
  Notification Process: Letter (preliminary), winners announced at competition

PINELLAS COUNTY ARTS COUNCIL (PCAC)

400 Pierce Boulevard
Clearwater, FL 34616
813-462-3327
CONTACT: MAGGIE MARR, SUPPORT SERVICES DIRECTOR

DIRECT SUPPORT PROGRAMS

➤ **ARTISTS RESOURCE FUND (ARF)**

Purpose: To provide a source of nongovernmental financial assistance to Pinellas County visual and performing artists for professional development

Eligibility:
  Residency: Pinellas County, 1 year
  Age: 18 or older
  Special Requirements: No students pursuing degrees; previous grantees ineligible for 3 years
  Art Forms: Dance, music, opera/musical theater, theater, visual arts, crafts, photography, media arts

Type of Support: Up to $1,000 for professional development project

Scope of Program: 10 awards, totalling $7,598, in FY 1990

Competition for Support: 38 applications in 1990

Application/Selection Process:
  Deadline: February 1
  Preferred Initial Contact: Call or write for application/guidelines
  Application Procedure: Submit application form, samples of work, resumé, project description and budget
  Selection Process: Peer panel of artists, board of directors
  Notification Process: Letter 6 weeks after deadline
  Formal Report of Grant Required: Yes

TECHNICAL ASSISTANCE PROGRAMS AND SERVICES

Programs of Special Interest: PCAC coordinates Arts-in-Education projects for county schools, maintains a resource library and mailing lists of artists, and publishes the Arts Advocacy Handbook and the annual Florida Festival Directory. The council offers workshops, seminars, and personal consultations on topics such as grantwriting and marketing.

THE PITTSBURGH NEW MUSIC ENSEMBLE, INC.

c/o Duquesne University School of Music
Pittsburgh, PA 15282
412-261-0554
CONTACT: EVA TUMIEL-KOZAK, EXECUTIVE DIRECTOR

PROFILE OF FINANCIAL SUPPORT TO ARTISTS
Total Funding/Value of In-Kind Support: $15,000
Competition for Funding: Total applications, 142; total individuals funded/provided with in-kind support, 11
Grant Range: $1,500

DIRECT SUPPORT PROGRAMS
➤ **HARVEY GAUL COMPOSITION CONTEST**
Purpose: To encourage young talent in composition and to show-case new American composers
Eligibility:
   Citizenship: U.S. (permanent residents also eligible)
   Special Requirements: Work must be unpublished and unperformed
   Art Forms: Music composition (chamber ensemble)
Type of Support: $1,500 and premiere by Pittsburgh New Music Ensemble
Scope of Program: 1 award biennially
Application/Selection Process:
   Deadline: April 1 (even-numbered years)
   Preferred Initial Contact: Call or write for application/guidelines (available 6 months before deadline)
   Application Procedure: Submit application form, $10 fee, score of work
   Selection Process: Jury
   Notification Process: Letter after May 31

➤ **CENTER FOR NEW MUSIC COMPOSERS' CONFERENCE FELLOWSHIPS**
CONTACT: DAVID STOCK, CONDUCTOR, PITTSBURGH NEW MUSIC ENSEMBLE
Purpose: To give emerging composers an opportunity to have their works read and performed by a professional ensemble
Eligibility:
   Art Forms: Music composition (ensemble of 6-16 performers)
Type of Support: Tuition-free, 1-week summer conference includ-ing daily rehearsals, readings, seminars, and evening concerts by the Center for New Music Contemporary Ensemble and the Pittsburgh New Music Ensemble; fellows responsible for room and board
Scope of Program: 10 fellowships in 1991

Application/Selection Process:
Deadline: Late April
Preferred Initial Contact: Call or write for guidelines
Application Procedure: Submit samples of work
Selection Process: Committee
Notification Process: Letter

THE PLAYWRIGHTS' CENTER

2301 Franklin Avenue East
Minneapolis, MN 55406
612-332-7481

PROFILE OF FINANCIAL SUPPORT TO ARTISTS
Total Funding/Value of In-Kind Support: $92,500+
Competition for Funding: n/a
Grant Range: Up to $10,000

DIRECT SUPPORT PROGRAMS
➤ **PLAYLABS**
Purpose: To serve playwrights and their plays by providing an intensive working conference with dramaturgs, directors, and professional actors
Eligibility:
Citizenship: U.S.
Special Requirements: Unproduced, unpublished scripts only; preference to full-length plays
Art Forms: Playwriting
Type of Support: 2-week summer workshop including room, board, travel, stipend; plays receive public readings (accepted playwrights must attend pre-conference workshop in May; travel paid)
Scope of Program: 4-6 awards per year
Application/Selection Process:
Deadline: December 1
Preferred Initial Contact: Write for application (available in October); enclose SASE
Application Procedure: Submit application form, script
Selection Process: Artistic staff
Notification Process: Letter in April
➤ **JEROME PLAYWRIGHT-IN-RESIDENCE FELLOWSHIPS**
Purpose: To provide emerging playwrights with funds and services to aid them in the development of their craft
Eligibility:
Citizenship: U.S. (permanent residents also eligible)

Special Requirements: Must not have had more than 2 works fully produced by professional theaters

Art Forms: Playwriting

Type of Support: 1-year fellowship including $5,000 stipend, use of the center's developmental programs of workshops and readings with professional actors, dramaturgs, and directors; fellows must spend fellowship period in Minnesota as Core Members of the Playwrights' Center (up to 3 months professional leave or extension may be requested)

Scope of Program: 6 per year

Application/Selection Process:

Deadline: January 15

Preferred Initial Contact: Write for application/guidelines (available November 15); enclose SASE

Application Procedure: Submit application form, samples of work, other materials as requested

Selection Process: Independent panel of judges

Notification Process: April

Formal Report of Grant Required: Yes

➤ **MCKNIGHT FELLOWSHIPS**

Purpose: To recognize playwrights whose work has made a significant impact on contemporary theater

Eligibility:

Citizenship: U.S.

Special Requirements: Must have had at least 2 works fully produced by professional theaters; previous grantees ineligible for 2 years

Art Forms: Playwriting

Type of Support: $10,000 1-year fellowship, up to $2,000 for workshops and staged readings of fellow's scripts, and funds to defray transportation and housing costs for playwrights living more than 150 miles from Minneapolis; fellows spend 1-2 months of fellowship period in residency at Playwrights' Center

Scope of Program: 3-5 awards per year

Application/Selection Process:

Deadline: Mid-December

Preferred Initial Contact: Write for application/guidelines (available October 15); enclose SASE

Application Procedure: Submit application form, samples of work

Selection Process: Independent panel of judges

Notification Process: Mid-March

Formal Report of Grant Required: Yes

➤ **MCKNIGHT ADVANCEMENT GRANTS**

Purpose: To recognize Minnesota playwrights whose work demonstrates exceptional artistic merit and potential by making grants that may be used to support a wide variety of activities that advance recipients' art and careers

Eligibility:
    Citizenship: U.S.
    Residency: Minnesota
    Special Requirements: Must have had at least 2 works fully produced by professional theaters; previous recipients ineligible for 2 years
    Art Forms: Playwriting
Type of Support: $7,500 grant, plus up to $2,000 for workshops and staged readings using the center's developmental program or for joint development or production purposes with a partner organization; grantees must participate in 1 community-related program and attend at least 1 reading or workshop per week at the center
Scope of Program: 3 per year
Application/Selection Process:
    Deadline: Early January
    Preferred Initial Contact: Write for application/guidelines (available November 1); enclose SASE
    Application Procedure: Submit application form, samples of work
    Selection Process: Independent panel of judges
    Notification Process: Letter by April 1
    Formal Report of Grant Required: Yes

TECHNICAL ASSISTANCE PROGRAMS AND SERVICES

Programs of Special Interest: The Playwrights' Center holds free lectures, seminars, and roundtables that are open to the public. Playwright Memberships are open to all, and members are eligible to apply to Stagetime, a script development program that provides unrehearsed public readings, using professional actors and followed by audience discussion. Playwrights accepted for Core or Associate Memberships have access to play development workshops with theater professionals and the Monday Night Reading Series, which includes readings by professional actors, followed by audience and private peer panel discussions. ($35 membership fee)

THE ROSA PONSELLE FOUNDATION

Windsor
Stevenson, MD 21153-9999
Fax: 301-486-0495
CONTACT: MISS ELAYNE DUKE, PRESIDENT

DIRECT SUPPORT PROGRAMS
➤ **ROSA PONSELLE INTERNATIONAL COMPETITION FOR THE VOCAL ARTS**
Purpose: To assist young developing artists with their training, and to provide young semi-professional and professional artists with cash awards and performance opportunities

Eligibility:
    Age: 18-25 (Developing Artists division), 21-32 (Semi-Professional and Professional division)
    Art Forms: Vocal performance (opera, concert, oratorio)
Type of Support: Semi-Professional and Professional division: 1st prize, $15,000; 2nd prize, $12,000; 3rd prize, $10,000; semi-finalists, $1,000; other $1,000-$2,000 cash prizes available; 75% of top cash prizes is awarded either as fees for 2 concert performances or as support for further study; Developing Artists division: $5,000 Study Grant awards
Scope of Program: Biennial competition (9 prizes, totalling $65,000, awarded in 1990)
Competition for Support: 125 applications in 1990
Application/Selection Process:
    Deadline: December
    Preferred Initial Contact: Request application/guidelines by letter or fax
    Application Procedure: Submit application form, $35 fee; audition required
    Selection Process: International panel of judges
    Notification Process: Letter (preliminaries)

PRIMARY STAGES COMPANY

584 Ninth Avenue
New York, NY 10036
212-333-7471
CONTACT: SETH GORDON, LITERARY MANAGER

DIRECT SUPPORT PROGRAMS
➤ **PRIMARY STAGES COMPANY**
Purpose: To develop new American plays by new American playwrights
Eligibility:
    Special Requirements: Scripts must be full-length and not have had a New York production
    Art Forms: Playwriting
Type of Support: Readings, productions (playwright receives stipend if work produced)
Scope of Program: 25 informal readings, 3 staged readings, 2 full productions in 1990-91 (scope varies from year to year)
Application/Selection Process:
    Deadline: Ongoing
    Preferred Initial Contact: Call or write for guidelines

Application Procedure: Submit cover letter, script
Selection Process: Literary manager, artistic director
Notification Process: Letter

PRINCE EDWARD ISLAND COUNCIL OF THE ARTS

Box 2234
94 Great George Street
Charlottetown, Prince Edward Island
Canada C1A 8B9
902-368-4410
CONTACT: JUDY MacDONALD

DIRECT SUPPORT PROGRAMS
➤ GRANTS PROGRAM—INDIVIDUAL GRANTS/
TRAVEL-STUDY GRANTS

Purpose: To assist individuals working in any of the arts disciplines
Citizenship: Canada (landed immigrants also eligible)
Residency: Prince Edward Island, 6 months
Art Forms: Music, dance, theater, writing/publications,
film/video, visual arts, crafts, environmental arts
Type of Support: $1,000-$2,000 individual grants; up to $800 travel-
study grants
Scope of Program: 28 grants, totalling approximately $45,000, in 1990
Competition for Support: 49 applications in 1990
Application/Selection Process:
Deadline: April 30, September 15, December 15
Application Procedure: Submit application form, 2 letters
of appraisal
Selection Process: Committee review
Notification Process: Letter 4 weeks after deadline
Formal Report of Grant Required: Yes

TECHNICAL ASSISTANCE PROGRAMS AND SERVICES
Programs of Special Interest: The council offers workshops, seminars, a referral service, a resource library, space for artists and arts
organizations, and office equipment for in-house use.

QUAD CITY ARTS (QCA)

106 East Third Street
Suite 220
Davenport, IA 52801
319-326-5190

DIRECT SUPPORT PROGRAMS

➤ ARTS DOLLARS INDIVIDUAL GRANTS

Purpose: To support specific professional development projects for the creation, completion, presentation, or production of a new work

Eligibility:
  Residency: Illinois (Rock Island, Mercer counties), Iowa (Scott, Clinton, Muscatine counties)
  Special Requirements: Must provide service to residents of the Quad City area
  Art Forms: All disciplines
Type of Support: Up to $500 for specific project
Scope of Program: 21 awards, totalling $6,500, in 1991
Competition for Support: 30 applications in 1991
Application/Selection Process:
  Call or write for information

TECHNICAL ASSISTANCE PROGRAMS AND SERVICES

Programs of Special Interest: QCA provides artist registry and information services.

RAGDALE FOUNDATION

1260 North Green Bay Road
Lake Forest, IL 60045
708-234-1063
CONTACT: MICHAEL WILKERSON, DIRECTOR

DIRECT SUPPORT PROGRAMS

➤ RESIDENCIES FOR ARTISTS

Purpose: To provide a peaceful place and uninterrupted time for writers, scholars, and artists who are seriously committed to a specific project

Eligibility:
  Art Forms: Music composition, visual arts, media arts, literature (including playwriting), interdisciplinary

Type of Support: 2-week to 2-month residencies include housing, work space, meals; residents asked to pay $10/day but financial assistance available
Scope of Program: 150 residencies in 1990
Competition for Support: 400 applications in 1990
Application/Selection Process:
  Deadline: January 15, April 15, September 15
  Preferred Initial Contact: Call or write for application/guidelines
  Application Procedure: Submit application form, samples of work, references, resumé, financial statement (if seeking fee waiver)
  Selection Process: Peer panel of artists
  Notification Process: Letter or phone call 7 weeks after deadline
  Formal Report of Grant Required: Yes

RHODE ISLAND STATE COUNCIL ON THE ARTS (RISCA)

95 Cedar Street
Suite 103
Providence, RI 02903
401-277-3880
CONTACT: EDWARD HOLGATE, DIRECTOR, INDIVIDUAL ARTIST PROGRAMS

PROFILE OF FINANCIAL SUPPORT TO ARTISTS
Total Funding/Value of In-Kind Support: $146,650 for FY 1990
Competition for Funding: Total applications, 311; total individuals funded/provided with in-kind support, 78
Grant Range: $250-$4,350

DIRECT SUPPORT PROGRAMS
➤ FELLOWSHIPS
Purpose: To encourage the creative development of originating artists by enabling them to set aside time to pursue their work and achieve specific career goals
Eligibility:
  Residency: Rhode Island, 1 year
  Age: 18 or older
  Special Requirements: Originating artists only; no students; previous recipients ineligible to apply in same category for 3 years; Artist Project awardees ineligible for 1 year
  Art Forms: Choreography, crafts, design, film/video, folk arts, literature, music composition, new genres, photography, visual arts

Type of Support: $500-$3,000 awards in 1991

Scope of Program: 24 awards in 1991

Application/Selection Process:

Deadline: April 1

Preferred Initial Contact: Call or write for application/guidelines

Application Procedure: Submit application form, samples of work, resumé

Selection Process: Panels of artists and arts professionals

Notification Process: Letter in mid-July

Formal Report of Grant Required: Yes

➤ **ARTIST PROJECTS/TRAVEL GRANTS**

Purpose: Artist Projects awards enable an artist to create new work or complete works-in-progress; Travel Grants provide funds to an individual artist for an impending out-of-state travel opportunity that will significantly impact the artist's work or career

Eligibility:

Residency: Rhode Island, 1 year

Age: 18 or older

Special Requirements: No students; previous recipients ineligible for same grant for 1 year

Art Forms: Choreography, crafts, design, film/video, folk arts, literature, music composition, new genres, photography, visual arts, performing arts (Travel Grants only)

Type of Support: Artist Projects, $2,000-$5,000 for specific project-related costs (completed work must be publicly presented in Rhode Island); Travel Grants, $100-$1,000 for out-of-state travel for opportunities such as creation, collaboration, or exhibition of work, project-oriented research or study, or attendance at a professional conference or workshop

Scope of Program: 22 Artist Projects awards, 19 Travel Grants in 1990

Application/Selection Process:

Deadline: October 1 (Artist Projects and Travel Grants), April 1 (Travel Grants only)

Preferred Initial Contact: Call or write for application/guidelines

Application Procedure: Submit application form, samples of work (Artist Projects), resumé, project or travel budget, documentation of travel opportunity (Travel Grants)

Selection Process: Panel of artists and arts administrators, board of directors

Notification Process: Letter 8-10 weeks after deadline

Formal Report of Grant Required: Yes

➤ **FOLK ARTS APPRENTICESHIPS**

CONTACT: WINIFRED LAMBRECHT, DIRECTOR, FOLK ARTS

Purpose: To foster the sharing of traditional artistic skills between a master artist and an apprentice who is already familiar with the genre

Eligibility:
  Residency: Rhode Island (out-of-state masters eligible in rare cases)
  Special Requirements: No students; master and apprentice must apply as a team
  Art Forms: Folk arts
Type of Support: $100-$2,000 for master's fees and materials and travel
Scope of Program: 18 apprenticeships in 1990
Application/Selection Process:
  Deadline: April 1, October 1
  Preferred Initial Contact: Call or write for application/guidelines (potential applicants usually identified from field work of Folk Arts staff)
  Application Procedure: Submit application form, supplemental information form, samples of work, resumé, project budget
  Selection Process: Panel of folk arts experts
  Notification Process: 8-10 weeks after deadline
  Formal Report of Grant Required: Yes

TECHNICAL ASSISTANCE PROGRAMS AND SERVICES
Programs of Special Interest: RISCA's Arts in Action workshop series educates artists in practical matters such as marketing, legal issues, and fiscal management. The council maintains an Arts in Education/Artist Roster that lists professional Rhode Island artists eligible for school and community residencies (application deadline, April 1). The Touring Program funds nonprofit organizations for public performances, exhibitions, and media events.

ROCKEFELLER FOUNDATION

1133 Avenue of the Americas
New York, NY 10036
212-869-8500

DIRECT SUPPORT PROGRAMS
➤ **MULTI-ARTS PRODUCTION FUND (MAP)**
CONTACT: ARTS AND HUMANITIES DIVISION

Purpose: To provide development or production support to projects that reflect bold and insightful approaches to intercultural or international representation in the performing arts
Eligibility:
  Special Requirements: Professional artists and arts organizations are eligible; application must be made through a nonprofit administering organization; projects should explore issues of cultural

pluralism, the aesthetic expressions of non-Western cultures, or the relationship of the individual to the cultural environment

Art Forms: Performing arts

Type of Support: $10,000-$40,000 for partial project support

Scope of Program: 31 grants, totalling $725,000, in 1990

Application/Selection Process:

Deadline: July 31

Application Procedure: Sponsor submits application cover sheet, project budget, financial statement, artist's resumé/biography, samples of artist's work (optional)

Selection Process: Panel of arts professionals

Notification Process: Mid-December

➤ **BELLAGIO STUDY AND CONFERENCE CENTER RESIDENCIES**

CONTACT: SUSAN E. GARFIELD, MANAGER, BELLAGIO CENTER OFFICE

Purpose: To provide a site for artists and scholars who have significant publications, compositions, or shows to their credit to work on projects, particularly projects that will result in publications, exhibition, or performances

Eligibility:

Special Requirements: Priority given to arts projects that increase artistic experimentation across cultures; previous recipients ineligible for 10 years

Art Forms: All disciplines

Type of Support: 5-week residency at the Bellagio Center in Milan, Italy, including room and board

Scope of Program: 135 residencies per year

Application/Selection Process:

Deadline: Quarterly, 1 year before residency

Preferred Initial Contact: Call or write for brochure

Application Procedure: Submit application form, project description, resumé, samples of work, reviews of work (if possible)

Selection Process: Committee

Notification Process: 2 months after deadline

TECHNICAL ASSISTANCE PROGRAMS AND SERVICES

Programs of Special Interest: The Playwrights-in-Residence Program provides funds for theaters for playwrights' residencies.

SAN ANTONIO DEPARTMENT OF ARTS AND CULTURAL AFFAIRS (DACA)

P.O. Box 839966
San Antonio, TX 78283-3966
512-222-2787
CONTACT: KATE MARTIN, PROJECT MANAGEMENT SPECIALIST

DIRECT SUPPORT PROGRAMS
➤ INDIVIDUAL ARTISTS GRANTS PROGRAMS

Purpose: To assist both emerging and established artists by supporting work of artistic merit, to encourage innovative projects (e.g., performance art, multi-disciplinary media, new genres), and to support projects by individuals who lack institutional support

Eligibility:
  Citizenship: U.S.
  Residency: Bexar County
  Special Requirements: Originating, professional artists only; no students; previous grantees ineligible for 1 year; project must take place in San Antonio; DACA encourages applications that represent the cultural and geographic diversity of San Antonio and that represent women and the disabled; collaborations encouraged
  Art Forms: Choreography, music composition, playwriting, performance art, visual arts, crafts, design arts, photography, media arts, literature, multi-disciplinary

Type of Support: Up to $2,000 for project that takes place in San Antonio and leads to a public presentation

Scope of Program: 12 awards, totalling $20,000, in FY 1991

Competition for Support: 81 applications in FY 1991

Application/Selection Process:
  Deadline: Spring (usually March)
  Preferred Initial Contact: Call or write for application form
  Application Procedure: Arrange for pre-application interview with DACA staff before deadline; submit application form, samples of work, resumé, project budget, letter of support
  Selection Process: Peer panel of artists
  Notification Process: Letter after panel meeting (July)
  Formal Report of Grant Required: Yes

TECHNICAL ASSISTANCE PROGRAMS AND SERVICES

Programs of Special Interest: DACA maintains a library and offers free workshops for artists on topics such as career development, legal issues, marketing, and public relations.

SANTA BARBARA COUNTY ARTS COMMISSION

112 West Cabrillo Boulevard
Santa Barbara, CA 93101
805-568-3430
CONTACT: PATRICK H. DAVIS, EXECUTIVE DIRECTOR

PROFILE OF FINANCIAL SUPPORT TO ARTISTS

Total Funding/Value of In-Kind Support: $17,000 for FY 1990-91
Competition for Funding: Total applications, 45; total individuals
funded/provided with in-kind support, 6
Grant Range: n/a

DIRECT SUPPORT PROGRAMS

➤ **INDIVIDUAL ARTISTS PROGRAM**

Purpose: To support the creative life of Santa Barbara County by
assisting emerging artists in establishing and developing their
professional careers in the arts

Eligibility:
  Citizenship: U.S.
  Residency: Santa Barbara County, 1 year
  Age: 18 or older
  Special Requirements: Originating, professional artists only; no
  full-time students pursuing degrees or previous recipients
  Art Forms: Choreography, music composition, theater, visual
  arts, photography, literature

Type of Support: $2,500 in FY 1990-91

Scope of Program: 3 awards in FY 1990-91

Application/Selection Process:
  Deadline: Fall
  Preferred Initial Contact: Call or write for application/guidelines
  Application Procedure: Submit application form, samples of
  work, resumé, artist's statement
  Selection Process: Peer panel of artists, arts professionals, and
  community arts advocates
  Notification Process: Letter 1 month after deadline
  Formal Report of Grant Required: No

➤ **NEW WORKS GRANTS**

Purpose: To encourage artists to present original and challenging
work to Santa Barbara County audiences and to enrich the creative
process by collaborating with other county artists or arts organizations

Eligibility:
  Residency: Santa Barbara County
  Special Requirements: Artist must be sponsored by a nonprofit
  organization; originating artists only

Art Forms: All disciplines
Type of Support: Up to $3,000 for specific project
Scope of Program: n/a
Application/Selection Process:
   Deadline: June 15
   Application Procedure: Sponsor submits application form, financial statement, project description and budget, artist's resumé, samples of work, support materials (e.g., letters of support, reviews)
   Selection Process: Panel of local citizens and arts experts
   Notification Process: 2 months after deadline
   Formal Report of Grant Required: Yes

SEATTLE ARTS COMMISSION (SAC)

305 Harrison Street
Seattle, WA 98109
206-684-7171
TDD: 206-587-5500
CONTACT: DIANE SHAMASH

DIRECT SUPPORT PROGRAMS
➤ SEATTLE ARTISTS PROGRAM
Purpose: To fund the development of new work or works-in-progress in all disciplines
Eligibility:
   Residency: Seattle
   Special Requirements: Originating artists only
   Art Forms: Visual arts, literature, choreography, music composition, media arts
Type of Support: $1,000-$5,000 grant for project
Scope of Program: $80,000 budget
Application/Selection Process:
   Deadline: Fall
   Preferred Initial Contact: Call or write for information

TECHNICAL ASSISTANCE PROGRAMS AND SERVICES
Programs of Special Interest: The Arts in Education (AIE) Program supports the use of professional artists and arts organizations in Seattle schools.

SEATTLE GROUP THEATER

3940 Brooklyn Avenue, NE
Seattle, WA 98105
206-685-4969

DIRECT SUPPORT PROGRAMS
➤ **MULTICULTURAL PLAYWRIGHTS' FESTIVAL**

Purpose: To develop the work of playwrights of color through workshops, readings, and opportunities to meet with professional writers, directors, and producers

Eligibility:
  Citizenship: U.S.
  Special Requirements: Applicants must be of African-American, Asian-American, Latino/Hispanic-American, or Native American ethnic background; scripts must not have been produced by any professional theater operating under contract with the Actors' Equity Association in the U.S.; musicals, children's plays, translations, and adaptations are ineligible
  Art Forms: Playwriting

Type of Support: 2-week summer residency; finalists receive professional workshop development of their work, 4 performances, $1,000 honorarium, housing, travel; semi-finalists receive professional, rehearsed readings of their work and possibly housing and travel

Scope of Program: 6-8 residencies per year (2 finalists, 4-6 semi-finalists)

Competition for Support: 157 applications in 1991

Application/Selection Process:
  Deadline: November 15
  Preferred Initial Contact: Write for guidelines
  Application Procedure: Submit cover letter, script, resumé
  Selection Process: Jury of local and national theater professionals
  Notification Process: Letter in May

SHENANARTS, INC.

Route 5, Box 167F
Staunton, VA 24401
703-248-1868
CONTACT: ROBERT GRAHAM SMALL, DIRECTOR, PLAY AND SCREENWRITING PROGRAMS

DIRECT SUPPORT PROGRAMS
➤ **SHENANDOAH PLAYWRIGHTS RETREAT**

Purpose: To provide young and established playwrights with a stimulating, challenging environment to test and develop new work

Eligibility:
Art Forms: Playwriting
Type of Support: 3-week summer residency including room, board, and travel; playwrights collaborate with dramaturgs, directors, and acting company to develop new work
Scope of Program: 4-7 residencies per year
Competition for Support: 225 applications in 1990-91
Application/Selection Process:
Deadline: March 1
Preferred Initial Contact: Call or write for guidelines
Application Procedure: Submit draft of proposed project, artist's statement
Notification Process: Letter

SIERRA ARTS FOUNDATION (SAF)

200 Flint Street
Reno, NV 89501
702-329-1324
CONTACT: VIRGINIA KEENEY, EXECUTIVE DIRECTOR

DIRECT SUPPORT PROGRAMS
➤ GRANTS PROGRAM
Purpose: To provide grants-in-aid to individuals, groups, or nonprofit organizations to support projects of educational and community significance as well as imaginative, innovative, or experimental projects
Eligibility:
Residency: Northern Nevada and neighboring Sierra Nevada region
Special Requirements: Preference given to applicants who present evidence of matching funds or comparable in-kind support; previous grantees ineligible for 1 year
Art Forms: All disciplines
Type of Support: Up to $2,000 for project
Scope of Program: 4 grants to individuals in FY 1991
Application/Selection Process:
Deadline: Quarterly
Preferred Initial Contact: Call to check on availability of funds, discuss project with Grants Coordinator/Program Director
Application Procedure: Submit application form, samples of work, project budget, resumé
Selection Process: Organization staff, Grants Committee including board members
Notification Process: Letter 1 month after deadline
Formal Report of Grant Required: Yes

TECHNICAL ASSISTANCE PROGRAMS AND SERVICES

Programs of Special Interest: The Arts-in-Education Program places professional artists in month-long residencies in Washoe County elementary schools. SAF cosponsors the Arts on the Move Festival in Reno and maintains an artist registry.

THE JOHN PHILIP SOUSA FOUNDATION

c/o U.S. Marine Band
8th and I Streets, SE
Washington, DC 20390-5000
CONTACT: CHAIRMAN, SUDLER INTERNATIONAL WIND BAND COMPOSITION CONTEST

DIRECT SUPPORT PROGRAMS

➤ **SUDLER INTERNATIONAL WIND BAND COMPOSITION CONTEST**

Purpose: To encourage the composition and performance of superior wind band music at the international level and to further the wind band as a serious medium of performance

Eligibility:
   Special Requirements: Work must have been written in the past 2 years and conform to the accepted wind band instrumentation of the composer's own country; collaborations ineligible
   Art Forms: Music composition (wind band)

Type of Support: $12,000 plus $500 for travel expenses to presentation ceremony

Scope of Program: 1 award every 2 years

Application/Selection Process:
   Deadline: October (odd-numbered years)
   Preferred Initial Contact: Write for application/guidelines
   Application Procedure: Submit application form, score and cassette of work, biography
   Selection Process: Preliminary screening, international jury of music professionals
   Notification Process: 2 months after deadline

SOUTH CAROLINA ARTS COMMISSION (SCAC)

1800 Gervais Street
Columbia, SC 29201
803-734-8696
CONTACT: DAVID URNESS, PERFORMING ARTS DIRECTOR

PROFILE OF FINANCIAL SUPPORT TO ARTISTS
Total Funding/Value of In-Kind Support: $106,588 for FY 1991
Competition for Funding: Total applications, n/a; total individuals funded/provided with in-kind support, 120
Grant Range: n/a

DIRECT SUPPORT PROGRAMS
➤ FELLOWSHIP PROGRAM
Purpose: To recognize the achievements of South Carolina artists
Eligibility:
  Citizenship: U.S.
  Residency: South Carolina, 6 months
  Special Requirements: No full-time, degree-seeking under-graduates; professional artists only; previous grantees ineligible for 5 years
  Art Forms: Visual arts, crafts, music performance, fiction, poetry
Type of Support: $7,500 in 1991
Scope of Program: 6 awards in 1991
  Deadline: September 15
  Preferred Initial Contact: Call or write for application/guidelines
  Application Procedure: Submit application form, samples of work
  Selection Process: Peer panel of artists, board of directors
  Notification Process: Letter
  Formal Report of Grant Required: No

➤ GRANTS-IN-AID
Purpose: To help support specific, planned activities such as the production of new work, marketing, and professional development
Eligibility:
  Citizenship: U.S.
  Residency: South Carolina, 6 months
  Special Requirements: No degree-seeking, full-time undergraduate students; professional artists only; matching funds required
  Art Forms: All disciplines
Type of Support: Up to 50% cost of specific project (usually no more than $7,500; the value of the artist's time may account for 1/2 of the matching requirement)
Scope of Program: 13 grants in 1991

Application/Selection Process:
Deadline: January 15
Preferred Initial Contact: Call or write for application/guidelines
Application Procedure: Submit application form, samples of work, resumé, project budget
Selection Process: Board of directors, organization staff, advisory panel
Notification Process: Letter
Formal Report of Grant Required: Yes

➤ SMALL GRANTS

Purpose: To help support short-term, small-budget projects that arise during the current year
Eligibility:
Residency: South Carolina, 6 months
Special Requirements: No students; matching funds required; organizations and individuals are eligible
Art Forms: All disciplines
Type of Support: Maximum $1,000 for up to 50% cost of specific project (the value of the artist's time may account for 1/2 of the matching requirement)
Scope of Program: 18 grants to organizations, totalling $11,000, in 1990-91
Application/Selection Process:
Deadline: Quarterly
Preferred Initial Contact: Call or write for information; in some areas, this program is administered by local arts councils
Application Procedure: Submit application form, resumé, samples of work, project budget
Selection Process: Staff, executive director
Notification Process: Letter
Formal Report of Grant Required: Yes

TECHNICAL ASSISTANCE PROGRAMS AND SERVICES

Programs of Special Interest: Individuals selected for the Approved Artist Roster are eligible for the Arts-in-Education, Visiting Artist, Rural Arts, and Mobile Arts programs. The annual Community Tour Artist Roster lists performing artists and ensembles approved by the SCAC for booking at community concerts, festivals, college and university series, churches, and service organization events; some SCAC fee support is available.

SOUTH DAKOTA ARTS COUNCIL (SDAC)

108 W. 11th Street
Sioux Falls, SD 57102
605-339-6646
CONTACT: SHIRLEY SNEVE, ASSISTANT DIRECTOR

DIRECT SUPPORT PROGRAMS

➤ **ARTIST FELLOWSHIPS/EMERGING ARTIST GRANTS**

Purpose: Artist Fellowships recognize and encourage the creative achievement of South Dakota artists of exceptional talent in any arts discipline; Emerging Artist Grants assist artists in the development of their careers

Eligibility:
　Residency: South Dakota
　Special Requirements: No students; previous grantees ineligible for 2 years (Fellowships) or 3 years (Emerging Artist Grants)
　Art Forms: All disciplines
Type of Support: $5,000 (Fellowships), $1,000 (Emerging Artist Grants)
Scope of Program: 5 Fellowships, 5 Emerging Artist Grants in 1991
Application/Selection Process:
Competition for Support: 79 applications in 1991
　Deadline: February 1
　Preferred Initial Contact: Call or write for application/guidelines
　Application Procedure: Submit application form, resumé, samples of work, support documentation (optional)
　Selection Process: Arts disciplines panels, the council
　Notification Process: April
　Formal Report of Grant Required: Yes

➤ **PROJECT GRANTS**

Purpose: To enable South Dakota artists to reach the public more effectively through special projects (particularly innovative or creative projects and projects that reach disabled, minority, rural, or new constituencies)

Eligibility:
　Residency: South Dakota
　Special Requirements: No students; no applicants for Emerging Artist or Fellowship Grants; matching funds required
　Art Forms: All disciplines
Type of Support: Up to 50% of total project costs
Scope of Program: n/a
Application/Selection Process:
　Deadline: February 1
　Preferred Initial Contact: Call or write for application/guidelines

Application Procedure: Submit application form, resumé, samples of work, support documentation (optional), project description and budget
Selection Process: Arts disciplines panels, the council
Notification Process: April
Formal Report of Grant Required: Yes

TECHNICAL ASSISTANCE PROGRAMS AND SERVICES

Programs of Special Interest: The SDAC endorses artists and provides fee support for Artists-in-Schools (deadline September 15) and Touring Arts (deadline February 1) programs.

SOUTHERN ARTS FEDERATION (SAF)

1293 Peachtree Street, NE
Suite 500
Atlanta, GA 30309
404-874-7244
CONTACT: BOB JOHNSON, PERFORMING ARTS PROGRAM ADMINISTRATOR

TECHNICAL ASSISTANCE PROGRAMS AND SERVICES

Programs of Special Interest: SAF develops a roster of performing arts touring artists from inside and outside the region; fee support grants are available to presenters in the region who sponsor performances and residencies in their communities (artist application deadline, February 1 of even-numbered years). The Jazz Program sponsors technical assistance workshops for artists and organizations, and is developing a jazz database of artists, presenters, and media. Meet the Composer/Southeast allows presenters to apply for a portion of the composer's participation fee for such activities as master classes, lectures, and interviews with local media. The Dance on Tour Program offers fee support to presenters of out-of-state dance artists/companies. The Southern Arts Exchange regional booking conference showcases performing artists/groups. The Southeastern Performing Arts Presenter Directory profiles 400 presenting organizations.

SPRINGFIELD AREA ARTS COUNCIL

510 East Monroe Street
Springfield, IL 62701
217-753-3519
CONTACT: MARGE CAMPANE, ASSISTANT DIRECTOR

DIRECT SUPPORT PROGRAMS
➤ **ARTIST ADVANCEMENT AWARDS**
Purpose: To assist committed visual, performing, literary, and interdisciplinary artists with in advancing their work and careers
Eligibility:
  Residency: Sangamon, Menard counties, 1 year
  Age: 21 or older
  Special Requirements: No students; artists who have received 2 consecutive awards are ineligible for 1 year
  Art Forms: All disciplines
Type of Support: Up to $500 for costs such as training, travel, documentation of work, services, or supplies
Scope of Program: 9 grants, totalling $3,450, in 1991
Competition for Support: 9 applications in 1991
Application/Selection Process:
  Deadline: October
  Preferred Initial Contact: Call or write for application/guidelines
  Application Procedure: Submit application form, samples of work, resumé, project budget
  Selection Process: Peer panel of artists
  Notification Process: Letter
  Formal Report of Grant Required: Yes

TECHNICAL ASSISTANCE PROGRAMS AND SERVICES
Programs of Special Interest: The council's programs include Arts-in-Education residencies and a registry of local artists.

STATE ARTS COUNCIL OF OKLAHOMA

2101 N. Lincoln Boulevard
Room 640
Oklahoma City, OK 73105
405-521-2931

TECHNICAL ASSISTANCE PROGRAMS AND SERVICES
Programs of Special Interest: The council maintains a resource library, and provides fee support for the Artists-in-Residence Program (some out-of-state artists eligible) and the Oklahoma Touring Program (Oklahoma artists only).

STEPPENWOLF THEATRE COMPANY

1650 North Halstead
Chicago, IL 60614
312-335-1888
CONTACT: ERIC SIMONSON, ARTISTIC ASSOCIATE

DIRECT SUPPORT PROGRAMS

➤ **NEW PLAYS PROJECT**

Purpose: To develop new material for the company and to work with new playwrights whose work is rich in character and story

Eligibility:

Art Forms: Playwriting

Type of Support: $1,000 to playwrights to complete 1st draft; $5,000 to playwrights selected for development workshop (program subject to change)

Scope of Program: 10 scripts received 1st draft support, 4 received workshop development support in 1991

Competition for Support: 500 applications in 1991

Application/Selection Process:

Preferred Initial Contact: Write for information

Application Procedure: Submit script idea, biography; selected playwrights asked to submit 15-30 pages of script

Selection Process: Panel of ensemble members

Notification Process: Letter

SUNDANCE PLAYWRIGHTS LABORATORY

R.R. 3
Box 624-D
Sundance, UT 84604
801-225-4107
CONTACT: MANAGING DIRECTOR

DIRECT SUPPORT PROGRAMS

Purpose: To give playwrights the chance to develop their work and explore their scripts

Eligibility:

Special Requirements: Must have letter of recommendation from the artistic director/literary manager of a nonprofit theater; lab's particular interests include ethnic artists and projects, artists from other disciplines who wish to write for theater, adapting work to film, and children's theater projects

Art Forms: Playwriting

Type of Support: July residency to develop script with professional theater artists and other artists (residents receive travel, room, and board)

Scope of Program: Four 3-week residences, six 5-day residencies

Competition for Support: 175 applications in 1991

Application/Selection Process:
Deadline: December 15
Preferred Initial Contact: Write for information; enclose SASE
Application Procedure: Submit letter of recommendation, script, resumé
Selection Process: Staff review, committee of theater professionals
Notification Process: Letter by April 15

EL TEATRO DE LA ESPERANZA

P.O. Box 40578
San Francisco, CA 94140
415-255-2320
CONTACT: EVE DONOVAN, GENERAL MANAGER

DIRECT SUPPORT PROGRAMS

➤ ISADORA AGUIRRE PLAYWRIGHTING LAB

Purpose: To help build a body of Latino dramatic literature in the U.S.

Eligibility:
Special Requirements: Applicants must be Latino; scripts must be full-length works-in-progress that reflect the Chicano experience; preference to bilingual scripts, but monolingual Spanish or English acceptable; preference to scripts requiring 6 or fewer actors
Art Forms: Playwriting

Type of Support: 6-week summer residency, including script development lab, staged public readings, $1,500 stipend; scripts are considered for future full production

Scope of Program: 1-3 residencies available in 1992

Competition for Funding: 25 applications per year

Application/Selection Process:
Deadline: March 15
Preferred Initial Contact: Call or write for guidelines
Application Procedure: Submit script, resumé
Notification Process: Letter by May 1

THE TEN-MINUTE MUSICALS PROJECT

Box 461194
West Hollywood, CA 90046
213-656-8751
CONTACT: MICHAEL KOPPY, PRODUCER

DIRECT SUPPORT PROGRAMS

Purpose: To foster the creation of complete short stage musicals
Eligibility:
  Special Requirements: Work must be 7-14 minutes in duration, with maximum cast of 9; adaptations of work in public domain or for which rights have been obtained are encouraged
  Art Forms: Musical theater
Type of Support: $250; possible further development of work
Scope of Program: Approximately 5 awards per year
Competition for Support: 100 applications per year
Application/Selection Process:
  Deadline: October 1
  Preferred Initial Contact: Call or write for guidelines
  Application Procedure: Submit script, scores on cassette, lead sheets
  Selection Process: Staff review
  Notification Process: December 1

TENNESSEE ARTS COMMISSION (TAC)

320 Sixth Avenue, N.
Suite 100
Nashville, TN 37243-0780
615-741-1701

DIRECT SUPPORT PROGRAMS
➤ INDIVIDUAL ARTISTS FELLOWSHIPS

Purpose: To recognize and support outstanding professional Tennessee artists
Eligibility:
  Residency: Tennessee
  Special Requirements: No students; professional artists only; previous fellowship winners ineligible
  Art Forms: Visual arts, theater, music, dance, literature, media arts, crafts (eligible categories within these disciplines rotate)
Type of Support: Up to $5,000
Scope of Program: 14 fellowships, totalling $52,000, in FY 1989

Competition for Support: 150 applications in 1989

Application/Selection Process:

   Deadline: January 8

   Preferred Initial Contact: Call or write for application/guidelines

   Application Procedure: Submit application form, samples of work, resumé, references

   Selection Process: Individuals outside of organization

   Notification Process: Letter in July

   Formal Report of Grant Required: Yes

TECHNICAL ASSISTANCE PROGRAMS AND SERVICES

Programs of Special Interest: Artists may seek residencies in schools through the Arts in Education Program (contact Director of Arts in Education; February deadline). Professional Tennessee performing artists may apply to the Touring Arts Program, which provides fee support to nonprofit organizations that present rostered artists (contact Director of Touring Arts Program).

TEXAS COMMISSION ON THE ARTS (TCA)

920 Colorado Street, 5th Floor
P.O. Box 13406, Capitol Station
Austin, TX 78711
512-463-5535 or 800-252-9415
CONTACT: JOHN PAUL BATISTE

DIRECT SUPPORT PROGRAMS

➤ ORGANIZATIONAL, PROJECT, AND TOURING SUPPORT—PERFORMING ARTS

Purpose: To support individuals and organizations through funding and touring opportunities

Eligibility:

   Residency: Texas

   Special Requirements: Individual artists must apply through a Texas-based nonprofit organization

   Art Forms: Dance, music, theater, multi-disciplinary, interdisciplinary, folk arts

Type of Support: Grants for organizational, project, and touring support

Scope of Program: 451 grants totalling $2,557,455

Competition for Support: 800 applications per year

Application/Selection Process:

   Deadline: January 15

   Preferred Initial Contact: Call or write for application/guidelines

   Application Procedure: Submit application form, additional materials as requested

Selection Process: Peer panel review
Notification Process: Letter
Formal Report of Grant Required: Yes

TECHNICAL ASSISTANCE PROGRAMS AND SERVICES
Programs of Special Interest: Individual artists may apply for residencies through the Arts in Education Program.

TEXAS COMPOSERS FORUM (TCF)

P.O. Box 670923
Dallas, TX 75367
214-231-1666
CONTACT: MARY DUREN, EXECUTIVE DIRECTOR

TECHNICAL ASSISTANCE PROGRAMS AND SERVICES
Programs of Special Interest: The Meet the Composer/Texas Grants Program assists Texas nonprofit organizations that commission new works or feature composers in performance-related activities such as conducting, performing, supervising rehearsals, or meeting audiences informally. TCF will assist in matching composers with sponsors. The Meet the Composer/Texas Sacred Music Project assists Texas religious institutions in the commissioning of new works. TCF Performance Assistance Grants provide support to Texas nonprofit organizations that present public performances of music by Texas composers. TCF is planning to develop an archive and discography of the music of Texas composers.

THEATRE ASSOCIATION OF PENNSYLVANIA

2318 South Queen Street
York, PA 17402
717-741-1269
CONTACT: MARCIA D. SALVATORE, EXECUTIVE DIRECTOR

➤ **PENNSYLVANIA PLAYWRIGHT FELLOWSHIP PROGRAM**
Purpose: To provide an opportunity for established or emerging artists of exceptional talent to set aside time for writing, research connected with a creative project, or other activities that will help the individual advance to a new level of artistic achievement
Eligibility:
  Residency: Pennsylvania, 2 years
  Special Requirements: No students; minimum 3 years' professional experience; originating artists only

Art Forms: Playwrighting, solo performance (e.g., mime, puppetry)
Type of Support: Up to $8,000
Scope of Program: 8-24 awards per year (15 in 1991)
Competition for Support: 60 applications in 1991
Application/Selection Process:
　Deadline: May 1
　Preferred Initial Contact: Call or write for application/guidelines
　Application Procedure: Submit application form, sample of
　work, project description, resumé
　Selection Process: Independent panel of judges
　Notification Process: Letter before September 1
　Formal Report of Grant Required: Yes

THEATRE COMMUNICATIONS GROUP (TCG)

355 Lexington Avenue
New York, NY 10017
212-697-5230

➤ **TCG/NEA DIRECTOR FELLOW PROGRAM**
Purpose: To assist early-career stage directors while they work with
senior artists to develop artistic skills or while they pursue an inde-
pendent program related to artistic development
Eligibility:
　Citizenship: U.S. (permanent residents also eligible)
　Special Requirements: No students; salaried staff directors at
　professional theaters generally ineligible; previous recipients
　ineligible; must be prepared to relocate
　Art Forms: Theater (directing)
Type of Support: $15,000
Scope of Program: $146,000 granted in 1989
Application/Selection Process:
　Deadline: January
　Application Procedure: Submit application form, resumé; semi-
　finalists submit 3 letters of recommendation; finalists are
　interviewed in May
　Selection Process: Panel of theater directors
　Notification Process: February (semi-finalists), April (finalists)

➤ **TCG/NEA DESIGNER FELLOWS PROGRAM**
Purpose: To assist early-career stage designers while they work
with senior artists to develop artistic skills
Eligibility:
　Citizenship: U.S. (permanent residents also eligible)

Special Requirements: Must have 2-5 years of professional experience; must be willing to relocate; full-time salaried staff designers at professional theaters generally ineligible; artists enrolled in training programs ineligible

Art Forms: Theater design (costume, lighting, set)

Type of Support: $15,000

Scope of Program: $150,000 awarded in 1989

Application/Selection Process:

Deadline: March

Application Procedure: Submit application form, samples of work, resumé; finalists present full portfolio and are interviewed

Selection Process: Panel of theater designers

Notification Process: Letter in June

UCROSS FOUNDATION

2836 U.S. Highway 14-16 East
Clearmont, WY 82835
307-737-2291
CONTACT: ELIZABETH GUHEEN, PROGRAM DIRECTOR

DIRECT SUPPORT PROGRAMS
➤ RESIDENCY PROGRAM

Purpose: To provide individual work space and living accommodations for selected artists and scholars so that they may concentrate, in an uninterrupted fashion, on their ideas, theories, and works

Eligibility:

Age: 18 or older

Special Requirements: Previous residents ineligible for 2 years

Art Forms: All disciplines

Type of Support: 2-week to 4-month residencies with no charge for room, board, or studio space

Scope of Program: 30-35 residencies per year

Competition for Support: 250 applications per year

Application/Selection Process:

Deadline: October 1, March 1

Preferred Initial Contact: Write for application/guidelines; enclose SASE

Application Procedure: Submit application form, samples of work, references, resumé

Selection Process: Peer panel of artists

Notification Process: Letter 8 weeks after deadline

Formal Report of Grant Required: No

UNITED ARTS

Resources and Counseling (R&C)
429 Landmark Center
75 West Fifth Street
St. Paul, MN 55102
612-292-3206
CONTACT: CHRIS OSGOOD, MANAGER OF ARTISTS' SERVICES

TECHNICAL ASSISTANCE PROGRAMS AND SERVICES
Programs of Special Interest: United Arts offers a variety of workshops for individual artists on topics such as fellowship and grant preparation, artists' live/work space, legal issues, and marketing; fees average $15.

UNITED ARTS COUNCIL OF GREENSBORO, INC.

Greensboro Cultural Center
200 North Davie Street
P.O. Box 869
Greensboro, NC 27402
919-333-7440
CONTACT: JUDITH K. RAY, COMMUNITY DEVELOPMENT DIRECTOR

DIRECT SUPPORT PROGRAMS
➤ EMERGING ARTISTS PROGRAM
Purpose: To encourage artists in their formative years by helping them cover the costs of professional development activities such as presenting their work for exhibits, training, travel, and production of new work
Eligibility:
    Citizenship: U.S.
    Residency: Guilford County
    Special Requirements: No students
    Art Forms: All disciplines
Type of Support: $250-$1,000 for specific activity
Scope of Program: 11 awards, totalling $6,000, in FY 1989
Competition for Support: 21 applications in 1989
Application/Selection Process:
    Deadline: March 1
    Preferred Initial Contact: Call or write for application/guidelines
    Application Procedure: Submit application form, samples of work, resumé, financial statement, project budget

Selection Process: Organization staff, board of directors, individuals outside of organization
Notification Process: Letter within 8 weeks of deadline
Formal Report of Grant Required: Yes

TECHNICAL ASSISTANCE PROGRAMS AND SERVICES

Programs of Special Interest: The council hires jazz musicians for its summer concert series and musicians and dancers to perform at the annual City Stage Festival. The Steinberger Artists Center provides low-cost studio space to artists.

UNIVERSITY OF LOUISVILLE

School of Music
Louisville, KY 40292
502-588-5996/6907
CONTACT: DAVID R. HARMAN, EXECUTIVE SECRETARY, GRAWEMEYER MUSIC AWARD COMMITTEE

DIRECT SUPPORT PROGRAMS

➤ GRAWEMEYER AWARD FOR MUSIC COMPOSITION

Purpose: To offer an international prize in recognition of outstanding achievement by a composer in a large musical genre

Eligibility:
Special Requirements: Composer must be nominated by a professional music organization or individual (performer or performing group, conductor, critic, publisher, or head of a professional music school or department); work must have had a premiere public performance in the past 5 years
Art Forms: Music composition (choral, orchestral, chamber, electronic, dance, opera, musical theater, extended solo work, song-cycle)

Type of Support: $150,000 paid in 5 annual installments

Scope of Program: 1 award per year

Competition for Support: 150 nominations in 1990

Application/Selection Process:
Deadline: Late January
Preferred Initial Contact: Nominator calls or writes for nomination form/guidelines
Application Procedure: Nominator submits nomination form, $30 fee, recording of nominated work, documentation of premiere public performance, supporting letter, composer's biography
Selection Process: University of Louisville jury, international jury, Grawemeyer Committee
Notification Process: Phone call to recipient in mid-April

UTAH ARTS COUNCIL (UAC)

617 East South Temple
Salt Lake City, UT 84102
801-533-5895

PROFILE OF FINANCIAL SUPPORT TO ARTISTS

Total Funding/Value of In-Kind Support: $498,770 for FY 1990

Competition for Funding: Total applications, 1,362; total individuals funded/provided with in-kind support, 448 (includes each artist participating in Utah Performing Arts Tour)

Grant Range: Up to $5,000

DIRECT SUPPORT PROGRAMS

➤ **VISUAL ARTS FELLOWSHIPS**

CONTACT: SHERRILL SANDBERG, VISUAL ARTS COORDINATOR

Phone: 801-533-5757

Purpose: To aid practicing artists of exceptional talent and demonstrated ability in their process of aesthetic investigation and creation of original works of art

Eligibility:
   Citizenship: U.S.
   Residency: Utah
   Age: 18 or older
   Special Requirements: No students pursuing degrees; previous recipients ineligible for 3 years
   Art Forms: Visual arts, crafts, video, photography, interdisciplinary, multi-disciplinary

Type of Support: $5,000

Scope of Program: 2 awards per year

Application/Selection Process:
   Deadline: Mid-April
   Preferred Initial Contact: Call for application/guidelines
   Application Procedure: Submit application form, samples of work, 3 references, resumé
   Selection Process: Individuals outside of organization
   Notification Process: Letter or phone call in October
   Formal Report of Grant Required: Yes

➤ **FOLK ARTS APPRENTICESHIP PROJECT**

CONTACT: CRAIG MILLER, APPRENTICESHIP PROJECT COORDINATOR

Phone: 801-533-5760

Purpose: To preserve and promote Utah's artistic and cultural traditions

Eligibility:
   Residency: Utah (apprentice)

Special Requirements: Master and apprentice should generally be from same community or background

Art Forms: Folk arts

Type of Support: Up to $2,500 for master artist's fees, supplies, and travel for 3- to 12-month apprenticeships

Scope of Program: $53,269 granted in 1990

Application/Selection Process:

   Deadline: December 1

   Preferred Initial Contact: Call or write for application/guidelines

   Application Procedure: Submit application form, samples of work, proposed lesson plan, project budget

   Selection Process: Panel of folk artists and folk arts experts

   Notification Process: Letter in late February

   Formal Report of Grant Required: No

TECHNICAL ASSISTANCE PROGRAMS AND SERVICES

Programs of Special Interest: Artists selected for the council's Artists Bank are eligible for school and community residencies (contact Sue Heath, Arts in Education Coordinator). The Utah Performing Arts Tour publishes a roster of performing artists/companies eligible for 1-day community residencies and performances; fee support is available to nonprofit organizations that present these artists (contact Susan Boskoff, Community/State Partnership Coordinator).

VERMONT COUNCIL ON THE ARTS (VCA)

136 State Street
Montpelier, VT 05602
802-828-3291
CONTACT: GRANTS OFFICER

PROFILE OF FINANCIAL SUPPORT TO ARTISTS

Total Funding/Value of In-Kind Support: $94,000 for FY 1990 (for Fellowships and New Works Grants)

Competition for Funding: Total applications, 388; total individuals funded/provided with in-kind support, 41

Grant Range: $500-$5,000

DIRECT SUPPORT PROGRAMS

➤ FELLOWSHIPS

Purpose: To support the creative development of Vermont artists

Eligibility:
Residency: Vermont
Age: 18 or older
Special Requirements: No students
Art Forms: All disciplines
Type of Support: $3,500 fellowships; $500 finalist awards
Scope of Program: 17 fellowships, 19 finalist awards in 1990
Application/Selection Process:
Deadline: March 15
Application Procedure: Submit application form, resumé, samples of work
Selection Process: VCA staff, advisory panels, VCA board of trustees
Notification Process: July
Formal Report of Grant Required: Yes

➤ **NEW WORKS GRANTS**

Purpose: To fund the creation and presentation of original and innovative work that challenges traditional perceptions of art forms and advances the development and exchange of ideas among artists and between artists and audiences

Eligibility:
Residency: Vermont (for collaborative projects, at least 50% of participants must be Vermont residents)
Special Requirements: Artists must apply with a partner non-profit organization; no full-time students; project must include plans for a public presentation in Vermont
Art Forms: All disciplines
Type of Support: $1,000-$10,000 for specific project
Scope of Program: 5 grants, totalling $25,000, in 1990
Application/Selection Process:
Deadline: February 15
Preferred Initial Contact: Discuss project ideas and application procedure with grants officer
Selection Process: New Works panel, VCA board of trustees
Notification Process: May
Formal Report of Grant Required: Yes

TECHNICAL ASSISTANCE PROGRAMS AND SERVICES

Programs of Special Interest: Community Arts Grants provide towns with funds to commission artists to create works of art that have special meaning to residents. Artists may apply to participate in the Arts in Education and Touring Artists programs; information about successful applicants appears in the Artists Register, which is provided to potential sponsors. The council maintains a job bank and lists of other opportunities for artists, as well as the Resource Center, a noncirculating library of information about the arts. The council holds informative workshops, including Grant Seekers Workshops for artists and organizations seeking VCA funding.

VIDEO FOUNDATION TO ASSIST CANADIAN TALENT (VIDEOFACT)

151 John Street
Suite 301
Toronto, Ontario
Canada M5V 2T2
416-596-8696
CONTACT: JULIE THORBURN, PROGRAM DIRECTOR

DIRECT SUPPORT PROGRAMS
➤ **PROJECT GRANTS**

Purpose: To support the number and quality of music videos produced in Canada through providing financial assistance toward the production of music videos

Eligibility:
  Citizenship: Canada (landed immigrants also eligible)
  Special Requirements: Producers, managers, artists, record labels, record or video production companies are eligible; video director or production company, or video production facilities must be located in Canada; 2 of the following must be located in Canada: composer, lyricist, principal performer, performance/production
  Art Forms: Music video

Type of Support: Up to 50% of project cost to a maximum of $12,500

Scope of Program: $950,000 available in 1990-91

Competition for Support: 107 out of 416 applications funded in 1989-90

Application/Selection Process:
  Deadline: 5 per year
  Preferred Initial Contact: Call or write for application/guidelines
  Application Procedure: Submit application form, samples of work, resumé, project budget
  Selection Process: Board of directors
  Notification Process: Phone call or letter 4 weeks after deadline
  Formal Report of Grant Required: Yes

VIRGINIA CENTER FOR THE CREATIVE ARTS (VCCA)

Mt. San Angelo
P.O. Box VCCA
Sweet Briar, VA 24595
804-946-7236
CONTACT: WILLIAM SMART, EXECUTIVE DIRECTOR

DIRECT SUPPORT PROGRAMS
➤ RESIDENCIES
Purpose: To provide a retreat where writers, visual artists, and composers may pursue their work, free from the distractions and responsibilities of day-to-day life
Eligibility:
  Age: Usually 20 or older
  Art Forms: Music composition (chamber, choral, new, orchestral), opera, theater (general, experimental), visual arts, architecture, photography, film, literature, interdisciplinary, multi-disciplinary
Type of Support: 1- to 3-month residencies including room, board, and studio; artists asked to pay $20 per diem fee if possible
Scope of Program: 280 residencies in 1990
Competition for Support: 3,000 applications in 1990
Application/Selection Process:
  Deadline: May 25, September 25, January 25
  Preferred Initial Contact: Call or write for application/guidelines
  Application Procedure: Submit application form, $15 application fee, samples of work, references, resumé
  Selection Process: Peer panel of artists
  Notification Process: Letter or phone call 2 months after deadline
  Formal Report of Grant Required: No

VIRGINIA COMMISSION FOR THE ARTS

James Monroe Building
17th Floor
101 North 14th Street
Richmond, VA 23219-3683
804-225-3132 (voice/TDD)
CONTACT: REGIONAL COORDINATORS

DIRECT SUPPORT PROGRAMS
➤ PROJECT GRANTS FOR INDIVIDUAL ARTISTS
Purpose: To encourage significant development in the work of individual artists and in the media in which they work and to support the realization of specific artistic ideas

Eligibility:
  Residency: Virginia
  Art Forms: All disciplines on a rotating basis
Type of Support: Up to $5,000 to support a specific project
Scope of Program: 25 awards, averaging $4,000, in FY 1991
Competition for Support: 57 applications in 1991
Application/Selection Process:
  Deadline: March 1
  Preferred Initial Contact: Call or write for guidelines/application
  Application Procedure: Submit application form, samples of work, resumé, project budget
  Selection Process: Peer panel of artists, VCA board
  Notification Process: Letter in June
  Formal Report of Grant Required: Yes

TECHNICAL ASSISTANCE PROGRAMS AND SERVICES

Programs of Special Interest: The Touring Assistance Program provides fee support to nonprofit organizations that present Virginia performing artists/ensembles listed in the annual Tour Directory (artist application deadline, June 15). The commission maintains a mailing list of artists categorized by discipline. The commission administers an Artists-in-Education Residency Program and provides information about its grant programs through an annual series of application assistance seminars.

VIRGIN ISLANDS COUNCIL ON THE ARTS (VICA)

P.O. Box 6732
41 Norre Gade
St. Thomas, VI 00802
809-774-5984

DIRECT SUPPORT PROGRAMS
➤ SPECIAL PROJECTS

Purpose: To financially assist individual artists' projects, including partial support for research, participation in professional development workshops or seminars, and materials for specific projects
Eligibility:
  Residency: Virgin Islands
  Special Requirements: Must have matching funds
  Art Forms: All disciplines
Type of Support: Maximum $5,000 to cover up to 50% of cost of specific project
Scope of Program: 15 grants, totalling $24,490, in FY 1990

Application/Selection Process:
Application Procedure: Submit application form, project narrative, supplemental materials
Selection Process: VICA staff and council, panelists
Notification Process: Letter within 2 weeks of council meeting
Formal Report of Grant Required: Yes

TECHNICAL ASSISTANCE PROGRAMS AND SERVICES
Programs of Special Interest: VICA staff assist individual artists seeking funding from other sources.

VOCAL RESOURCE CENTER OF MICHIGAN

3975 Cass Avenue
Detroit, MI 48201
313-278-2508

TECHNICAL ASSISTANCE PROGRAMS AND SERVICES
Programs of Special Interest: The Vocal Resource Center provides a free referral service for professional Michigan vocalists. The Open Stage Series gives singers of art songs and folk songs an opportunity to receive critiques of their performances.

LUDWIG VOGELSTEIN FOUNDATION, INC.

P.O. Box 4924
Brooklyn, NY 11240-4924

DIRECT SUPPORT PROGRAMS
➤ GRANTS PROGRAM
Purpose: To provide grants to individuals in the arts and humanities who demonstrate merit and need
Eligibility:
Special Requirements: No students; preference to projects with no other source of funding
Art Forms: Prose, poetry, biography, playwriting, visual arts, music composition (except popular music and musicals); unaffiliated scholars and scholars from small schools also eligible; eligible disciplines vary from year to year
Type of Support: Average $2,300 in 1990 for specific project
Scope of Program: 23 grants, totalling $52,900, in 1990

Application/Selection Process:
Deadline: Spring (writers, scholars, composers); summer (visual artists)
Preferred Initial Contact: Write for guidelines
Application Procedure: Submit project proposal and budget, copy of IRS return, resumé, samples of work
Selection Process: Board
Notification Process: Letter

WASHINGTON STATE ARTS COMMISSION (WSAC)

110-9th and Columbia Building
Mail Stop GH-11
Olympia, WA 98504-4111
206-753-3858
CONTACT: MARY FRYE

DIRECT SUPPORT PROGRAMS
➤ ARTIST FELLOWSHIP AWARDS

Purpose: To provide artists with funds to create new work, improve skills, or pursue artistic development
Eligibility:
Residency: Washington State
Special Requirements: Must demonstrate at least 5 years' professional achievement; no students enrolled in degree programs; preference to artists who have not won WSAC fellowship in past 5 years; originating artists only
Art Forms: Disciplines rotate on 2-year cycle; performing arts (music composition, choreography, playwriting), 3-dimensional visual arts eligible in odd-numbered years; literature, 2-dimensional visual arts eligible in even-numbered years
Type of Support: $5,000
Scope of Program: 6 awards per year
Application/Selection Process:
Deadline: August 31
Application Procedure: Submit application form, samples of work, resumé
Selection Process: Peer panel of artists, commission
Notification Process: Letter in December
Formal Report of Grant Required: Yes

WESTBETH THEATRE CENTER, INC.

151 Bank Street
New York, NY 10014
212-691-2272

DIRECT SUPPORT PROGRAMS

➤ **AMERICAN PLAYWRIGHT PROGRAM**

Purpose: To encourage the development and production of new American plays through readings and in-house production

Eligibility:

Special Requirements: Full-length plays only; no musicals; plays must not require more than 10 characters, large physical production, or expensive costume plots

Art Forms: Playwriting

Type of Support: Script development and readings allowing playwrights to work with professional actors, directors, and dramaturgs; some plays are selected for in-house production

Scope of Program: 3-5 readings per year

Competition for Support: 150 applications per year

Application/Selection Process:

Deadline: Ongoing

Preferred Initial Contact: Write for guidelines

Application Procedure: Submit cover letter, complete script

Selection Process: Staff

Notification Process: Letter 2-6 months after application

WESTERN STATES ARTS FEDERATION (WESTAF)

236 Montezuma Avenue
Santa Fe, NM 87501-2641
505-988-1166

CONTACT: CRAIG SMITH, DIRECTOR OF PROGRAM DEVELOPMENT

TECHNICAL ASSISTANCE PROGRAMS AND SERVICES

Programs of Special Interest: Performing artists/companies may apply for inclusion on the Western States Performing Arts Tour Roster; WESTAF assists presenters with fee support for these artists. Meet the Composer/West assists presenters in bringing composers together with audiences to present their music. WESTAF publishes the National Arts JobBank and provides or offers assistance in training opportunities such as conferences, workshops, and seminars.

WEST VIRGINIA DIVISION OF CULTURE AND HISTORY

Cultural Center
Capitol Complex
Charleston, WV 25305
304-348-0220
CONTACT: Ms. LAKIN RAY COOK, EXECUTIVE DIRECTOR, ARTS & HUMANITIES SECTION

DIRECT SUPPORT PROGRAMS
➤ TRAVEL FUND

Purpose: To provide artists and arts administrators with financial assistance to attend out-of-state seminars, workshops, conferences, and showcases important to their field of expertise (in-state events of national scope may be funded in some cases)

Eligibility:
    Residency: West Virginia
    Special Requirements: Professional artists and arts administrators only; previous recipients ineligible for 1 year
    Art Forms: All disciplines

Type of Support: 50%, up to $200, of travel costs

Application/Selection Process:
    Deadline: At least 6 weeks before event (early application encouraged)
    Preferred Initial Contact: Call or write for application/guidelines
    Application Procedure: Submit application form, financial statement
    Notification Process: Within 3 weeks of application

TECHNICAL ASSISTANCE PROGRAMS AND SERVICES

Programs of Special Interest: Music, theater, opera, or dance groups may request assistance to support extraction of parts, additional rehearsal costs, partial costume costs, or other costs associated with the unique aspects of new works by American composers, playwrights, and choreographers. Performing arts organizations may request assistance to encourage the creation of new works by American playwrights, composers, writers, and choreographers; the commissioning is usually competitive, and a prospectus is sent to West Virginia artists working the appropriate media. The Artist/Arts Administrator Opportunities File holds information on contests, workshops, and job opportunities. The selective West Virginia Artists List and Register profiles individual artists. Artists interested in the Arts in the Community, Artist in Residence, Presenting West Virginia Artists, or Touring programs should develop a proposal with a sponsor who will apply for funding.

WISCONSIN ARTS BOARD (WAB)

131 West Wilson Street
Suite 301
Madison, WI 53703
608-266-0190
CONTACT: BETH MALNER, PERCENT FOR ART AND INDIVIDUAL
ARTISTS COORDINATOR

DIRECT SUPPORT PROGRAMS
➤ **INDIVIDUAL ARTIST PROGRAM**

Purpose: Fellowships assist artists in advancing their careers; New Work Awards allow artists to pursue specific projects; Development grants assist artists in developing their skills as professionals

Eligibility:
  Citizenship: U.S.
  Residency: Wisconsin, 6 months
  Special Requirements: No students pursuing degrees; recipients of New Work Awards and Development Grants must match grants in cash or in-kind support
  Art Forms: Literary arts (including playwriting), visual arts eligible every year; other disciplines rotate on 2-year cycle between music composition/media arts and choreography/interarts (conceptual art, installations, interdisciplinary, performance art, theater)

Type of Support: Fellowships ($5,000 unrestricted grants), New Work Awards ($3,500 matching grant for pursuit of a project-oriented activity), Development Grants ($1,000 matching grant for professional development activity)

Scope of Program: 7 awards each (2 Fellowships, 2 New Work Awards, 3 Development Grants) in music composition, choreography, and interarts in eligible years

Competition for Funding: 540+ applications (all disciplines) in 1989

Application/Selection Process:
  Deadline: September 15
  Preferred Initial Contact: Call or write for application/guidelines
  Application Procedure: Submit application form, samples of work, resumé, artist's statement (optional); artists chosen for New Work Awards and Development Grants must submit project description before receiving grant
  Selection Process: Peer panel of artists, board of directors
  Notification Process: Letter in January
  Formal Report of Grant Required: Yes

TECHNICAL ASSISTANCE PROGRAMS AND SERVICES

Programs of Special Interest: The Wisconsin Touring Program provides support for organizations to sponsor performances by Wisconsin professional touring artists. WAB sponsors workshops in such areas as grantwriting, audience development, and marketing. Artists selected for inclusion in the *Arts-in-Education Artists Directory* are eligible for school and community residencies. The WAB also publishes *Working Together*, a directory of Wisconsin organizations that present the performing arts; the *Directory of Wisconsin Performing Touring Artists*; the *Wisconsin Folk Artists Registry*; and *A Guide to Planning Your Residency*.

THE HELENE WURLITZER FOUNDATION OF NEW MEXICO

P.O. Box 545
Taos, NM 87571
505-758-2413

DIRECT SUPPORT PROGRAMS
➤ **RESIDENT GRANTS**
Purpose: To provide creative artists with rent-free housing in Taos, New Mexico
Eligibility:
 Special Requirements: Originating artists only
 Art Forms: All disciplines
Type of Support: 1-6 months' rent-free housing (living and work space) in Taos during spring and summer
Scope of Program: 30 grants per year
Application/Selection Process:
 Deadline: Ongoing
 Preferred Initial Contact: Write for application/guidelines
 Application Procedure: Submit application form; selected applicants are put on waiting list (housing is booked through 1994)
 Selection Process: Board of directors
 Notification Process: Letter

WYOMING ARTS COUNCIL

2320 Capitol Avenue
Cheyenne, WY 82002
307-777-7742
CONTACT: RENÉE BOVÉE, COMMUNITY SERVICES COORDINATOR

DIRECT SUPPORT PROGRAMS
➤ **FELLOWSHIPS/INDIVIDUAL ARTIST GRANTS**
Purpose: Fellowships are designed to assist emerging Wyoming artists at crucial times in their careers; Individual Artist Grants

support specific projects that promote, preserve, encourage, and stimulate culture in the state

Eligibility:
Residency: Wyoming
Age: 18 or older
Special Requirements: No students; previous Fellowship winners ineligible for 4 years; Individual Artist Grants require matching funds
Art Forms: All disciplines

Type of Support: Fellowships, $2,500; Individual Artist Grants, up to $1,000 1:1 matching grant for specific project

Scope of Program: 12 Fellowships (4 each in visual arts, literature, performing arts); 10 Individual Artist Grants in 1990

Competition for Support: 120 applications per year

Application/Selection Process:
Deadline: September 1 (Visual Arts and Performing Arts Fellowships), August 1 (Literary Fellowships), August 15 (Individual Artist Grants)
Preferred Initial Contact: Call or write for application/guidelines
Application Procedure: Submit application form, samples of work, references, resumé (Individual Artist Grant), project budget and description (Individual Artist Grant), artist's statement (Fellowship)
Selection Process: Peer panel of artists and board of directors
Notification Process: Letter in October/November
Formal Report of Grant Required: Yes

TECHNICAL ASSISTANCE PROGRAMS AND SERVICES

Programs of Special Interest: The council sponsors Artspeak, an annual gathering of artists that includes workshops and a regional performing arts showcase. Artists selected for inclusion in the Arts in Education Program Artist Roster are eligible for school and community residencies.

YADDO

Box 395
Saratoga Springs, NY 12866
518-584-0746
CONTACT: ADMISSIONS COMMITTEE

DIRECT SUPPORT PROGRAMS
➤ RESIDENCIES
Purpose: To provide a working retreat for artists
Eligibility:
Special Requirements: Professional artists only
Art Forms: Literature, visual arts, music composition

Type of Support: 2- to 8-week residencies, including room, board, working space; residents encouraged to pay $20/day, but qualified applicants accepted regardless of ability to pay

Scope of Program: 176 residencies in 1986

Application/Selection Process:

Deadline: January 15, August 1 (for October-May residencies only)

Preferred Initial Contact: Write for application

Application Procedure: Submit application form, $20 application fee, samples of work, names of sponsors, professional and biographical information

Selection Process: Peer panel of artists

Notification Process: April 1, late September

THE YARD

890 Broadway
Fifth Floor
New York, NY 10003
212-228-0911

CONTACT: JOHN DODSON, ADMINISTRATIVE DIRECTOR

PROFILE OF FINANCIAL SUPPORT TO ARTISTS

Total Funding/Value of In-Kind Support: $26,850 for FY 1990-91

Competition for Funding: Total applications, 175; total individuals funded/provided with in-kind support, 14

Grant Range: $700-$8,750

DIRECT SUPPORT PROGRAMS

➤ PAUL TAYLOR FELLOWSHIP

Purpose: To provide 1 choreographer and up to 6 additional artists with a residency on Martha's Vineyard to create, rehearse, and perform a new work

Eligibility:

Special Requirements: Applicants must have been professionally performing their work for at least 3 years; no students; artists perform new work on Martha's Vineyard and in New York City

Art Forms: Modern dance

Type of Support: 3-week spring residency including housing, sole use of The Yard's rehearsal spaces, and $8,750 project fee to cover choreographer's fee, transportation and living stipend for choreographer and accompanying artists, rehearsal and performance fees for New York performances, and production costs (e.g., costumes, music, sets, special lighting)

Scope of Program: 1 award per year

Application/Selection Process:

Deadline: Early December

Preferred Initial Contact: Call or write for guidelines

Application Procedure: Submit cover letter, resumé, letter of recommendation, samples of work, information about upcoming performances that selection committee members might attend; 3 finalists selected to audition

Selection Process: Peer panel of artists, staff, Paul Taylor

Notification Process: Finalists notified in January; winner notified by phone by February 1

Formal Report of Grant Required: Yes

➤ **SESSION FOR CHOREOGRAPHERS**

Purpose: To provide choreographers and dancers with an 8 1/2-week residency on Martha's Vineyard to create, rehearse, and perform new works

Eligibility:

Special Requirements: Professional artists only; no students; choreographers must have professionally produced work for at least 3 years; artists perform new works on Martha's Vineyard and in New York City

Art Forms: Modern dance

Type of Support: 8 1/2-week summer residency including housing, $1,200 living stipend, $250 performance fee for week in New York, up to $400 production budget for choreographers

Scope of Program: 4 choreography residencies, 8 performer residencies per year

Application/Selection Process:

Deadline: December (choreographers), February (dancers)

Preferred Initial Contact: Call or write for guidelines

Application Procedure: Submit cover letter, resumé, letter of recommendation, information about upcoming performances that selection committee members might attend; all finalists are interviewed; dancer semi-finalists audition in New York City

Selection Process: Peer panel of artists, staff

Notification Process: Early February (choreographers), late March (dancers)

Formal Report of Grant Required: No

➤ **ARTIST-IN-THE-SCHOOLS RESIDENCY**

Purpose: To select a teacher/choreographer for a 3- to 4-week residency to teach dance/movement in the Martha's Vineyard public schools

Eligibility:

Special Requirements: Professional artists only; no students; teaching experience required

Art Forms: Modern dance

Type of Support: 3- to 4-week fall residency requiring about 20 hours of teaching; resident receives $700 fee, housing, and use of The Yard's rehearsal space

Scope of Program: 1 residency per year
Application/Selection Process:
  Deadline: December
  Preferred Initial Contact: Call or write for guidelines
  Application Procedure: Submit cover letter, samples of work, letter of recommendation, resumé; applicants are interviewed
  Selection Process: Peer panel of artists, staff
  Notification Process: Phone call to recipient in mid-February
  Formal Report of Grant Required: Yes

BRUCE YARNELL AWARD

15 West 82nd Street, #4B
New York, NY 10024
212-799-4267

DIRECT SUPPORT PROGRAMS
➤ **BRUCE YARNELL AWARD**
Eligibility:
  Citizenship: U.S., Canada
  Age: Up to 35
  Art Forms: Male vocal performance (bass, bass-baritone, baritone)
Type of Support: Cash award ($2,000 minimum)
Scope of Program: 1 award per annual or biennial competition
Competition for Support: 60 applications per competition
Application/Selection Process:
  Preferred Initial Contact: Write for information
  Application Procedure: Submit application form; auditions held throughout the U.S.; semi-finals and finals held in New York
  Selection Process: Panel of music professionals
  Notification Process: Letter or phone call (preliminaries)

YELLOW SPRINGS INSTITUTE (YSI)

1645 Art School Road
Chester Springs, PA 19425
215-827-9111
CONTACT: VESNA TODOROVIC MIKSIC, DIRECTOR OF PROGRAM AND DEVELOPMENT

DIRECT SUPPORT PROGRAMS
➤ **ARTISTS' RESIDENCY PROGRAM**
Purpose: To strengthen the role played by art and artist in time of cultural change through active support of experimentation

Eligibility:
Special Requirements: 3 years experience as professional artist;
no students
Art Forms: Modern dance, new music, experimental theater,
experimental visual arts, performance art, audio art, interdisci-
plinary, multi-disciplinary
Type of Support: 2- to 3-week residency including room, board,
rehearsal and production facilities, technical assistance
Scope of Program: 13 ensembles in 1990
Application/Selection Process:
Deadline: Late December
Preferred Initial Contact: Call or write for application/guidelines
Application Procedure: Submit application form, samples of
work, project proposal
Selection Process: Organization staff, peer panel of artists
Notification Process: Phone call and follow-up letter 2 months
after deadline

YOUNG CONCERT ARTISTS, INC. (YCA)

250 West 57th Street
Suite 921
New York, NY 10019
212-307-6655
CONTACT: MARK HAYMAN, AUDITIONS DIRECTOR

DIRECT SUPPORT PROGRAMS
➤ YOUNG CONCERT ARTISTS INTERNATIONAL AUDITIONS
Purpose: To discover and launch the careers of extraordinary
young musicians
Eligibility:
Special Requirements: Must be at the beginning of professional
concert career; must not be under U.S. management (except vocalists)
Art Forms: Music performance (chamber, new, solo/recital,
orchestral)
Type of Support: New York and Washington, D.C., recitals; several
years of complete career management, including concert bookings
across the U.S. in solo recitals, appearances with orchestras, perfor-
mances at music festivals, educational residencies, debut recordings,
and publicity and promotional materials
Scope of Program: 3 new musicians accepted in 1991 (number of
winners varies from year to year)
Competition for Support: 300 applications in 1991
Application/Selection Process:
Deadline: October 15

Preferred Initial Contact: Call or write for application/guidelines (available in late summer)

Application Procedure: Submit application form, $30 fee (refunded to musicians not selected to audition), 2 recommendations; preliminary auditions held in New York City in November and December (applicants living more than 200 miles from New York may submit preliminary audition on tape); semi-final and final auditions in New York in January

Selection Process: Jury of professional musicians

Notification Process: Letter in December to semi-finalists; winners announced at final auditions

THE LOREN L. ZACHARY SOCIETY FOR THE PERFORMING ARTS

2250 Gloaming Way
Beverly Hills, CA 90210
CONTACT: MRS. NEDRA ZACHARY

DIRECT SUPPORT PROGRAMS

➤ **NATIONAL VOCAL COMPETITION FOR YOUNG OPERA SINGERS**

Purpose: To help launch the careers of opera singers by assisting them in finding employment in European opera houses

Eligibility:

Age: 21-33 (females), 21-35 (males)

Special Requirements: Must have operatic training; previous top award winners ineligible; top winners must acquire basic knowledge of German language before departure; vocalists who have had a contract with a European opera house are ineligible

Art Forms: Opera

Type of Support: Round-trip flight to Europe for auditioning, $3,000 (top awards); at least $1,000 (finalists)

Scope of Program: 2 top awards, 8 finalists in FY 1989-90

Competition for Support: 181 applications in 1989-90

Application/Selection Process:

Deadline: February (for New York auditions), April (for Los Angeles auditions)

Preferred Initial Contact: Write for application/guidelines; enclose SASE

Application Procedure: Submit application form, $25 fee, resumé; applicants must audition in preliminaries and semi-finals in New York or Los Angeles; final auditions held in Los Angeles (New York finalists receive travel and housing)

Selection Process: Panel of artists and arts professionals

Formal Report of Grant Required: No

ALPHABETICAL INDEX OF ORGANIZATIONS

250

MONEY FOR FILM & VIDEO ARTISTS

INDEX OF ORGANIZATIONS BY DISCIPLINE

INDEX OF ORGANIZATIONS BY GEOGRAPHIC AREA

INDEX OF ORGANIZATIONS BY TYPE OF SUPPORT

PERFORMANCE OPPOR-
TUNITIES

PRESENTERS, INFORMATION

PRODUCTION/DEVELOPMENT
ASSISTANCE & RESIDENCIES

PROFESSIONAL DEVELOPMENT/
TECHNICAL ASSISTANCE
GRANTS

PROJECT SUPPORT

REGISTRIES

SHOWCASES/BOOKING CONFERENCES

STUDY GRANTS

TOURING OPPORTUNITIES

West Virginia Division of Culture and
History, 237
Wisconsin Arts Board, 238

TRAVEL GRANTS

Alaska State Council on the Arts, 6
Arts International, 36
Canada Council, The, 52, 54, 56, 58, 60
Dance Theater Workshop, 78
Jerome Foundation, 112

Manitoba Arts Council, 128
New Brunswick Department of Tourism,
Recreation and Heritage—Arts
Branch, 165
Prince Edward Island Council of the
Arts, 202
Rhode Island State Council on the Arts,
205
West Virginia Division of Culture and
History, 237

ABOUT THE AMERICAN COUNCIL
FOR THE ARTS

The American Council for the Arts (ACA) is one of the nation's primary sources of legislative news affecting all of the arts and serves as a leading advisor to arts administrators, individual artists, educators, elected officials, arts patrons, and the general public. To accomplish its goal of strong advocacy of the arts, ACA promotes public debate in various national, state, and local forums; communicates as a publisher of books, journals, *Vantage Point* magazine and *ACA UpDate*; provides information services through its extensive arts education, policy, and management library; and has as its key policy issues the needs of individual/originating artists, public and private support for the arts, arts education, multiculturalism, and international cultural relations.

Gramley Library
Salem College
Winston-Salem, NC 27108